# Biographies

## IN AMERICAN FOREIGN POLICY

*Joseph A. Fry, University of Nevada, Las Vegas*
Series Editor

The Biographies in American Foreign Policy Series employs the enduring medium of biography to examine the major episodes and themes in the history of U.S. foreign relations. By viewing policy formation and implementation from the perspective of influential participants, the series seeks to humanize and make more accessible those decisions and events that sometimes appear abstract or distant. Particular attention is devoted to those aspects of the subject's background, personality, and intellect that most influenced his or her approach to U.S. foreign policy, and each individual's role is placed in a context that takes into account domestic affairs, national interests and policies, and international and strategic considerations.

The series is directed primarily at undergraduate and graduate courses in U.S. foreign relations, but it is hoped that the genre and format may also prove attractive to the interested general reader. With these objectives in mind, the length of the volumes has been kept manageable, the documentation has been restricted to direct quotes and particularly controversial assertions, and the bibliographic essays have been tailored to provide historiographical assessment without tedium.

Producing books of high scholarly merit to appeal to a wide range of readers is an ambitious undertaking, and an excellent group of authors has agreed to participate. Some have compiled extensive scholarly records while others are just beginning promising careers, but all are distinguished by their comprehensive knowledge of U.S. foreign relations, their cooperative spirit, and their enthusiasm for the project. It has been a distinct pleasure to have been given the opportunity to work with these scholars as well as with Richard Hopper and his staff at Scholarly Resources.

# THOMAS
# JEFFERSON

## Westward the Course of Empire

# THOMAS
# JEFFERSON

## Westward the Course of Empire

### Lawrence S. Kaplan

A Scholarly Resources Inc. Imprint
Wilmington, Delaware

Scholarly Resources Inc.
104 Greenhill Avenue
Wilmington, DE  19805-1897

**Library of Congress Cataloging-in-Publication Data**

Kaplan, Lawrence S.
    Thomas Jefferson : westward the course of empire /
Lawrence S. Kaplan.
        p.    cm.
    Includes bibliographical references and index.
    ISBN 0-8420-2629-0 (alk. paper). — ISBN 0-8420-2630-4 (pbk. :
alk. paper)
    1. Jefferson, Thomas, 1743–1826—Views on foreign relations.
2. United States—Foreign relations—1775–1783.  3. United
States—Foreign relations—1783–1815.  I. Title.
E332.45.K34    1998
973.4'6'092—dc21                                                98-7364
                                                                    CIP

⊛ The paper used in this publication meets the minimum require-
ments of the American National Standard for permanence of paper
for printed library materials, Z39.48, 1984.

*In Memory of Colby Teachers*

*William J. Wilkinson*
*1874–1950*

*Paul A. Fullam*
*1907–1955*

*Carl G. Anthon*
*1911–1996*

# About the Author

---

Lawrence S. Kaplan (Ph.D., Yale, 1951) is University Professor Emeritus at Kent State University and Adjunct Professor of History at Georgetown University. His studies in the Jeffersonian era include *Jefferson and France* (reprint ed., 1980); *Colonies into Nation: American Diplomacy, 1763–1800* (1972); and *Entangling Alliances with None: American Foreign Policy in the Age of Jefferson* (1987).

# Contents

# Preface

Rather than end this preface with a conventional acknowledgment of the help others have given me in the preparation of this volume, I wish to begin with an expression of special appreciation for the heroic efforts of Andy Fry, the general editor of this series, in providing commentaries at every stage of this essay on Jeffersonian foreign policy. It is rare that an editor, whose primary mission is to locate authors and offer general encouragement, will take the time and energy to provide the service he has given to this project. He was able to draw from his own familiarity with the early national period of the republic to make substantive as well as editorial recommendations.

Rick Hopper's invitation to write this book continues a long-standing relationship with Scholarly Resources that began with my meeting Dan Helmstadter in 1966. It also opened the way for me to revisit a subject that has interested me for almost half a century. I am grateful for the opportunity to rethink some of the judgments I had made in the past, and to respond to some of the criticisms offered in the interim.

This is an occasion as well to recognize the institutions and individuals that have supported me over the years. My journey into Jeffersoniana began with Samuel Flagg Bemis's seminar at Yale in 1948. Fellow graduate students in that seminar, Bob Ferrell and Art Richmond, encouraged my studies then and later, along with such friends as Al Bowman of the University of Tennessee at Chattanooga and Alex DeConde of the University of California at Santa Barbara. I appreciate, too, the constant support of Ronald L. Hatzenbuehler, one of the few former doctoral students who has followed a Jeffersonian path. In Washington, my colleagues in *The Emerging Nation* of the NHPRC—editor Mary A. Giunta, coeditor J. Dane Hartgrove, Norman A. Graebner, and Peter Hill—have offered insights into Jefferson's role as diplomatist which have been of great service to this project. I received sustenance from the American Council on Learned Societies, the American Philosophical Society, and the Woodrow Wilson International Center for Scholars. Most notable has been continuing encouragement from Kent State University, particularly in the early days of its doctoral program. My thanks go to Marge Evans and Ellen Denning for putting up with my handwriting for so many years, and a special note of thanks to Donna Walker for her gift of the Princeton edition of Jefferson's writings as I was beginning this project.

This volume encompasses such issues as Haitian relations, the Barbary Wars, and Indian affairs that I had not included in earlier studies of Jefferson's foreign policies. In undertaking the book I have used portions of my earlier writings reworked as extended quotations and passages as well as rephrased and transposed excerpts. They are taken from the following articles and chapters, arranged in chronological order.

"The Philosophes and the American Revolution." *Social Science* 31 (January 1956): 31–36.

"Jefferson, the Napoleonic Wars, and the Balance of Power." *William and Mary Quarterly*, 3d ser., 14 (April 1957): 196–218.

"Jefferson's Foreign Policy and Napoleon's Ideologues." *William and Mary Quarterly*, 3d ser., 19 (July 1962): 344–59.

*Jefferson and France: An Essay on Politics and Political Ideas.* New Haven: Yale University Press, 1967; reprint, Westport, CT: Greenwood Press, 1980.

"The Consensus of 1789: Jefferson and Hamilton on American Foreign Policy." *South Atlantic Quarterly* 71 (January 1972): 91–105.

*Colonies into Nation: American Diplomacy, 1763–1800.* New York: Macmillan, 1972.

"Thomas Jefferson: The Idealist as Realist." In *Makers of American Diplomacy*, 2 vols., ed. Frank J. Merli and Theodore A. Wilson, 1:53–79. New York: Scribner's, 1974.

"Toward Isolationism: The Rise and Fall of the Franco-American Alliance, 1778–1800." In *The American Revolution and a "Candid World,"* ed. Lawrence S. Kaplan, 134–60. Kent, OH: Kent State University Press, 1977.

"Reflections on Jefferson as a Francophile." *South Atlantic Quarterly* 79 (Winter 1980): 28–50.

"The Founding Fathers and the Two Confederations: The United States of America and the United Provinces of the Netherlands, 1783–1789." In *A Bilateral Bicentennial: A History of Dutch-American Relations, 1782–1982*, ed. J. W. Schulte Nordholt and Robert P. Swierenga, 33–48. New York: Octagon Books, 1982.

"Thomas Jefferson and Foreign Relations." In *Thomas Jefferson: A Reference Biography*, ed. Merrill D. Peterson, 311–30. New York: Scribner's, 1986.

"Jefferson and the Constitution: The View from Paris." *Diplomatic History* 11 (Fall 1987): 321–35.

"Jefferson as Anglophile: Sagacity or Senility in the Era of Good Feelings?" *Diplomatic History* 16 (Summer 1992): 487–94.

# Chronology

**1743**

Born (April 13) at Shadwell, Albemarle County, Virginia

**1757**

Death of his father; studies with the Reverend James Maury

**1760**

Enrolls in the College of William and Mary, Williamsburg

**1767**

Takes up the practice of law after studies with George Wythe

**1769**

Represents Albemarle County in Virginia's House of Burgesses; begins construction of Monticello

**1772**

Marries Martha Wayles Skelton; birth of first child, Martha

**1774**

Publishes *Summary View of the Rights of British America*

**1775**

Attends Second Virginia Convention, Williamsburg; named delegate to Second Continental Congress, Philadelphia

**1776**

Drafts Declaration of Independence, Philadelphia; returns to Virginia legislature and sponsors bills ranging from the abolition of primogeniture to land reform to religious toleration

**1779**

Elected governor of Virginia for one-year term (and again in 1780); British troops under Lord Cornwallis invade the state during his second term

**1781**

Completes *Notes on Virginia*

**1782**

Death of his wife

**1783**

Elected to Congress, where he pushes through the Treaty of Paris and drafts a plan of organization for the Northwest Territory

**1784**

Sent by Congress to Paris to join John Adams and Benjamin Franklin in negotiating commercial treaties

**1785**

Succeeds Franklin as U.S. minister to France

**1786**

Meets Tripoli's ambassador in London to discuss depredations against American ships by the Barbary states

**1788**

Travels with Adams to Holland to request loans from Dutch bankers for the new nation

**1789**

Leaves France to return to the United States; urges the additions of a Bill of Rights to the Constitution

**1790**

Takes office as secretary of state in President George Washington's first Cabinet; differs strongly in his views from Federalist Alexander Hamilton, secretary of the treasury; outlines policy for the navigation of the Mississippi River

**1794**

Resigns from the Cabinet and returns to Monticello

**1796**

Wins election against Federalist candidate John Adams for the vice presidency; deals with repercussions of Jay's Treaty

**1797**

Elected president of the American Philosophical Society, Philadelphia

**1798**

Leads attack against the Federalists' Alien and Sedition Acts, which curb freedom of speech and the press; drafts Kentucky Resolutions; addresses Francophobia following the XYZ affair

**1800**

Elected president of the United States

**1801**

Launches four-year campaign against the Barbary states following Tripoli's declaration of war

**1803**

Promotes the purchase of the Louisiana Territory from France after negotiations with France and Spain over Louisiana and the Floridas; dispatches Meriwether Lewis and William Clark to explore the headwaters of the Missouri River and on westward

**1804**

Reelected to a second term as president; attempts to keep his country neutral during the conflict between France and Great Britain

**1807**

Rejects Monroe-Pinkney Treaty; pushes the Embargo Act through Congress

**1809**

Returns to Monticello; works on plans to create a university in Virginia at Charlottesville (which opens in 1825)

**1821**

Writes his "Autobiography"

**1826**

Dies (July 4) at Monticello

*Westward the course of empire takes its way;*
*The Four first Acts already past,*
*A fifth shall close the Drama with the day:*
*Times's noblest offspring is the last.*

Bishop George Berkeley
"On the Prospect of Planting Arts and Learning in America"
Rhode Island, circa 1730

# 1

## The "Candid World" of Thomas Jefferson

### 1743–1776

When the military band of General Lord Charles Cornwallis played the old march "The World Turned Upside Down" at the surrender field in Yorktown on October 19, 1781, it symbolized European bewilderment over the events of his generation. The American Revolution had been the occasion for rude colonials to upset the world as it was in the eighteenth century. If this was true on the battlefield, it was equally true in the chancelleries. The new nation seemed to hold ideas about the outside world that would overturn established international relations. Thomas Jefferson's career as diplomatist embodied this outlook, and while he was not the first explicator of American foreign relations nor the sole formulator of American diplomacy, his voice was the most pervasive in the first generation of the republic's history.

Jefferson's voice may also have been the most paradoxical. Following his trajectory as a guide to the development of the nation's foreign policy requires confrontation with a series of apparent contradictions. An eloquent defender of nonentanglement with European powers, he advocated, it seemed, an informal alliance with France in the Embargo Act of 1807 and with Britain on the eve of the Monroe Doctrine in 1823. An articulate spokesman for an agrarian republic in the 1790s, he supported manufactures during his presidency to ensure independence from European economic control. A believer in the efficacy of peaceful coercion, he employed military force against the Barbary powers in 1804 and advocated war against Britain in 1812. The foregoing does not exhaust the number of paradoxes that a critic can compile. This book will attempt to seek coherence both in Jefferson's life as a maker of foreign policy and in the foreign relations of the new nation.

## Early Influences

Jefferson's foreign policies had their beginnings in the world of his youth. Whatever disagreements there have been among biographers, they are one in this respect: he was a child of the eighteenth-century Enlightenment. The culture in which he was reared, and that produced the American Revolution, was shaped by an international elite anticipating a future when the rule of Reason would govern human society in the manner that the rule of Nature governed the physical world. By the time of Jefferson's birth Newton had already displaced Thomas Aquinas and Descartes as the oracle of the age. Enlightened despots reigned in Europe, their power tempered by the philosophers who guided them. Frederick the Great of Prussia and Catherine of Russia paid at least lip service to the principles of the Enlightenment. The illogic of despotic rule may have been apparent to sages such as Bolingbroke and Voltaire, but they had little doubt that natural law, once fully recognized, would bring about ever greater progress to mankind even under the agency of benevolent monarchs. Neither Rousseau and the romanticists with their challenge to reason nor the new apostles of the old order—the Burkes and de Maistres—had arrived on the scene to disturb the optimism of the philosophers of the Enlightenment. From 1750 to 1767, Jefferson the student absorbed the teachings of his age when it had its greatest faith in the destiny of Reason.

Over the years scholars have attempted to parse Jefferson's numerous references to writings of such varied philosophers as the Scottish Lord Kames, the French Montesquieu, the English Locke, and to figures from the Roman republic whom he had admired. His *Commonplace Book* contained quotations from a wide spectrum of political philosophers, many of them primarily English—but hardly to the exclusion of French writers. Montesquieu alone is cited in twenty-seven separate quotations. An invoice of books purchased from London in 1769, the year Jefferson was first elected to public office, suggests the breadth of his interests. They include treatises by Burlamaqui and Locke as well as by Montesquieu. His deistic beliefs—a rational approach to religion—can be linked to the works of Lord Bolingbroke and Lord Kames. But Jefferson's literary mentors were not tied to the eighteenth century; his education in the classics was an early and lasting influence. He expressed his indebtedness to his father for his classical learning. As he wrote to Joseph Priestley in 1800, "I thank on my knees, Him who directed my early education; for having put into my possession this rich source of delight; and I would not exchange it for anything which I could then have acquired, and have not since acquired."[1]

There is always the temptation to single out one or two of these authorities to explain the intellectual justification of Jefferson and his contemporaries for the American Revolution and for the form of government they would fashion in the first generation of the new republic. The national origin of individual European thinkers had little effect on the philosophy of the Revolution. What the rebellious colonists wanted were philosophic assurances that the universe was governed by natural law, that all men possessed certain inherent rights, that their governments depended on the consent of the governed, and that when rulers failed in their duties, they should be dismissed. With their eyes fixed on these tenets, the colonial leaders cited authorities not for a particular philosophic principle, but for the broad moral support their names and their ideas would give to the American cause. Jefferson himself in his old age claimed that the Declaration of Independence "was intended to be an expression of the American mind. All its authority rests then on the harmonizing sentiments of the day, whether expressed in conversation, in letters, printed essays, or the elementary books of public right, as Aristotle, Cicero, Locke, Sidney, etc." As Carl Becker observed a half-century ago, "where Jefferson got his ideas is less a question than where he could have got away from them."[2]

Becker's acceptance of the Enlightenment's synoptic influence did not put to rest questions about whose were the primary influences on Jefferson and the Founding Fathers. The need to separate intellectual strands is as strong at the end of the twentieth century as it has ever been. The current preoccupation with the issue of liberalism versus republicanism in the Revolutionary era is a case in point. There is no doubt that the civic virtues of classical Rome were very much alive in Thomas Jefferson and James Madison's image of a new nation guided by selfless public servants. In this view, commerce was seen as a corrupting influence, and isolation from Europe was equated with isolation from selfish individualism. The small agrarian republic seemed to be the antithesis of the alliance of government and finance and the division of society between the haves and have-nots.

Jefferson's place in the conflict over the direction of the new nation is obviously a significant part of any understanding of his foreign policies. Among the many seeming inconsistencies identified with him is his vision of a nation of small yeoman farmers under a limited government, freed from the corrupt practices of the Old World, as opposed to a statesman who would take advantage of the weaknesses of European adversaries to advance American commercial interests. Jefferson's record will continue to challenge the historian into the next century, and nowhere in his career is the challenge more daunting than in his management of foreign relations.

His introduction to the transatlantic world of letters began with his father. Biographers have made a point of contrasting the high social position of Jefferson's maternal ancestors with the humble origins of Peter Jefferson. But even those who admitted that the father's cultural baggage was not that of the average backwoodsman felt it necessary to emphasize that he could be classified as a gentleman despite his limited formal education. Their confusion was largely the result of exaggerating the distinctions between Tidewater and Piedmont Virginia. While the frontiersman may have carried with him only the rudiments of the English tradition, the contrast between the aristocrats of the plantations and the ambitious Peter Jefferson of the uplands represented a difference in time—little more than a generation—rather than in space. Nor did his marriage into the Randolph family signify a unique bridging of a social gap.

The bare facts of Peter Jefferson's life suggest that his educational attainments were at least equal to those of the Tidewater gentry, and the range of his intellectual curiosity was considerably greater. It is worth noting that he had been chosen along with Joshua Fry, professor of mathematics at the College of William and Mary, to survey the boundary line between Virginia and North Carolina. This event had considerable significance, according to Herbert Baxter Adams, historian of the college: "through association with a Williamsburg professor the father of Thomas Jefferson became inclined to give his son a liberal education and to train him to the art of surveying."[3] Whatever the extent of Peter Jefferson's abilities as a surveyor may have been, he set his son on a path out of the Piedmont and into a larger world.

Before his untimely death in 1757 at the age of fifty, the elder Jefferson had made plans to give the boy a classical education. The executors of his estate, following his instructions, placed Thomas in the school of the Reverend James Maury, a "correct classical scholar" who far surpassed his previous teacher, William Douglas, in the knowledge of Greek and Latin. Douglas, also a clergyman, taught Jefferson some French but not enough of anything else to warrant more than a patronizing line in his "Autobiography." [4] Maury's influence may have been more profound than Jefferson recognized, for it was at his school that the young man learned the classics and learned them well. Familiarity with classical civilization was one of the keys to cultural eminence at a time when the republican virtues of Athens and the moral character of Cicero were emulated.

Although it is tempting to find Jefferson's roots in Maury's school, his primary connection with the ideas of the Enlightenment did not begin until 1760, when he left Maury's tutelage—and Albemarle County—to study at the College of William and Mary in Williamsburg. A serious student, he was not quite seventeen when he identified the advantages that he saw in going to the college. Among them was the opportunity to "get a more universal Acquaintance, which may hereafter be serviceable to me."[5] While he wrote to friends of his wish to travel to Europe, the world beyond the Virginia forests was opened to him in Williamsburg, not only by the brilliance of the capital's social life (although he certainly enjoyed that), but also by his relations with three of the most stimulating minds in the colony.

One of the three, Professor William Small, initiated the young Jefferson into the world of the Enlightenment. The only member of the faculty without a clerical background and a recent immigrant from Scotland, he was Jefferson's mentor in Newtonian physics and his guide to the mechanistic universe so prized by deists. Small's two friends, George Wythe and Francis Fauquier, soon enriched the student's store of knowledge. Wythe, already a promising young lawyer in Williamsburg, was even then displaying the wisdom that was to make him the dean of American teachers of law before the end of the century. In addition to a sound legal training, he gave Jefferson a deeper appreciation of the classics. No less influential was the presence of the controversial Lieutenant Governor Fauquier, who had a reputation as a wit and "philosophe." Although he also had a reputation as a gambler, which made him a little out of place in the circle, his humanitarian spirit and broad tolerance displayed another side of the Enlightenment to Jefferson.

Under Wythe's tutelage, Jefferson began the study of law in the manner that he undertook most intellectual matters. The path to the bar could be walked in six months, as Patrick Henry demonstrated. In Virginia, unlike in England, becoming a lawyer was an informal matter of apprenticeship combined with some reading of Sir Edward Coke's *Institutes of the Laws of England*. For Jefferson it was a five-year journey, from 1762 to 1767, an opportunity to study the range of history from Rome to England along with speculations gleaned from philosophers and moralists about the meanings behind laws. He was fortunate in enjoying the benefits of his father's estate, which permitted the leisure to pursue the course of study a less-favored student could not have afforded. Making a living from the law was not a priority for him.

Jefferson's habit of copying snatches from writings that he admired during this time has given posterity some insights into his ideas and values during his formative years. These works deal with morals, political theory, natural law, natural rights, and the particular rights of Englishmen. He was also attracted to the challenges to religious orthodoxy found in pagan writers and in the work of the skeptical Lord Bolingbroke. Eternal verities, he discovered, were not to be found in a literal interpretation of the Bible, but rather from an informed observation of Nature. The philosophers and poets reinforced his convictions. When he quoted the naive queries of Bolingbroke about the location of Heaven or about the putatively incestuous relationship between Adam and Eve, he was seeking truths that would be in conformity with Reason and Nature rather than abandoning received values. Doubt about the meaning of a biblical passage did not mean doubt about the existence of a beneficent God. Jefferson exploited Homer's wisdom, not his mythology, to show that the moral sense of right and wrong transcended a particular time and place.

What was developing from the studies of the young Virginian was an ideology comprised of an attachment to the British tradition of individual rights that was expanded by the teachings of British and French contributors to the Enlightenment. Although Jefferson later renounced Montesquieu when the French Revolution made the philosopher appear to be an exponent of conservatism and monarchism, a younger Jefferson found in his work rationalizations against Parliamentary interference in the affairs of the colonies. The principle of a federal empire composed of equal states under the rule of a common king, a major element of his ideas at the First Continental Congress in 1774, may be found in extensive quotations from Montesquieu recorded in the *Commonplace Book*. The budding lawyer paid special attention to a passage in

Montesquieu's influential treatise *L'Esprit des lois* (1748), which stated that laws establishing the right of suffrage in a democratic government were fundamental "because," he added in the margin, " by their votes the people exercise their sovereignty."[6]

## Toward Independence

It was inevitable that Jefferson's studies increasingly reflected more than abstract verities from classical writers or from seventeenth-century authorities. The colonial world was in turmoil during most of his stay in Williamsburg. The Peace of Paris in 1763 forced a confrontation between the British Parliament and the American colonies that had been dormant during most of the past century of benign neglect. The defeat of France and its withdrawal from the continent removed the colonies from long-standing dependence upon British military forces. At the same time, it focused British attention on the sacrifices that the mother country had made in the wars with France that were not shared by the colonists. The succession of British wars attempting to enforce an antiquated navigation system led to conflicts that Jefferson the student could not ignore. His deep admiration for so many aspects of British civilization was marred by a sense that the mother country was repressing rights of overseas Englishmen.

There was also a change in America's views of France. No matter how broad the common ground between French and British exponents of the Enlightenment, France had been the common enemy of Britain and the colonies. The French and Indian War that had begun in 1754 two years before it spread to Europe was American in origin. The mother country was dragged into conflict once again, with more reluctance than it had exhibited in earlier wars with France. But once France was no longer an enemy it could be used as a counterpoise to Britain, an objective that Jefferson was to follow all his public life. As for the philosophers of the Enlightenment, British or French, they could offer authority impartially for colonial actions against Britain.

Jefferson took up the practice of law in 1767, the year of the Townshend Acts that imposed duties on products imported not from foreign sources, as in all preceding navigation laws, but on British products. The young lawyer could not help but be influenced by the climate of his times, especially when it was heated by the dynamic personality of Patrick Henry. As a student in Williamsburg, Jefferson had attended the debate over the Stamp

Act in 1765 and claimed that he had never heard such a splendid display of oratory from any other man: "He appeared to me to speak as Homer wrote."[7] Years later, Jefferson was critical of Henry's intellectual limitations and of his casual knowledge of the law. But he was impressed in 1765 with the eloquence of Henry's denunciation of the Stamp Act, and while his method of expression would have differed from his older contemporary, he shared Henry's sentiments about representative government.

It was not surprising that Jefferson was successful as a lawyer. With his social connections, his methodical habits, and his keen mind he quickly built a substantial practice. It was also not surprising that he was more interested in the philosophy of the law than in its practice. Jefferson, however, was not a prisoner of any particular philosophical or legal school. Even in his early years he was willing and able to place a principle in the service of his immediate objective. He once gave an idiosyncratic meaning to the concept of natural law when he summoned it to help him in a court case over the issue of slavery. "Under the law of Nature," he claimed in *Howell v. Netherland*, "all men are born free, everyone comes into the world with a right to his own person, which includes moving and using it at his own will."[8]

Although Jefferson lost this case in 1770, he showed his appreciation for the qualities of the term "natural law" by elaborating on its theme four years later before the Continental Congress in his pamphlet *Summary View of the Rights of British America*. He was primarily interested in one interpretation of natural law, the right to self-defense, which the colonists might have to invoke if the king's ministers persisted in harrying them. Before he was finished, however, Jefferson had demonstrated that almost all the colonial demands against England fell under the rubric of natural law—from the desire for free trade to the abuse of royal authority.

That Jefferson would be drawn into the colonial conflict with Britain was as inevitable as his entry into public life. He was, after all, a rising young lawyer, a substantial landholder, and well connected with the leading lights of the colony. In 1769 he was elected to represent Albemarle County in the Virginia Assembly as his father had done before him. It was an assembly of notables who recognized and appreciated his talents as a serious legislator with a gift for elegant expression. His name was attached to resolutions at every stage of the growing conflict with the mother country. Emotionally close to Patrick Henry as the House of Burgesses requested action in response to the Massachusetts General Court circular appeal against the Townshend Acts, Jefferson joined his colleagues in framing what they considered to be moderate resolutions asserting Virginia's exclusive right to impose internal taxes on its citizens. When Royal Governor Lord Botetourt dissolved the Assembly, the legislators moved to the Raleigh Tavern where they created the "Association," agreeing not to import enumerated goods from England until Parliament revoked its measures. Jefferson was one of the signatories.

The crisis ended with a new election that returned all the protesters to office; and the repeal of the Townshend laws in 1770, with the exception of the tax on tea, brought back a semblance of normality. Unlike many of his colleagues, Jefferson was not satisfied with a status quo that permitted Parliament to override the authority of the American legislatures. The duty on tea was a reminder of Britain's authority to tax, an issue that continued to disturb him. He signed another Association agreement in June 1770 that was supposed to be in effect until the Tea Act was repealed. Apparently, Jefferson's sense of grievance did not prevent Lord Botetourt from installing him as commander of the militia in Albemarle, nor his accepting the commission.

While Anglophobic sentiment was gradually building in Virginia, events in New England in 1773 and 1774 stoked passions that had never fully dissipated. The attack against the British revenue cutter *Gaspée* in Narragansett Bay by a Rhode Island mob as it attempted to capture smugglers resulted in British threats to bring the accused to England for trial. Once again, colonial liberties appeared to be at stake. Jefferson recorded in his "Autobiography" that the older members of the House of Burgesses were not "up to the point of forwardness & zeal which the times required"; therefore, a group of younger burgesses, including Henry and himself, met once again at the Raleigh Tavern to establish a committee of correspondence with patriots from other colonies "to consider the British claims as a common cause to all, and to produce a unity of action."[9] It is worth noting that the group wanted Jefferson to draw up the resolutions. He graciously deferred to Dabney Carr, his brother-in-law and new member of the Assembly, rather than accept the honor for himself.

The colonies' focus in 1773 was on Parliament's Tea Act, which permitted the East India Company to market its product in America through company agents rather than through established American tea merchants. Britain thereby unwittingly stimulated a colony-wide reaction, with the most notable clash occurring in Boston where tea was ceremoniously dumped into the harbor. The next step for Virginians was to respond to the Port Act that the British imposed on Boston in reprisal for the Tea Party, thereby punishing Massachusetts by cutting off its trade with the world, and incidentally destroying the economy of the colony. Jefferson and his colleagues agreed that they "must boldly take an unequivocal stand in the line with Massachusetts."[10] Jefferson wrote these words in 1820, but his memory was accurate. He first advised his constituents to set aside a day of fasting and prayer in light of the hostile invasion of a sister colony. Subsequently, he was appointed on July 26, 1774, to represent Albemarle County at a convention of deputies to be held at Williamsburg that would take such measures as breaking off "commerce with every part of the British empire which shall not in like manner break off their commerce with Great Britain."[11]

Jefferson's draft of instructions to the Virginia delegates to the Continental Congress reflected not only a leadership role but also a summation (the *Summary View*) of his outlook on the larger world informed by a combination of education and experience. His stance, unlike that of Patrick Henry or Samuel Adams, was not that of a radical revolutionary. He was not asking for a separation from the mother country; rather, he was asking the king to redress the wrongs inflicted "by the legislature of one part of the empire, upon those rights which god and the laws have given equally and independently to all."[12] He reminded the king that Americans were overseas Englishmen possessed of the same rights of self-government as those living in Britain. His image of Saxon emigration to Britain being replicated in America carried with it the idea that the settlement of the colonies was made by Americans themselves, not by "the British public."[13] Each colony had its own representative government, just as Parliament represented the mother country. Jefferson's selective history of the British in America placed Parliament in the position of usurper, attempting to inhibit the natural right of free trade with all parts of the world. If the British representative body was superior in any fashion to its American counterparts, it was as a regulator for the empire. In essence, Jefferson seemed to suggest that the only viable future for the colonies was a recognition on the part of Britain of a federal system in which the colonial assemblies possessed legislative authority equivalent to that of Parliament.

While the *Summary View* professed loyalty to the Crown, "an humble and dutiful address . . . to his majesty begging leave to lay before him as chief magistrate of the British empire" the complaints of his American subjects,[14] the subsequent text did little to confirm humility or loyalty. It is difficult to find much humility in Jefferson's suggestion that the king reflect "that he is no more than the chief officer of the people, appointed by the laws, and circumscribed with definite powers."[15] The rights the colonists claimed were the rights of Nature, not "the gift of the chief magistrate," nor is there much respect implicit in his cry: "Open your breast Sire, to liberal and expanded thought. Let not the name of George the third be a blot in the page of history."[16] The *Summary View* in essence was a message that neither kings nor parliaments could abuse the laws of Nature or the rights of Englishmen, and both required that self-government be accepted by the mother country if the colonies were to remain within the empire.

Publication of this pamphlet in England gave Jefferson the reputation of being one of the leaders of sedition, and rightly so. When war broke out, he helped to organize the Virginia militia and represented the colony in the Second Continental Congress in 1776. His correspondence between April 1775, when Massachusetts confronted British regulars at Lexington Green, and July 1776, when independence was declared, revealed conflicted emotions toward the mother country. Writing to John Randolph in England in August 1775, he expressed a hope that "the returning wisdom of Great Britain will e'er long put an end to this unnatural contest." He would rather be dependent, he claimed, upon Britain, "properly limited than on any nation upon earth, or than on no nation." These words may have been chosen to appease the feelings of a potentially estranged Tory friend, but they were counteracted immediately afterward by his admission that he was "one of those too who rather than submit to the right of legislating for us assumed by the British parliament . . . would lend my hand to sink the whole island in the ocean."[17] Three months later his language was even more extravagant. Writing again to Randolph, he exclaimed: "Believe me Dear Sir there is not in the British empire a man who more cordially loves a Union with Gr. Britain than I do. But by the god that made me I will cease to exist before I yield to a connection on such terms as the British parliament propose, and in this I think I speak the sentiments of America."[18]

The transition from the *Summary View* to the Declaration of Independence was not difficult for Jefferson. The essential themes of that pamphlet remained in place. New British abuses were added, but the principle of colonial self-government was paramount,

justified as it was by the natural rights philosophy of the Enlightenment and by his attachment to the Whig interpretation of English constitutional history. Deism was represented in "Nature's
God," and natural rights were enshrined in "self-evident" truths.
Locke's influence was reflected in the right of the people to change
their government "whenever any form of government becomes
destructive" of their unalienable rights. But there is no reason to
doubt Jefferson's claim that no single philosopher guided the framing of the Declaration. He neither aimed "at originality of principles or sentiments, nor yet copied from any particular and
previous writing."[19] Jefferson was using ideas common to the Enlightenment to resolve an essentially American issue: namely, that
government was the business of the governed. And he did so in a
synoptic fashion by blending the rights of Englishmen celebrated
in the Glorious Revolution of the seventeenth century with the natural rights philosophy predominant among the literati of the eighteenth century.

More striking was the substitution of the king for Parliament
as the reason for the separation from Britain: "The history of the
present King of Great Britain is a history of repeated injuries and
usurpations, all having in direct object the establishment of an ab-
solute tyranny over these States." Until 1776, Jefferson and his colleagues had laid the blame for Britain's behavior on Parliament,
but in the Declaration of Independence it was the Crown itself that
was personally responsible for America's sufferings. Indeed, nowhere in the document is Parliament specifically identified. There
is a reference to "their Legislature" as if it were a foreign entity,
and a charge that "he [the king] has combined with others" to sub-
jugate the American states without suggesting that the "others"
had been effectively governing the colonies for over a century. But
while declaring independence was a bold step, the substitution of
king for Parliament was not. It was prefigured in warnings clearly
made in the *Summary View*.

If independence was the objective of the Continental Congress,
there was no alternative to addressing the head of state. There was
an additional reason, however, for de-emphasizing the colonial relationship with the British Parliament, and this was implicit in the
appeal to "let Facts be submitted to a candid world." Up until the
outbreak of hostilities the outside world had hardly figured in
Jefferson's universe. The scholars celebrating natural law or deistic principles may have been French, German, and Italian in
nationality, but they shared the common language of the Enlight-

enment. As the new nation faced the formidable military power of the former mother country, it had to pay attention to Britain's European rivals, which would be needed to help the United Colonies maintain independence.

Thomas Paine's *Common Sense* had pointed the way six months earlier when it assumed that the importance of the American market would guarantee European assistance to the colonial war effort. Nor did Americans overlook the opportunities their departure from the empire would give to France to seek revenge for its losses in earlier wars with Britain. Even the conservative John Dickinson could claim in 1775: "Our cause is just. Our union is perfect. Our preparations are nearly completed. Our internal resources are great; and our Assurance of foreign Assistance is certain."[20] It was the certainty of foreign assistance that was the primary source of Dickinson's confidence. Similarly, two months after the Declaration, John Adams's Treaty Plan anticipated military alliances with European powers without obligations on the part of the United States.

It was in the context of revolution and the need to find help abroad that France as a national entity entered into Jefferson's Weltanschauung. It is fair to suggest that before the Revolutionary War, Jefferson, the Virginian, a beneficiary of the British empire, had no expectations of an American alliance with France under any terms. France had been Britain's, and hence the colonies', enemy through his formative years. It was Virginia, after all, that precipitated the Seven Years' War by challenging France's movement from Quebec into the Ohio Valley in midcentury. This was not the France of the philosophes but rather the power representing a religious and political authority that would deny British America access to the West.

## A New Role for France

The Revolution increased Jefferson's awareness of the vital role France could play in achieving independence and the use to which that country might be put in strengthening the national economy by replacing Britain as a trading partner. This was one of the messages signaled in the Declaration of Independence. But in 1776 Jefferson did not realize any more than his fellow countrymen just how important France would be to the winning of the war. While they welcomed the prospect of a friendly France providing assistance because of its own interest in reducing British power, they assumed that their service to the French Crown in producing a rift in the British empire was fully as great as any help France might give the United States in the course of the war. These assumptions seemed justified at first by the willingness of the Comte de Vergennes, the French foreign minister, to send an unofficial envoy to Philadelphia in 1775 to assure Americans of his government's disinterested concern for their success.

With no illusions about France's motives in making overtures to the colonies, the Continental Congress created in November 1775 the Committee of Secret Correspondence "for the sole purpose of corresponding with our friends in Great Britain, Ireland, and other parts of the world."[21] This embryonic Foreign Office intended to exploit France's interest by sending abroad Silas Deane as a commercial agent to procure supplies and, if possible, political and military assistance. The Declaration of Independence enabled Congress to act even more boldly by dispatching a more official mission to Paris with an outline of a model treaty. There was nothing supplicatory about the American attitude in 1775 and 1776. No binding military alliance was anticipated. There was no need for concessions to extract aid from France since the very act of separation from the mother country should have been sufficient reason for the French to support a common cause.

Jefferson fully shared these expectations in the summer of 1776. Writing to his boyhood friend John Page on August 20 from his vantage point in Philadelphia, he observed that the Dutch as well as the French were rallying behind the new nation. He reported news from the Dutch island of Saint Eustatius that Holland had refused both to renew the prohibition on the exportation of powder to the colonies and to furnish the British with troops, despite pressure from London. Jefferson delighted in the reports that when Britain in response seized several Dutch ships, Holland armed forty warships and was raising as many as 20,000 troops. It seemed possible that the Dutch would go to war on the side of America. But the weight of France on America's side was more critical, and in August this prospect seemed imminent. Writing a week later to his friend Edmund Pendleton, a member of the Continental Congress, Jefferson claimed that "we have assurance (not newspaper, but Official) that the French governors of the West Indies have received orders not only to furnish us with what we want but to protect our ships. They will convoy our vessels, they say, thro' the line of British cruisers."[22]

Although these actions were certainly gratifying to him, they were only to be expected from a country that would benefit from the success of the American Revolution. In the same spirit he regarded the services of individual Frenchmen who wanted to enlist in the struggle as a natural by-product of their nation's interest in the outcome. In fact, he speculated that the Continental army had more French volunteers than it needed. As he suggested to John Page, "I would not advise that the French gentlemen should come here. We have so many of that country, and have been so much imposed upon, that the Congress begins to be sore on that head."[23] Because they did not bring their horses with them, these volunteers aggravated the problem of supplying American cavalrymen. Valid as these points were, they showed no appreciation for foreign aid at this juncture, and no realization of a need to propitiate the country from which the volunteers came.

Jefferson's reasons for declining the honor of serving with Benjamin Franklin and Silas Deane as a commissioner to the French court reflected family problems, notably his wife's illness, rather than a distaste for European travel. His concerns about his wife's health were genuine, and yet it is worth speculating about the importance he placed on a French connection in September 1776. Had he not been so confident of the inevitability of Europe's attachment to the American cause he might have paid more attention to the judgment of Richard Henry Lee, one of a committee of four appointed to draft letters of credence to the three newly elected commissioners. Lee was convinced that "the most eminent services that the greatest of her sons can do America will not more essentially serve her and honor themselves, than a successful negotiation with France. With this country, every thing depends upon it."[24] If Jefferson regretted his decision, it seemed that a missed opportunity to enjoy the company of French literati was the primary reason. A French alliance was of lesser magnitude as he prepared to return to Virginia.

Jefferson's worldview was formed in his youth, and it did not change substantially over his long career. Shaped by the Enlightenment, it was always broader than the Virginia Piedmont or Tidewater. By the time he entered the Continental Congress, his vision was firmly transatlantic. The youthful statesman saw Britain and France, and even Spain, as sources of a culture he shared. Of all the European nations, Britain was the most influential. But the spirit that moved him toward revolution made France as significant a font of the spirit of reason as the mother country. If he identified France as an ally in these years, it was largely because Britain had turned its back on its own great traditions of freedom. What the Virginian found in France was less a supporter of the concepts of the Enlightenment than a useful collaborator in the struggle for American independence.

## Notes

1. TJ to Joseph Priestley, January 27, 1800, in Andrew E. Lipscomb and Albert E. Bergh, eds., *The Writings of Thomas Jefferson*, 20 vols. (Washington, DC: Thomas Jefferson Memorial Association, 1903–04), 10:147 (hereafter cited as Lipscomb and Bergh).

2. TJ to Henry Lee, May 8, 1825, Lipscomb and Bergh, 16:118–19; Carl Becker, *The Declaration of Independence: A Study in the History of Political Ideas* (New York: Alfred A. Knopf, 1945), 27.

3. Herbert B. Adams, *The College of William and Mary* (Washington, DC: Government Printing Office, 1887), 36.

4. TJ, "Autobiography," Lipscomb and Bergh, 1:1.

5. TJ to John Harvie, January 14, 1760, in Julian P. Boyd, ed., *The Papers of Thomas Jefferson*, 24+ vols. (Princeton: Princeton University Press, 1950), 3 (hereafter cited as Boyd).

6. Gilbert Chinard, ed., *The Commonplace Book of Thomas Jefferson* (Baltimore: Johns Hopkins University Press, 1926), 269.

7. TJ, "Autobiography," Lipscomb and Bergh, 1:5.

8. Paul L. Ford, ed., *The Works of Thomas Jefferson*, 12 vols. (New York: G. P. Putnam's Sons, 1904–05), 1:474.

9. TJ, "Autobiography," Lipscomb and Bergh, 1:7.

10. Ibid., 9.

11. "Resolutions of the Freeholders of Albemarle County," Boyd, 1:118.

12. TJ, *A Summary View of the Rights of British America*, ibid., 121, 122.

13. Ibid., 122.

14. Ibid., 121.

15. Ibid.

16. Ibid., 134.

17. TJ to John Randolph, August 25, 1775, ibid., 241–42.

18. TJ to John Randolph, November 29, 1775, ibid., 269.

19. TJ to Henry Lee, May 8, 1825, Lipscomb and Bergh, 16:118.

20. John Dickinson's draft of the "Declaration of the Causes," Boyd, 1:211.

21. Worthington C. Ford et al., eds., *Journals of the Continental Congress, 1774–1789*, 24 vols. (Washington, DC: Government Printing Office, 1905), 3:392.

22. TJ to Edmund Pendleton, August 26, 1776, Boyd, 1:505.

23. TJ to John Page, July 30, 1776, ibid., 482.

24. Richard Henry Lee to TJ, September 27, 1776, ibid., 522.

# 2

## The Alliance in Wartime

### 1777–1783

### The Trials of Governor Jefferson

Jefferson was not wholly absorbed in local affairs during his service in the House of Delegates from October 1776 through June 1779. Not only was the war in the north constantly on his mind, but the "candid world" was also a continuing factor in his hopes for the success of the Revolution. He still entertained a wish (rather than a hope) in 1777 that the British court would "return to its senses in time to seize the little advantage which still remains within their reach from this quarter." British friends of America might still win over a government that had turned its back on its own heritage. If only Parliament would acknowledge the independence of the United States, a mutually beneficial commercial treaty, and "even a league of mutual offence and defence might be approved by our people."[1] Such were the sentiments he expressed to Benjamin Franklin in August 1777.

To John Adams he stated his concerns about the need for credits abroad, and not just from France and Holland. He had heard that the Grand Duke of Tuscany was "well disposed" to the American cause. With some ten million crowns "lying dead in his coffers," Jefferson thought it possible that perhaps one million pounds in specie might be available on loan.[2] And if it should be prudent to sound out the Grand Duke in advance of a solicitation, he knew a native of the duchy, in Virginia to cultivate vines and olives, who could serve as agent. Jefferson made this recommendation at a time when the fortunes of General Washington's army were on the decline and funds were

in short supply. His concerns for the new nation increased exponentially as the war came closer to his home state.

By 1779, when he was elected governor of Virginia, Europe had
assumed an even more important role, and foremost among the
potential European supporters was France. Any expectation that
Britain would come to its senses was long gone. As British forces
moved into Virginia, the alliance with France, consummated by
treaty in February 1778, became indispensable to the survival of
the new nation.[3] Jefferson or Adams could no longer consider an
alliance without obligations, or shop around Europe picking and
choosing at leisure among donors presumably eager to lend financial or military assistance. Instead, the American negotiators in Paris
discovered that they had to convince a reluctant French court to
enter the war as an ally. This did not take place until France was
assured that the Americans could defeat the British, as they had at
Saratoga in the fall of 1777, and until a Spanish fleet was ready to
join the French fleet in an effort against the common enemy. The
result was not a simple commercial alliance but an entangling connection that required a commitment on the part of the United States
to bind itself to France's foreign policy objectives. The young republic found itself obligated by the terms of the Treaty of Alliance
of 1778 to remain at war until its senior partner agreed to conclude
peace negotiations. France's subsequent treaty with Spain in 1779
meant that America would have to pay the price of Spain's align-
ment—namely, the retrocession of Gibraltar to the Spanish Crown.

Jefferson shared fully in the shift in mood about the role of
France in the war against the former mother country. As a member
of the Virginia legislature and as governor, he felt an increasing
dependence upon French aid and a corresponding bitterness toward Britain. The Treaty of Alliance placed France in the role of
*deus ex machina,* assuring a success that had seemed doubtful in
the dark days of 1777. "If there could be a doubt before as to the
event of the war," he informed an Italian correspondent in June
1778, "it is now totally removed by the imposition of France and
the generous alliance she has entered into with us."[4] It is unlikely
that he would have considered the terms "generous" in 1776 when
he envisioned all Europe offering material support for American
independence without reciprocal concessions on the part of the new
nation. And a year later Governor Jefferson would not be as san-
guine about the impact of French participation in the war.

Once the alliance was made, however, his hopes were
buoyed. The contrast between the French friend and the British en-

emy was stark. The horrors of war descended on Jefferson in 1780 after a British fleet landed one thousand men at Hampton who returned to their ships after committing "horrid depredations." When he urged General Horatio Gates to "send out a swift boat from some of the inlets of Carolina to notify the french Admiral that his enemies are in a net," he was pleading as much for revenge as for military aid.[5]

His two years as governor were marked by personal danger and frustration. A British invasion forced him to flee from Richmond to Charlottesville and then to Staunton, as the enemy moved deeper into his state. The low point of his unhappy term as governor was his hasty exit from his own home at Monticello, barely escaping capture by Colonel Banastre Tarleton's dragoons. But the necessity for flight, while no more reprehensible than the equally precipitate flight of his colleagues, invited charges of cowardice, or at least of incompetence, on the part of the head of the state. The scars from this encounter never fully healed, as his elliptical account of his experience as governor in the "Autobiography" suggests. He resigned in 1781 in favor of "a Military commander, being invested with the Civil power also, both might be wielded with more energy, promptitude and effect for the defence of the State."[6]

When Jefferson reflected in 1788 that "History will never relate the horrors committed by the British army in the *southern* states of America," he was referring as much to his own sufferings at the hands of the enemy as he was to those of his fellow citizens.[7] Hatred of British behavior, inspired by fear and humiliation, was a powerful factor in shaping his attitude toward Britain's continental enemy, and served as a stimulus to find reasons for Francophilia that had not been present before the war. An increased sense of dependence accounted for the bitter tone of reproach to those congressmen who would seek reconciliation with the mother country at the expense of France. He had heard that "their conduct on this head has been so dissatisfactory to the French minister that he thinks of returning to his own country, ostensibly for better health, but in truth through disgust. Such an event would be deplored here as the most dreadful calamity."[8]

French Minister Conrad Gérard did leave a few months later without the recriminations Jefferson had feared. With obvious relief the Virginia governor was pleased to welcome a French military force to his state "with the utmost cordiality and [shall] spare nothing which shall be within our power to aid and accommodate them in whatever situation they shall chuse."[9] He counted on the intervention of the French fleet to frustrate a British invasion of Virginia spearheaded by Benedict Arnold. As the number of British troops in Virginia increased, he looked upon France as a mighty host, the counterweight to British power.

Repeated failure did not shake Jefferson's faith. The Chevalier de la Luzerne, Gérard's successor, did aid Virginia to the extent of dispatching Admiral Destouches from Newport, Rhode Island, with a few vessels. Notwithstanding Destouches's brief visit to Virginia waters, British forces had little trouble in disembarking in Virginia to reinforce Arnold. Jefferson was disappointed, but expressed his appreciation for French efforts even when they were inadequate. He made a special point of telling Luzerne in his next application for aid just how greatly indebted the United States was to France. Although the governor would not have exhibited resentment as long as there was the prospect of future assistance, there was no cynicism in his sentiments. Besides seeing France as America's arsenal for the immediate needs of the war and a prop for his own lowered morale in the dark days of 1781, he anticipated in French aid an opportunity to secure for the United States economic as well as political independence from Britain.

## Jefferson and George Rogers Clark

Distracted though he was by the problems of a wartime governor, Jefferson was never diverted from a vision of an American West that France's evacuation of the Mississippi Valley offered to Virginians. Foreign Minister Vergennes was more perceptive than he realized when he shared his doubts about Jefferson's appointment as peace commissioner in 1781 in a letter to Luzerne. Admitting that he did not know Jefferson or John Jay, he did know that "they belong to two States that have exorbitant claims, and I fear that the general good strikes them less than the particular interest of their respective provinces."[10] On balance, the French foreign minister was mistaken about the damage that the Virginia governor might do to French interests, at least in this period, but he did touch upon problems Virginians could pose for France's Spanish ally.

Long before he became governor, Jefferson had been privy to a Virginia scheme to capture from Britain the country between the Appalachian Mountains and the Mississippi River. The objectives were the posts of Kaskaskia, Vincennes, and Detroit. Sir Henry Hamilton, Lieutenant Governor of Detroit, was leading Indian raids against Virginia frontiersmen. Under the direction of the youthful

George Rogers Clark, Virginians worked out a plan for taking possession of the entire territory west of the mountains and relieving frontiersmen of the Indian threat. Governor Patrick Henry in 1777 listened to Clark's persuasive argument that the handful of British troops could not withstand a bold thrust in the West. Henry was persuaded, and induced a group of influential leaders, including George Mason, George Wythe, and Jefferson, to support Clark.

Jefferson was kept fully abreast of the progress of Clark's expedition against Kaskaskia, Vincennes, and then Detroit in 1778. He recognized the important role French settlers in the West might play in removing the British from the Northwest Territory. Although Clark realized that these *habitants* were not an altogether reliable force on which the Virginians could depend, the young colonel assumed that with appropriate coaching they would make docile subjects, if not willing allies. After capturing Kaskaskia in July 1778 in a surprise attack, he moved on to Vincennes. With the help of a prominent French priest, he succeeded in convincing the residents to renounce their ties to Britain by showing them the treaty of alliance recently signed between the United States and France.

Clark's striking success in handling the French population had a heartening effect upon Virginians when the news reached Richmond. It seemed to guarantee the friendship and cooperation of the only civilian group of white men in the West. Not that their support should have occasioned particular surprise: these settlers, after all, had been under the British flag for less than fifteen years, since the 1763 Treaty of Paris ending the French and Indian War transferred the territory to Britain. Clark's presence revived the hostility to Britain that lay just below the surface. In displaying their willingness to fight alongside the Americans, *habitants* might also bring along their Indian allies. The Richmond inner circle envisioned immediate advantages for both the American cause and for Virginia's ambitions. As Jefferson prepared to succeed Henry as governor in 1779 he recognized that the French alliance, among its many benefits, might be the instrument to Americanize the West.

There is no doubt that the Clark expedition inspired dreams of a rising American empire. It also awakened hopes of undoing Generals Montgomery and Arnold's defeat in French Canada in 1775, when the countryside failed to rise up and join the American invaders. Such was Patrick Henry's hope when he told Clark how Admiral Comte d'Estaing had recently urged French Canadians to take up arms against Britain and link their cause to America's. Such reports, often nothing more than rumors, circulated before and during Jefferson's term of office, and they had a tonic effect on him at a time when bad news at home served to exaggerate good news abroad. The following rumor of French activity was sent to Jefferson by Nathaniel Randolph in 1780: "There is a report prevailing here that the French has laid Seige to Quebeck and carried it." They "will so effectually subdue British power in that whole Country, that the Savage will become allies to the French, if what is reported be true; there is nothing more likely, for there is no people we know, can do more than half as much with Indians as the French."[11]

The British conquests of New France and the trans-Appalachian West were not all that drew Jefferson's attention to Clark's expedition. Even before the war his vision had extended beyond the mountains to the Mississippi and Louisiana, then under Spanish rule. The governor revealed some of his hopes in a letter to Colonel Clark advocating the construction of a military post at the juncture of the Ohio and Mississippi rivers to protect the future New Orleans trade by controlling traffic on the Mississippi. The importance of such a strategically placed fort was obvious. John Todd, the county lieutenant in Kaskaskia, subsequently observed that the command of trade on both sides of the river "might Serve as a Check to any Incroachments from our present Allies the Spaniards whose growing power might justly put us upon our guard and whose fondness for engrossing Territory might otherwise urge them higher up the River on our side than we would wish."[12] The tone of this letter sounded, to be sure, a defensive rather than an offensive note, but it appeared that no distinction was made between defense against the British enemy, an immediate problem, and defense against a cobelligerent, a future problem. Jefferson shared with Todd ambitions that would eventually pit the United States against Spain. It is not unreasonable to speculate that the "incroachments" Todd referred to represented a projection of American future territorial expansion.

Jefferson's sights in 1780, however, were set more on surviving the war with Britain than on pursuing conflict with Spain. Continuing dependence upon France made it unlikely that the beleaguered Virginia governor would challenge France's ally, Spain, by threatening its hold on Louisiana. Even if prospects for the termination of the war with Britain had been brighter, the new nation would still need French help to break Britain's economic control of American trade. Clark's expedition opened the way for trade with France via the Mississippi River and New Orleans, enabling the export of tobacco to France in return for articles needed by the Continental Army. Such an arrangement required the cooperation of Spain, which would have been difficult to secure if the American westward advance endangered its interests. Jefferson's choice of language in addressing the Spanish governor of Louisiana suggested appeasement, not confrontation. When he learned of Spain's entry into the war on France's side in 1779, the Virginia governor expressed his hope that "the weight of your powerful and wealthy Empire" would hasten victory over the common enemy. He added: "Our Vicinity to the State over which you immediately preside; the direct channel of Commerce by the River Mississippi, the nature of those Commodities with which we can reciprocally furnish each other, point out the advantages which may result from a close Connection, and correspondence, for which on our part the best Foundations are laid by a grateful Sense of the Favors we have received at your Hands."[13]

As the war progressed, Jefferson's projection of Europe in the future of the United States grew exponentially more sophisticated. There was less of the Virginian and more of the American in the waning months of his tenure as governor. France was as indispensable to the nation's survival and prosperity after the war as it was in waging war on the side of the United States. But while his faith in an expanding America would conflict eventually with the interests of the French ally and the Spanish neighbor, he was discreet enough to avoid overt challenges while the support of both countries was needed to complete the process of independence. France could be of service in clinching America's control of the West, but this was a service that was not to be solicited in 1781.

The failure of Clark's final Detroit campaign did not weaken Jefferson's loyalty to the man who had opened his eyes to the many opportunities in Western expansion. He importuned Clark in 1782 to gather specimens of archaeological and anthropological interest and, not incidentally, as much information as he could about the territory between the Mississippi and "the South sea." Still smarting from criticism for his conduct as wartime governor, he reminded Clark to expect no appreciation from his country for the services he might render from his explorations. Still, the former governor urged him to go ahead. Despite his expression of disillusionment with politics, a sentiment that was to crop up periodically during difficult moments of his long career in public service, Jefferson concluded his letter by urging Clark to continue doing "good to your country and honour to yourself."[14]

This advice he would apply to himself, particularly when it involved the West. After receiving some geological specimens from Clark, he disclosed that a major reason for the need to stake out western territories for the United States was not French suspicion or Spanish hostility, but the knowledge that the former mother country, having recently concluded a peace treaty with the United States, was raising money to form a western expedition: "They pretend it is only to promote knolege. I am afraid they have thoughts of colonizing into that quarter."[15] Although Jefferson considered it unlikely that the United States would be wise enough to raise the money needed for its own expedition, he hoped that Clark would lead such a venture if the unexpected happened.

## The Continental Congress

The formal end of the war did not alter the fears and hopes that Jefferson had experienced during the struggle for independence. He still feared Britain, and he still had hopes of support for the new nation from France. The memories of British behavior in the war, even when they were not personal, had lasting results. In 1779, when Clark brought back Lieutenant Governor Henry Hamilton, the scourge of western settlers, in chains, Jefferson uncharacteristically kept him in that condition. Under normal circumstances, Hamilton should have been paroled and eventually exchanged, since Clark had made a capitulation agreement with the Detroit governor in the course of his capture. It required General Washington's intervention and the threat of British retaliation to make the Virginia governor relent and permit Hamilton to leave for New York under parole. Had Jefferson known how General Cornwallis would ravage his properties two years later, he might have been even harsher in his treatment of Hamilton.

Following his term as governor, Jefferson's return to private life was brief. Asked once again in 1781 to join the peace commission in Paris, he demurred once more in order to attend his wife during her terminal illness and to defend his reputation as governor. After her death in the following year, the Congress of the Confederation renewed its offer. He accepted, but by the time he was ready to embark for France the provisional treaty had been signed, making his presence unnecessary. Jefferson went back to Congress as head of the Virginia delegation, where he played a key role as a member of the committee in 1783 that wrote the report seeking immediate ratification of the Treaty of Paris.

During his service in the Confederation's Congress in 1783 and 1784, Jefferson displayed considerable sophistication about the new nation's relations with friends and enemies. While his emotions concerning Britain and France were highly charged, they did not prevent him from assessing the American role in the balance of power with considerable objectivity. It might have followed from his growing Francophilia that he would have joined those who denounced John Jay and John Adams for signing conditional and preliminary articles of peace in 1782 without a final consultation with Vergennes, thereby violating Congress's injunction that the envoys accept the French foreign minister's leadership in peace negotiations. James Madison was among those who condemned those Congressmen who voiced their suspicions of France's good faith, even though he would not go so far as to issue a specific rebuke to the commissioners for disobeying the instructions of Congress. Jefferson was remarkably silent during the debate over the articles of peace. He said nothing to deplore the behavior of the plenipotentiaries toward France or even to question Madison's implicit criticism of the anti-French sentiments of the American commissioners. The completion of peace arrangements was too important to allow divisions to fester in Congress that might jeopardize the objective. He shared the concern of the majority of Congressmen that the British government might void the treaty, signed on September 3, 1783, if it was not approved by March 3, 1784, when the exchange of ratifications was to take place in Paris.

Jefferson nevertheless advised against rushing pell-mell into ratifying the treaty when only seven states were represented in Congress (the Articles of Confederation called for nine states to approve a treaty). His caution about ratification, no less than his acceptance of the American commissioners' actions, signified either confidence in Britain's good faith in respecting terms of the treaty or suspicion of France's motives in wanting to control the commissioners. With respect to Britain he worried that a treaty ratified by only seven of the thirteen states in violation of the Confederation's own constitution would be an invitation for Britain to interpret the treaty to its own advantage, or even to repudiate it if war in Europe was renewed. Fortunately, two of the missing states took their seats in January 1784, making unnecessary the compromise Jefferson had worked out whereby the commissioners would request a three-month delay before the exchange of ratifications.

Jefferson's view of France was more complicated. It was dictated as always by his hopes of using that nation to further

American interests—and American interests at this moment demanded immediate peace. Conceivably, had Vergennes objected more vigorously to essentially separate Anglo-Ameican negotiations, Jefferson's reaction might have been different; but Vergennes accepted Franklin's lame explanation of American behavior without excessive strain on the bonds between the two allies. While Jefferson never forgot how vital a factor the French were in winning American independence and how important they would be in maintaining it, he did not overlook the position of the United States in the larger world. He sensed that France's European diplomacy might entangle the United States in an unwanted transatlantic war before the peace negotiations were completed. If Vergennes remained in power, that subtle statesman might drag the United States into a conflict over Turkey. The consequences of such a situation might include a stiffening of British peace terms on their assumption that a war on the continent would immobilize America's powerful ally. If only for this reason, rather than for any special animus toward Vergennes, he advocated ratification of the peace with Great Britain as rapidly as possible. "Happy for us that we have got into port just as this storm is rising,"[16] or so Jefferson hoped in December 1783.

Notwithstanding France's distractions in Europe, Jefferson tried to keep the United States in a position to utilize French support to safeguard the new nation from British designs upon its independence. But he recognized that this support could be secured only if the United States was strong enough to fulfill its contractual obligations, such as repaying its debts to French creditors. As a member of the Confederation's Congress in 1783 and 1784 the Virginia leader urged a strengthening of the central government. He knew that French sympathy would evaporate rapidly unless debts contracted during the war were paid. This problem was still unsolved when he left for Paris, and was not to be solved under the aegis of the Confederation. That body had only the funds the individual states would supply, and there was no agency for forcing states to fulfill their obligations. He noted that Virginia, Maryland, and Pennsylvania had granted Congress certain powers enabling it to counteract British commercial discrimination. But those powers "were all different," he complained. If the states would give Congress a uniform mandate, it could be in a position "to make it the interest of every nation to enter into equal treaties with us."[17] In particular, Congress should be empowered to collect revenue from the states by taxation (rather than by requisition) and to regulate commerce between the states and foreign nations. If the Confederation failed to manage these problems, jealousy among the states would allow Britain to assert its sovereignty once again. It seems that three and one-half years before a constitutional convention met to deal with these very matters, Jefferson had anticipated the indispensability of an empowered central government. Influenced by events in France, he initially had doubts in 1787 about such a transfer of power. It took all of Madison's persuasive abilities to win his friend back to the position he had held in 1784.

The period between the end of Jefferson's service as governor of Virginia and his departure for France as minister plenipotentiary to the Court of Versailles has often been identified as a hiatus in his life, a difficult time when he had to defend his record as governor and to witness the sufferings of his terminally ill wife. It was a difficult but not a barren time. Before he entered the Confederation Congress he had written the lengthy and revealing *Notes on Virginia* in response to the request of François de Marbois, the secretary of the French legation in Philadelphia, for information about the state. In this lengthy memoir, Jefferson did much more than provide a guidebook to geography and natural history. It gave him an opportunity to speak for America as well as for Virginia in challenging European naturalists such as the Comte de Buffon, who expounded the theory of animal, and even human, degeneracy in the New World. Jefferson's rebuttal took the form of citing Benjamin Franklin and astronomer David Rittenhouse as the American Newtons. His treatise on Virginia became a vehicle for the expression of his national pride.

The *Notes* was also the occasion for Jefferson to glorify the yeoman farmer of rural America in contrast to the city dweller. Few of his perorations are more quoted than his paean to "those who labor in the earth." They were "the chosen people of God if ever He had a chosen people, whose breasts He has made His peculiar deposit for substantial and genuine virtue." In an ideal world the "husbandman" deserved to be idealized for his self-reliance, his diligence, and his civic pride. Jefferson would have the workshops remain in Europe where "lands are either cultivated, or locked up against the cultivator." Such was not the case in Virginia, and by extension anywhere in America, where land was abundant. The price the Europeans paid for their industrial society was subservience of the lower class to elite landowners and venality of all the classes. "The mobs of great cities," he claimed, "add just so much to the support of pure government, as sores do to the strength of the human body."[18] In fact, the degeneracy that European scientists had wrongly attributed to animal and human life in America applied more accurately to the unhappy lives of residents of urban centers.

The glorification of the virtuous American farmer occupied only a small part of the *Notes on Virginia*. The intent of this lengthy reflection was to distinguish America from Europe, and to this end Jefferson's ode to the "husbandman" complemented his appreciation of the virtuous Indian. While his intention was to describe Virginia, it was the nation that was essentially his subject. When he mentioned great men, they were the Pennsylvanians Franklin and Rittenhouse as well as the Virginian Washington. The Mississippi and Missouri rivers were described as well as the James and the Nansemond rivers. The West was American, not simply an extension of Virginia. This sense of nation manifested itself during his brief but impressive service in the Congress of Confederation in 1784. His draft of an ordinance of government for the Northwest Territory provided for the cession of claims of his own state to lands west of the Appalachians as well as those of Massachusetts or Connecticut. His specific plan failed, but its principle of equality under the Union was the basis for the successful Northwest Ordinance of 1787.

Jefferson's national pride was particularly evident in his attitude toward the instructions that he took to Europe in 1784. Congress decided once again to offer him an opportunity to represent the United States in Paris, to join John Adams and Benjamin Franklin in attempting to negotiate trade agreements with European partners. He was in full accord with the policy, as he wrote in the *Notes*, "to throw open the doors of commerce, and to knock off all its shackles, giving perfect freedom to all persons for the vent of whatever they may chuse to bring into our ports, and asking the same in theirs."[19] Given the low state of the American economy in 1784, the need to open new markets was more imperative than ever. Hard money was scarce, imports exceeded exports, New England's shipbuilding and whaling industries had not recovered from the war, and Virginia's tobacco economy was still under the control of British merchants. The economic troubles once again were blamed on the former mother country, which seemed intent on exploiting the weakness of the Confederation. The exclusion of American carriers from the British West Indies, decreed by an Order in Council in 1783, symbolized Britain's hostility. No matter how sincere was Jefferson's preference for an autarchic society anchored in self-sufficient agriculture and isolated from the corruption of the Old World, he knew this was an ideal only. It was not the real world, nor was it the world that his own state ever inhabited. Virginia's prosperity as well as America's prosperity in general depended upon finding markets for their products, whether it was tobacco from Virginia or whale oil from New England.

The answer lay in trade with the customers beyond British reach. Free trade with open markets was the objective; and if this was impossible, then Jefferson would and did support retaliatory measures against those nations, notably Great Britain, that discriminated against American commerce, even if it meant instituting mercantilist navigation laws. Before departing for France, Jefferson helped draft the instructions he would carry out as minister plenipotentiary. Each of the two nations would impose duties that would be no greater than those imposed on any other nation. The ships of each nation would carry goods into the other's ports in their own bottoms. This was not quite free trade in the purest form, but it did advance the principle of reciprocity and by implication accorded an equal status to the United States. Sixteen European powers, along with the Barbary states, were Congress's target for commercial treaties. Each successful treaty of amity and commerce would be another step toward freedom from British economic domination.

Two parts of the instructions to the commissioners deserve special attention. The first was the inclusion of Great Britain as one of the sixteen nations with which Congress wanted treaties of amity and commerce. Whether a positive response was expected is another matter. Despite all the rebuffs from Britain in the past, Jefferson still entertained some hope that right-minded British liberals such as the Earl of Shelburne, an influential Cabinet minister, would see the light. The second noteworthy element was a promise to the Comte de Vergennes "that he may be assured it will be our constant care to place no people on more advantageous ground than the Subjects of his Majesty."[20] These instructions were written in part by Jefferson himself, and he took care to emphasize the priority that the United States placed in the treaty of amity and commerce with France in 1778. That country was more important than all the others combined in maintaining the new nation's independence and assuring it economic prosperity.

## Deepening the French Connection

Between the years 1776 and 1784, Jefferson had come to appreciate that a community of interests important enough to affect many of his ideas about domestic as well as foreign affairs existed between the United States and France. His attachment to that country rested for the most part on the practical advantages that close relations with France had given to the United States. Additionally, an important component of his attitude was informed by emotional factors—namely, gratitude for French support and anger at British behavior during the Revolution. While the intensity of his emotions may have blurred his vision of the limits of France's service to the new republic, it did serve to open a receptivity to French culture as opposed to the generalized culture of the Enlightenment, as had not been the case in his formative years.

War provided the Virginia statesman with opportunities to meet Europeans who normally would never have visited America—men conveying to him the way of life of French aristocrats. Soldiers such as General Lafayette, diplomats such as the Chevalier d'Anmours, and philosophers such as the Marquis de Chastellux all showed him a style of living that Jefferson had known only from his books. He adapted happily to many customs ordinarily considered uncongenial to Anglo-Saxons and often pejoratively advertised as French, such as an appreciation of good food and wine, a taste for abstract philosophy, and a love of art and music. The Virginia planter was already predisposed to these pursuits; intimacy with French friends developed them further. His culinary tastes offended some Virginians such as Patrick Henry, who accused Jefferson of having "abjured his native victuals" in favor of French cuisine.[21]

Frenchmen were welcome everywhere in America after the alliance was signed, for the entry of France into the war on America's side seemed to be the logical culmination of that tentative friendship that had its beginnings in 1763. The colleges quickly followed the salons in showing their appreciation of the French language. One of Jefferson's proudest boasts as governor was the introduction of French into the curriculum of his alma mater, the College of William and Mary. The importance he attached to this action may be seen in the prominence he gave it in his "Autobiography." While excluding most of the troubled events of his administration in those years, he emphasized that he had changed the organization of that institution by abolishing the two professorships of Divinity and

Oriental Languages and establishing in their place a professorship of Modern Languages.

It is not surprising in these circumstances that the Marquis de Chastellux, traveling from New England to the South during the war, found so many new Francophiles, like the one so enthusiastic for all French fashions that he wanted only the termination of "this little revolution" to effect a still greater one in the manners of the country.[22] Such adulation inspired a note of condescension, if not contempt, in this distinguished visitor. The beauty of Jefferson's Monticello, on the other hand, filled Chastellux with wonder and admiration for the artistic sensibility of at least one American.

Jefferson and Chastellux, like Jefferson and almost every Frenchman he met at this time, took delight in each other. The French found in him their American counterpart but with virtues they lacked. He was a man of Continental culture who retained the innocence of the "noble savage." Jefferson's tribute to Chastellux might be applied to all his French friends: "No circumstance of a private nature could induce me to hasten over the several obstacles to my departure more unremittingly than the hope of having Chevalr. de Chattlux as a companion in my voiage. A previous acquaintance with his worth and abilities had impressed me with an affection for him which under the then prospect of never seeing him again was imprudent."[23]

These warm sentiments bestowed on a man whom he had known for only a very short time were distributed in equal abundance to other French acquaintances. The most striking example was the relationship between Jefferson and Lafayette begun in the midst of the British invasion of Virginia. Despite the constant potential for friction brought on by the difficult military situation, they treated each other with courtesy and consideration. Not once did the dashing young general allude to France's great service to the American cause, and not once did he criticize the beleaguered governor's management of the war in Virginia. Instead, he displayed his eagerness to meet the author of the Declaration of Independence and deplored the inability of the French fleet to give Virginia more support in 1781. Jefferson was more than willing to meet Lafayette halfway. He was ashamed of the poor impression that his state must have made upon this representative of its powerful patron and hence all the more grateful for whatever aid France chose to give to the United States. Out of these brief encounters came a lifelong friendship.

The increasing attraction of France and Frenchmen was a major factor in Jefferson's pleasure over his new assignment as minister plenipotentiary to the Court of Versailles. It was not that his rejection of earlier invitations signified indifference to France; the obstacles to his accepting were genuine enough. It was simply that his ardor had increased over the years. It would not have been surprising if Minister Jefferson had blossomed into an indiscriminate Francophile over the next few years. That he did not was in good measure because the allures of French culture were counterbalanced by his continual awareness of shortcomings in the government's dealings with the United States. To use the image he invoked in 1786 in his correspondence with his intimate friend Maria Cosway, the Heart would always incline him toward France, but the Head would see to it that the inclination would serve the interests of his own country.

## Notes

1. TJ to Benjamin Franklin, August 13, 1777, in Julian P. Boyd, ed., *The Papers of Thomas Jefferson*, 24+ vols. (Princeton: Princeton University Press, 1950), 2:26–27 (hereafter cited as Boyd).

2. TJ to John Adams, August 21, 1777, ibid., 27–28.

3. Two treaties were signed in Paris on February 6, 1778: 1) a treaty of amity and commerce governing economic relations between France and the United States; and 2) a treaty of alliance between the two countries in the event of war between Britain and France.

4. TJ to Giovanni Fabbrioni, June 8, 1778, Boyd, 2:195.

5. TJ to Horatio Gates, October 28, 1780, ibid., 4:78.

6. TJ, "Autobiography," in Andrew A. Lipscomb and Albert E. Bergh, eds., *The Writings of Thomas Jefferson*, 20 vols. (Washington, DC: Thomas Jefferson Memorial Association, 1903–04), 1 (hereafter cited as Lipscomb and Bergh).

7. TJ to William Gordon, July 16, 1788, Boyd, 13:364.

8. TJ to William Fleming, June 8, 1779, ibid., 2:288.

9. TJ to Chevalier D'Anmours, November 10, 1779, ibid., 3:173.

10. Charles Gravier, Comte de Vergennes to Chevalier de Luzerne, September 7, 1781, in Mary Giunta and J. Dane Hartgrove, eds., *The Emerging Nation: A Documentary History of the Foreign Relations of the United States under the Articles of Confederation, 1780–1789*, 3 vols. (Washington, DC: National Historical Publications and Records Commission, 1996), 1:231.

11. Nathaniel Randolph to TJ, November 22, 1780, Boyd, 4:148.

12. John Todd to TJ, June 2, 1780, ibid., 3:416.

13. TJ to Bernardo de Gálvez, November 8, 1779, ibid., 4:167–68.

14. TJ to George Rogers Clark, November 26, 1782, ibid., 6:204–5.

15. TJ to George Rogers Clark, December 4, 1783, ibid., 371.

16. TJ to Benjamin Harrison, December 17, 1783, ibid., 389.

17. TJ to Benjamin Harrison, April 30, 1784, ibid., 7:139.

18. TJ, *Notes on Virginia*, Lipscomb and Bergh, 2:229–30.

19. Ibid., 240.

20. "Instructions to the Commissioners for Negotiating Treaties of Amity and Commerce, Enclosure III," Boyd, 7:267, 269.

21. Quoted in Henry S. Randall, *The Life of Thomas Jefferson*, 3 vols. (New York: Derby and Jackson, 1858), 3:508.

22. François Jean, Marquis de Chastellux, *Travels in North-America, in the Years 1780, 1781, and 1782*, trans. Howard C. Rice, Jr., 2 vols. (Chapel Hill: University of North Carolina Press, 1963), 1:135.

23. TJ to Madison, November 26, 1782, Boyd, 6:207.

# 3

## The European Years

### 1784–1789

Jefferson had every reason to look forward with pleasure to his often postponed visit to France when he
embarked from Boston in July 1784. All the omens seemed
favorable; he would renew friendships with Frenchmen
he had met in Virginia and find many more kindred spir-
its among influential sympathizers in Paris; he could expect a warm welcome from old colleagues and fellow
commissioners Franklin and Adams; and, above all, he
anticipated early favorable results in securing treaties of
amity and commerce with all the countries identified in
Congressional instructions. On the assumption that the
French government would be an active partisan for the
American cause, he foresaw Britain ultimately reopening
its West Indian ports to American commerce.

These expectations were too high. They reflected a
euphoria that could not last, and a seeming naiveté about
the ways of Europe. Two months before Jefferson left for
France, Minister Luzerne in Philadelphia dispatched to
Vergennes a shrewd assessment of Jefferson that was not
much wide of the mark, at least not in 1784. Luzerne noted
that he had won a reputation "of an enlightened man of
integrity and of an excellent Citizen, but one incapable
of holding the tiller in stormy weather." He further noted
that Jefferson "loves his country a great deal, but he is
too philosophical and too peaceful to have hatred or affection for any other nation, unless the United States are
interested therein." The French minister appreciated
Jefferson's "principle that it is important for the happiness and the prosperity of the 13 States to keep themselves as far from England as the condition of peace will

allow, that it is appropriate for them . . . to attach themselves to France." There was a tone of condescension in the assertion that "Mr. Jefferson does not join to his theoretical knowledge much experience and practice of affairs."[1]

## The London Mission: A Hopeless Cause

Luzerne's judgment about Jefferson's naiveté might have been accepted at face value had it been known by Patrick Henry, who considered Jefferson to have been a captive of Francophilia by the end of the decade, or by Federalist leaders, including John Adams, a decade later. But this was not Adams's view in 1784, or at any time when both men were working together over the next few years in Paris, London, or The Hague. And for good reason. Adams communicated his doubts to Jefferson about winning over Britain to an equitable relationship with the United States, and both men knew the reason why. Britain's aim was to divide the American states, to continue to enjoy the fruits of American trade without reciprocity. This knowledge did not prevent either statesman from using whatever influence he had with British friends of America to mitigate the damage inflicted by the Orders in Council of 1783.

In David Hartley, the British ambassador in Paris and signatory of the treaty with the United States, the Americans seemed to have had an ally. There was no doubt about his interest in restoring an Anglo-American relationship at the expense of the Franco-American alliance. Nor was there any doubt that the British ministry subverted Hartley's intentions by the Order in Council cutting off American reentry into the commerce of the British West Indies. While praising Hartley along with the Marquis of Lansdowne and Dr. Richard Price as part of "a very small circle" of supporters, Jefferson recognized that they "cannot introduce a connection with us as a topic of declamation. In short the madness is much more universal now than it was during the war."[2]

Jefferson would have been mistaken had he dismissed the series of British actions against the United States, from refusal to evacuate the Northwest posts to refusal to allow American trade with Britain's colonial ports, as a sign of "madness." There was method in this madness, and the American ministers abroad came to understand it. As long as there was no central authority to force compliance, the British would continue their practices. This was not a principle that Jefferson discovered in Europe. Upon receiving his appointment on May 7, 1784, to join Adams and Franklin in

Paris as commissioner on foreign commercial negotiation, he wrote Madison that he intended to "pursue there the line I have pursued here"—namely, increasing the powers of the Confederation. Article 3 of the instructions to the commissioners, drafted by Jefferson himself, stipulated that "these U.S. be considered in all such treaties and in every case arising under them as one nation upon the principles of the foederal Constitution."[3] It did not take Jefferson long to appreciate that "with England nothing will produce a treaty but an enforcement of the resolutions of Congress proposing that there should be no trade where there is no treaty."[4]

Although the states failed to grant the Confederation the authority to threaten Britain with a credible navigation law, Jefferson did not give up all hope of winning some concessions. As he wrote General Washington in December 1784, "the disposition of Gr. Britain does not seem very favourable to us. All information from thence represents the people and still more the merchants as extremely hostile." He suggested that he might have to go to the Court of St. James's personally to "bring their intentions to a decisive issue."[5] Adams's dour personality usually made him more suspicious of British behavior than his Virginia colleague. Both men were convinced that the British were behind rumors of an impending breakup of the United States, and that they were confident of profiting indefinitely from the lack of unity among the American states. Still, neither man had given up on the possibilities of influencing the British. If only they could be convinced that Americans "were capable of foregoing commerce with them," the British would be more likely to consent to an equal commerce. There was a world outside Britain "to supply us with gew-gaws, and all the world to buy our tobacco."[6] Adams for his part found hope in the British foreign minister's proposing that a consul general be sent to the United States. He speculated that this appointment "is a still Stronger Indication of a real Wish in the Ministry, that this Measure be pursued, and of a Secret Consciousness that they shall be obliged to treat."[7]

Conceivably, the elevation of both diplomats in the winter and spring of 1785—Jefferson as Franklin's successor as minister plenipotentiary to France, and Adams as minister plenipotentiary to England—may have contributed to a delusory optimism. If so, it did not last long. It was quickly dispelled by personal experience in London on the part of both men. Adams's congenital suspiciousness was deepened by the snubs he encountered in his dealing with the Foreign Ministry. His judgment, rendered before news arrived of his appointment as minister, was more prescient than he could have anticipated when he wrote Jay that "whoever goes will neither find it a lucrative or a pleasant Employment, nor will he be envied by me. I know that for Years if he does his Duty, he will find no personal Pleasure or Advantage."[8] He found the British, with only a few exceptions, pleased with the control they exercised economically over the new nation and without interest in opening up negotiations for a new commercial treaty. Throughout the 1780s, American exports to Britain were between one-half and one-third the value of imports from the former mother country.

Jefferson's hostility carried more emotional baggage. Scars from his encounters with the British while governor of Virginia made him easily susceptible to Anglophobia, even as his exposure to Frenchmen inclined him toward Francophilia. Therefore, his six-week visit to England in March 1786 only confirmed his prejudices about many things English, not the least of which was its cuisine. Even before his visit, he had fancied in a lighthearted letter to Abigail Adams that "it must be the quantity of animal food eaten by the English which renders their character insusceptible of civilization. I suspect it is in their kitchens and not in their churches that their reformation must be worked, and that Missionaries of that description from hence would avail more than those who should endeavor to tame them by precepts of religion or philosophy."[9] Once he arrived in London the matter grew more serious. He found himself on one occasion eating in a chophouse of the kind described by James Boswell a few years earlier, whose fare no self-respecting Frenchman or Francophile could stomach with equanimity. In fact, one of the chophouses mentioned by Boswell, Dolly's on Paternoster Row, was the subject of an uncharacteristic bit of Jeffersonian doggerel. The apparently extemporaneous verse opened with: "One among our many follies / Was calling in for steaks at Dolly's."[10]

His six weeks offered few opportunities for levity. The atmosphere was as depressing as the weather. There were few friends, outside the small circle of philosophers, such as Dr. Price, to pierce the hostility that he and Adams perceived everywhere in London. He expressed his aversion to most everything he found in Britain (its gardens excepted), most particularly to London's architecture ("in the most wretched stile I ever saw") and in the extravagance of the privileged classes ("a more baneful evil than toryism was during the war").[11] While he acknowledged the superiority of British governance over that of France, this appreciation was more likely a tribute to the British legacy to America of self-government than a reflection of the political situation he found in London in 1786, where a selfish oligarchy supported by an equally selfish manufacturing class ruled the nation. He left England convinced that the "nation hates us, their ministers hate us, and their king more than all other men."[12] Jefferson no more forgave the disrespect he encountered from the king in London than he forgot the embarrassing flight from his home during the war. His brief stay in Britain deepened his prejudices.

His bruised feelings notwithstanding, Jefferson did not confine his criticisms to British behavior. He was well aware of the inability of the Confederation to honor the obligations incurred under the Treaty of Paris in 1783, and he blamed its weakness for nullifying any progress the American commissioners might have made with the Foreign Ministry. He was convinced that some arrangement might have been agreed upon with British merchants seeking payment on debts dating back to the colonial years. As a Virginia debtor, he accepted these claims and believed that a compromise might have succeeded over the waiving of interest accumulated in the war years.

Nothing came of these overtures. But had the Confederation compelled the states to respect their obligations, the American position would have been stronger. As he plaintively presented the case to Monroe after his return to Paris: "Since it is left for each nation to pursue their own measures in the execution of the late treaty, may not Congress recommend a mode of executing that article respecting the debts, and send it to each state to be passed into law? . . . these debts must be paid, or our character stained with infamy among all nations and to all times."[13] Jefferson's distress over the Confederation's shortcomings matched the shrill tone of his accusations against Britain. There was still another dimension to his despair. Even as he sought in London and elsewhere opportunities to pry open the colonial ports of European powers, he wondered if entry into the West Indies was worth the vassalage to Great Britain that American dependence on British manufactures encouraged.

Relations with Great Britain was not the only failure to confront Jefferson and Adams. The primary reason for the visit to London was news from Adams that a minister from Portugal was in London with powers to enter into a treaty on behalf of his state. Moreover, there were possibilities of some arrangement with the Barbary states of Tripoli and Tunis if Jefferson and Adams jointly exercised their commission to take up negotiations. Adams estimated that a Portuguese treaty could be brought to a conclusion in three weeks. While a treaty was indeed signed by the Americans, the Chevalier de Pinto lacked the authority to add his signature to the document. The treaty failed of ratification in Lisbon, possibly because of Portuguese opposition to the importation of American flour, as Jefferson noted in his "Autobiography." More likely, Portugal's Cabinet politics were responsible for its unwillingness to ratify. While Jefferson was dissatisfied with the failure of the treaty to include admission of American trade to Portuguese possessions, successful conclusion of the negotiations at least would have been evidence of the acceptance of the United States into the international community of nations.

## Dealing with the Barbary States

The possibility of coming to an arrangement with at least some of the Barbary states was among the reasons that brought Jefferson to London in the spring of 1786. The prospect of a reasonable settlement was not dim in that year. Tripoli's ambassador to Britain did make recommendations, but they involved costly payments to keep its corsairs from seizing American ships and imprisoning American sailors. The relationship with the Barbary states, particularly Algiers, was the source of anguish and frustration for Jefferson that was far greater than any he felt in negotiations with any other country. Britain's hostility was clear and often personal, but it was not criminal in the way that Jefferson and Adams regarded the pirate nations of the Maghreb to be. The city-states of Algiers, Tunis, Morocco, and Tripoli in the eighteenth century were nominally part of the Ottoman Empire, but in reality were self-governing principalities. They prospered through piracy and kidnapping, extracting ransom from the victims' governments and demanding tribute that ranged from naval stores to jewels. To enjoy peace with these marauders of the Mediterranean required continual payments at a price determined by the ruling despots.

Outrageous as this behavior was, the willingness of the major European powers to pay the extortioners the price required to ensure safe passage as well as trading privileges was equally scandalous. Even more distressing was the encouragement Britain and France gave to the pirate states as they preyed on weaker maritime rivals who could not afford to pay the bribes or ransoms demanded when their ships and sailors were captured. Rather than use their military and naval strength to punish the pirates, the leading European nations maintained consulates in the Barbary states and profited from the plight of the smaller nations. For example, Sweden and Tuscany were expected to surrender trade in the Mediterranean to the powers that could afford to pay.

Abandonment of the Mediterranean trade was an option that Jefferson examined and quickly rejected. Yet such a course would have been consistent with his elevation of agrarian life over that of the merchant and manufacturer. Problems with the Barbary states might have set the stage for just such a withdrawal. Only two days after dispatching instructions to Captain John Lamb, en route to Algiers to negotiate the emancipation of American crews, Jefferson wrote to a young Dutch friend about "the expediency of encouraging our states to be commercial. Were I to indulge my own theory, I should wish them to practice neither commerce nor navigation, but to stand with respect to Europe precisely on the footing of China. We should thus avoid wars, and all our citizens would be husbandmen." This widely quoted letter has been cited as evidence of Jefferson's deeply held feelings about isolationism and agrarianism. But in the same letter he made it clear that "this is theory only, and a theory which the servants of America are not at liberty to follow. Our people have a decided taste for navigation and commerce. They take this from their mother country, and their servants are duty bound to calculate all their measures on this datum."[14]

There is no doubt that Jefferson fulfilled this obligation, and he seemed to fulfill it with very few reservations. Nowhere did his drive for aggressive action to open the ports of the world to American commerce manifest itself more vigorously than in his attitude toward the Barbary powers. As a diplomat his method should have been to negotiate. But, from the beginning of his service in France, he doubted the efficacy of diplomacy. What he saw was the escalating cost of payments needed to satisfy the Barbary leaders, and he judged that they would be exorbitant. It would be less expensive and more satisfying to employ force: "Would it not be better to offer them an equal treaty. If they refuse, why not go to war with them? . . . We ought to begin a naval power, if we mean to carry our own commerce. Can we begin it on a more honorable occasion or with a weaker foe? I am of opinion that [John] Paul Jones with half a dozen frigates would totally destroy their commerce: not by attempting bombardments as the Mediterranean states do wherein they act against the whole Barbary force brought to a point, but by constant cruising and cutting them to peices by peicemeal."[15] Here is the civilian statesman not only urging war but also offering advice as a naval strategist on the correct way of winning such a war.

This bellicosity was not an aberration. Securing peace through force rather than through purchase was a Jeffersonian theme that periodically surfaced over the years. His actions as president twenty years later were just the climax of a position he had taken as minister to France. The question of Algiers in particular was one of the few over which he differed with his colleague in London during this period. Adams understood Jefferson's feelings and did not reject the use of force on principle. Their experience in London with the ambassador of Tripoli confirmed their pessimism about the chances of an accommodation with the Barbary states. The ambassador suggested some 30,000 guineas for peace with Tripoli and an equal amount for Tunis. When Jefferson considered the additional demands of Algiers for the release of the crewmen being held hostage, he recognized that the paltry sum of $80,000 authorized by Congress in the spring of 1785 would only be "as a drop to the bucket."[16] Moreover, Captain Lamb, the agent Congress had sent to Algiers with the $80,000, had failed in his mission, partly through his own mishandling of negotiations, but mostly because the amount of the ransom was far more than Lamb could offer.

Adams reluctantly decided in July 1786, following Jefferson's return to Paris, to pay the monies as quickly as possible. No help would come from any European power, and the longer the delay, the higher the price would be. Jefferson disagreed. His calculations suggested that war would be a cheaper way to secure peace than trying to buy it. Besides, he supposed that Naples and Portugal would join the United States in standing up to the pirates, limiting the cost of mounting an operation. Adams was attracted to Jefferson's position but judged it unrealistic. The trouble was with Congress, which would not bear the cost of such an enterprise. As for building a navy, Adams was in full agreement but he feared that his agitated friend was underestimating the force required to defeat the Algerines. And even if Algiers were contained, it would still leave American shipping exposed in other Barbary waters.

Jefferson did not give up his hope of coercing the Algerines into freeing American captives and respecting American maritime rights. Although he recognized that the French government was uninterested in supporting the United States on this issue, he did win the full support of the most enthusiastic Americanophile in France, the Marquis de Lafayette himself, for a proposed confederation of smaller maritime powers against the Barbary states. The

French nobleman lobbied both the French court and the American Congress to back a concert of nations that would "compel the pyratrical states to perpetual peace, without price, and to guarantee that peace to each other."[17] The "Antipiratical Confederacy," which Lafayette was willing to head, never materialized, even though Congress directed the minister plenipotentiary in France to form a confederacy with the European nations at war with the Barbary states. John Jay's caution as the Confederation's secretary for foreign relations accounted for American inaction, while Lafayette's concern about France's official reaction was justified: "The devil of it will Be to make it Agreable to this ministry that I should meddle with the war."[18]

The Barbary question was never resolved during Jefferson's term as minister. It was always on his mind, not least because of the deplorable condition of American captives. Their plight helped to account for the energy he expended in trying to raise loans in Paris and in Amsterdam. If he could not raise an American navy or a new version of a league of armed neutrality, at least he could do whatever was possible to ransom and ameliorate the lot of his unfortunate compatriots. From time to time, however, he succumbed to the visions of the naval hero of the Revolution, John Paul Jones, who was in the service of Russia at this time. Jones's ideas included an alliance with the Russians in a common cause against the Turks and Algerines. Jefferson's belligerence toward the Barbary powers suggests that the label of pacifist never fitted the Virginia diplomat. At most, he was what Reginald Stuart has called a "half-way" pacifist.[19] Jefferson's hope in foreign relations was to promote a world free from the ravages of war, with markets open to all. His model treaties embodied this ideal, and it was reflected in the treaties that were made in the 1780s. But when confronted with hostile powers unable or unwilling to deal equitably with the United States, he had no hesitation about the use of force, especially when the rogue powers were weak enough for a league of victims to defeat them. This man of the Enlightenment accepted a role for limited war when other means failed, at least when applied to weak powers.

There was one apparent success with the Barbary states. While waiting for Lamb to find his way to Algiers, Adams and Jefferson agreed to send Thomas Barclay, the American consul general in Paris, to Morocco, where he concluded a treaty in 1787 that freed the captives and relieved the United States of annual tributes. The cost was a modest $30,000, and considerable credit went to

Spanish intercession on America's behalf. Although this was a successful negotiation, it was an unusual event. When he left France in 1789, Jefferson was still trying to free the captives in Algerine jails, hoping that the religious order of the Mathurins would negotiate for ransom of the prisoners. But the Mathurins' intervention required funds that Congress was hesitant to supply. The only other treaty negotiated during Jefferson's tenure in France was a treaty of amity and commerce with Prussia in 1785. Any connection with the Prussia of Frederick the Great would lift America's standing in Europe, particularly when the treaty provided for American access to Prussian ports in wartime. But trade with Prussia was minimal, and like the Moroccan treaty it stood out as an isolated event.

What impressed Jefferson and Adams more was the indifference of European powers, large and small, to American interests. Even when those interests coincided with their own, the smaller nations had no confidence in plans hatched by representatives of a weak new republic. When a larger country such as Spain did come to America's aid, it was only to assure American agreement to the Spanish control of the Mississippi River. What the United States needed was a strong central government to command the respect of all Europe. In its absence the American diplomatists in Europe had to turn to the two countries that could make a difference in coping with British domination—the Netherlands and France.

## Failure of the Dutch Model

Whatever frustrations Jefferson experienced from encounters with Britain, with the Barbary states, or even with the more benevolent Portugal and Prussia, he should have expected compensation from relations with the Netherlands. There seemed to have been a common destiny to unite the two nations. The Dutch were members of a republic, in fact a confederation not substantially different in organization from the American confederation; they were cobelligerents in the American Revolution and fellow opponents of British control of the seas. Their bankers provided funds to allow the fragile new republic to pay its many debts, and they were the first country after France to sign a treaty of amity and commerce with the United States, a recognition in 1782 that excluded a military connection but emphasized peace and friendship between the two countries and free entry into each other's ports. Although this benevolence did not include equal access to the colonial ports of the Netherlands, the treaty seemed to signal that America had an ally in Europe more in tune with its values than those of monarchical France.

In the years following the 1783 Treaty of Paris, financial support of Dutch bankers preoccupied Jefferson and Adams in their respective positions in Paris and London. Adams, minister to the Netherlands as well as to Britain, was fully aware of the significant position Dutch bankers occupied in the life of the American Confederation. The success of his mission, he and Jefferson believed, depended upon the ability of the United States to pay interest on its debts to the powerful French patron, and this could be accomplished only through the assistance of the Amsterdam financial community. Failure to secure new loans would damage America's credit in the world, perhaps irreparably, and could even be a harbinger of the failure of the republican experiment itself.

Adams had labored under enormous handicaps during the American Revolution to initiate loans in the face of the unwillingness of the Stadtholder, William, Prince of Orange, and his Anglophile faction to embarrass the British by supporting rebellious colonists as well as by the caution of bankers worried about the safety of their investments. Not until the States-General, the legislative arm of the United Provinces of the Netherlands, had recognized the United States in 1782 were American sympathizers—and France's friends—in the financial community of Amsterdam able to respond to Adams's importunities. America's chief banker was the van Staphorst family, who also served as the agent of Versailles. Of the $10 million in American foreign debt, almost half was owed to Dutch bankers. In short, the credit of the United States abroad rested as much in Dutch hands as in those of its original benefactor, France. The difficulties of a confederal government in New York unable to collect sufficient revenues to pay even the interest on its debts plagued its diplomats abroad during the life of the Articles of Confederation.

In this context, Jefferson's philosophical speculations about the virtues of Dutch republicanism could not conceal his nervousness that even the most sympathetic of America's Dutch friends would place financial interests above ideological ties. He recommended that Dutch financiers be encouraged to purchase American debts to France on the assumption that defaulting to France would be more dangerous to America's position in the world than defaulting to private bankers in Amsterdam. He explained to John Jay in 1786: "If there be a danger that our payments may not be punctual, it might be better that the discontents which would thence arise should be transferred from a court of whose good will we have so much need to the breasts of a private company."[20] Jefferson and Adams nevertheless were uncomfortable in their knowledge that Dutch speculators had exploitative interests in the American economy. If they were able to buy up the nation's domestic debt, they could control the direction of its economic future. Congress took this warning seriously. Concerned about the risk to American credit in the Netherlands, it turned down the plan.

The problem of excessive dependence was underscored by the sluggishness of Dutch bankers in floating a new loan in 1786 and 1787 at a time when Congress could not pay interest on previous loans. This reluctance to respond to America's needs left Jefferson with the burden of finding new ways of meeting unfulfilled payments to French veteran officers of the Revolution as well as the expenses of his own diplomatic mission in Paris. The solution suggested in Amsterdam was to take payment of a year's interest on certificates of the American domestic debt held by Dutch speculators as a precondition for the completion of the current foreign loan. This issue provoked a crisis in 1787 for the two American diplomats, and particularly for Jefferson, who felt intimidated by the intricacies of money questions and who was discomfited further by the prospect of Adams leaving him alone with the bankers as he returned to Massachusetts. It seemed that the so-called friends of America in Amsterdam—the Willinks brothers and the van Staphorst brothers—had maneuvered the diplomats into a corner.

Adams did leave Europe in April 1788 but not before meeting Jefferson in March at The Hague (where Adams intended to pay a farewell courtesy call as American minister to the Netherlands) and at Amsterdam. They managed to win a reprieve of three years for the United States in the form of a new loan to meet pressing obligations in Europe. Despite Adams's anger and Jefferson's anguish there was little doubt about the eventual outcome of these negotiations. The Amsterdam bankers had too much at stake to permit the destruction of American credit, as Adams recognized. Moreover, they were well aware that a new government then coming into being in New York would repay their investment at full value.

There was a happy ending to the problem of American credit in Holland, and certainly a satisfactory arrangement for those financiers who anticipated redemption of debts by the new federal government. But these outcomes were not obtained before Jefferson, the first secretary of state, became thoroughly troubled and not a little confused by the financial machinations, American as well as

Dutch, that he witnessed around him. In New York in 1790 he claimed that he always had been of the opinion that "the purchase of our debt to France by private speculations would have been an operation extremely injurious to our credit; and that the consequence foreseen by our bankers, that the purchasers would have been obliged, in order to make good their payments to deluge the market of Amsterdam with American paper and to sell it at any price, was a probable one."[21] The secretary of state obviously had changed his mind since 1786, when he deemed such an arrangement entirely appropriate.

His education in the mysteries of high finance yielded some cynical insights by the time he left France. He reported to Jay in 1789 that bankers would be able to borrow to fill subscriptions just enough to pay interest, "just that and no more or so much more as may pay our salaries and keep us quiet. . . . I think it is possible they may chuse to support our credit to a certain point and let it go no further but at their will; to keep it so poised as that it may be at their mercy."[22] Small wonder that Jefferson had an animus against speculators and feared their influence on the economy. The Netherlands, it became obvious, was no different from any other European nation. If the most-favored-nation clause in the 1782 commercial treaty with that state had any meaning, it was only in the symbolic value granted by the fact of an agreement itself, not by a Dutch departure from the restrictive economic system of Europe. Given the weakness of the power of Congress to regulate commerce under the Confederation, France and the Netherlands would follow the British example—namely, play one state against another, thereby encouraging disunion as they freely discriminated against American shipping. On occasion the Dutch appeared even more obdurate than their European rivals. Jefferson noted gloomily in 1785 that "Holland is so immovable in her system of colony administration, that as propositions to her on that subject would be desperate, they had better not be made."[23] Jay added a year later that the Netherlands' fear of competition made it "look as if the Dutch regret our having found the Way to China, and that will doubtless be more or less the Case with every Nation with whose Commercial Views we may interfere."[24]

These comments were hardly the final judgments of American policymakers about the role of the Netherlands in thwarting commercial development. They were essentially manifestations of unhappiness with both the weakness of the Confederation and the shortsightedness of its potential European partners that permitted

Britain to exploit the American trade without fear of retribution. To the end of this period, Jefferson still nursed hopes that France or Holland would replace Britain as America's chief trading partner, if only out of its own self-interest. Hence, he deplored both the actions of individual states in violating treaty agreements with the Continental nations and the provisions in the Articles of Confederation that permitted states to pass their own navigation acts. These provisions provided excuses for Europeans to continue in their old ways.

France and the Netherlands not only failed to help the United States against Britain, but they failed as well to help each other against a common adversary. In 1787, Prussia invaded Holland to avenge an insult to the Princess of Orange, the king's sister, by the Francophile Patriots. The Patriot party, a combination of aristocrats, democrats, intellectuals, and businessmen, looked to America for inspiration and to France for sustenance. France failed its Dutch friends; the French, intimidated by British influence with the Stadtholder and by the ineptitude of the Patriot defenses, repudiated their alliance. The aristocratic elements among the Patriots then deserted to the pro-British Orange party, and the pro-American republicans were sentenced to defeat and exile.

The impact of these events upon Jefferson and Adams was traumatic. They underscored the growing concern about the interference of the major European powers in Dutch affairs that was the subject of so much of Jefferson's correspondence to Jay between 1785 and 1788. If the plight of the Netherlands moved them, it was not only because the victims were identified as friends of America and the oppressors as supporters of the Anglophilic Stadtholder, but it was also because the troubles of the Dutch Confederation could become the troubles of the American Confederation. Civil war invited foreign intervention.

The experience of the Netherlands was a powerful argument to American witnesses of the evils of the balance of power and the inadequacies of alliances with great powers. Europe was a dangerous place and its history was a warning to the United States. While there may have been temporary advantages in joining one side or another (or occasionally imperative reasons to do so), it was always perilous and never to be sought after by the weaker power. "Wretched indeed is the nation in whose affairs foreign powers are once permitted to intermeddle!" Jefferson exclaimed in 1787. Holland was that wretched nation, a "frog between the legs of two fighting bulls," as Adams saw it.[25]

The Dutch republic was not just a case study of a failed aristocratic republic, however. The words of the American diplomats in Europe as well as those of their correspondents at home conveyed their distress over the sufferings of a kindred people with kindred institutions. They were often annoyed by Dutch selfishness and shortsightedness, particularly in the refusal of the Netherlands to open its colonial ports to American shipping. Yet their annoyance appeared to mask fears that America's fate might be much the same in the future. The sufferings of Holland provided a "crowd of lessons," as Jefferson put it, "never to have an hereditary officer of any sort: never to let a citizen ally himself with kings: never to call in foreign nations to settle domestic differences: never to suppose that any nation will expose itself to war for us, etc."[26]

## The French Ally

Jefferson had been in France for over three years when he pronounced those lessons. With some confidence he could believe that Americans had already learned most of them. Certainly, there was a clear consensus against "a hereditary officer" in the manner of the Stadtholder. And while he was to fear in later years Anglophilic "monocrats," such fears never related to the French monarchy. France was a vitally useful ally as a counterweight to malevolent Britain, but he never conceived that nation to be a model for Americans to emulate, nor would he place his trust in France's benevolence toward the United States. From time to time during his tenure in Paris, Jefferson expressed his suspicions about French intentions and criticized French behavior toward the United States. He was aware of France's unwillingness to support American policy toward the Barbary states, and resented it. He was also aware that the Anglo-French commercial treaty of 1786 gave Britain economic concessions, particularly in fisheries, at the expense of the American ally. This too was resented.

He also feared the revival of a French empire in North America. This mistrust was as important an incentive as trade with China in otter skins when he promoted the visions of the young Connecticut adventurer John Ledyard to mount an expedition to the Pacific Northwest. And when he learned of the planned expedition, sponsored by the king, of seasoned French naval officer Jean François de La Pérouse to explore the northwest coast of America, he expressed his alarm to Jay. While he acknowledged that scientific knowledge may have been one of the objectives, he wondered

whether the French "are perfectly weaned from the desire of pos-
sessing continental colonies in America. Events might arise which
would render it very desireable for Congress to be satisfied they
have no such wish. If they would desire a colony on the Western
side of America, I should not be quite satisfied that they would
refuse one which should offer itself on the eastern side."[27]

Jefferson's sensitivity about France's intentions was reflected
in his response to Jay's desire to enlist its support of America's
claims on the British-held posts in the Northwest. Despite the terms
of the 1783 Treaty of Paris, the British did not evacuate posts in
those territories on the grounds that other parts of the treaty, such
as America's obligation to repay debts to British creditors, had not
been honored. The question for Jefferson was not how far the French
ally considered itself bound to insist that Britain deliver the posts.
Rather, he was worried that such a question "would infallibly
produce another, How far we consider ourselves as guarantees of
their American possessions, and bound to enter into any future war
in which they may be attacked. The words of the treaty of alliance
seem to be without ambiguity on either head. Yet I should be afraid
to commit Congress by answering without authority."[28]

This constant wariness underlay Jefferson's diplomacy in
France. Yet it did not inhibit him from making every effort to shape
France into a form that would serve the new nation. Although ap-
pearances seemed to suggest otherwise, Jefferson was not in Paris
as a political reformer or as a man of culture indulging his taste for
the company of fellow intellectuals. He consciously made all his
social activities serve the needs of America's foreign policy. In essence his goals centered on France's role as a counterbalance to
Britain's economic stranglehold over the nation. By negotiating
commercial arrangements that would open up French markets to
American products, Jefferson sought to serve France as well as his
own country. The United States would be freed from its entanglement with British commerce, and France would prosper at Britain's
expense.

To achieve this objective, Jefferson intended to exploit many
links to sympathetic Frenchmen in positions of influence—friends
from the Revolution, admirers of Franklin, and an intelligentsia
fascinated by the American experiment. Few in these circles were
republicans and even fewer were democrats. But they all hoped to
give their nation a more satisfactory system of government that
would secure for the French the happiness, if not all the freedoms,
of the liberated Americans. Many of these liberal aristocrats were

political philosophes with whom the American minister enjoyed a free exchange of ideas and an appreciation of the refinements of civilized society. The common denominator of all of his friendships in France was good will toward the United States. It was this factor that Jefferson hoped to use to his country's advantage.

Jefferson's opponents in his lifetime and beyond considered his Francophilia and the connections it produced not as a service to the United States but as evidence of his weakness for things French. The warmth of his friendships was indisputable. Such luminaries as Lafayette, Chastellux, Jacques-Pierre Brissot de Warville, and the Marquis de Condorcet presented themselves as disciples, looking upon the American experience as a model for France to follow. Jefferson found himself in demand as an adviser to the moderate reformers who were to dominate the first stages of the French Revolution. He thoroughly enjoyed the vibrant social life of the salons, where the conversation was always lively and intelligent, and he was usually the object of lionization. He often professed to miss the simple life of rural Virginia, but it is hard to take seriously his claim that his friend Francis Hopkinson's Wednesday evenings in the company of Franklin and Rittenhouse "would be more valued by me more than the whole week in Paris."[29]

Whether or not the ideas of his French friends influenced him was quite another matter. Stimulating as their company was, his enthusiasm for their views was restricted to philosophical and political positions that agreed with his own judgments of what would serve American interests. He applied the ideas of the physiocrats to an American frame of reference, accepting only so much of physiocratic doctrine as his experience confirmed. Physiocracy itself was part of the general repudiation of mercantilism best expressed by Adam Smith in Britain. Like other intellectual phenomena of the eighteenth century, physiocracy appealed to natural law for its legitimacy. Under the leadership of François Quesnay and the Marquis de Mirabeau, the physiocrats devised a system of society in which all moral as well as economic values rested on land and agriculture.

There was much in physiocracy that Jefferson approved—veneration of the farmer, dislike of government interference in economic activity—but his chief bond with the physiocrats was their admiration for the United States and the use to which this admiration might be put in the service of American economic policies. In most respects their ideals and ambitions were different from his. Essentially, they were dogmatists, while he was a pragmatist; his judgments were colored by an awareness of his country's needs. While he applauded the physiocrats' efforts in fighting the tobacco monopolists, he looked askance at the low-tariff Anglo-French treaty of 1786 even though that treaty conformed with physiocratic principles. Even the identification of Jefferson with physiocrats through their common concern for the farmer is fallacious. They were not speaking of the same "farmer." The French envisioned the advancement of aristocratic values inherent in the nobleman's estate, while Jefferson measured the small farm in terms of democratic values.

The American minister to France was no more an agrarian than he was a physiocrat. His awareness of the frailty of the infant republic had modified his genuine interest in the farmer before he arrived in France, as his *Notes on Virginia* revealed. Ideally, a self-sufficient society of yeomen farmers would insulate Americans from the lures of British commerce. But this was never a practical option. His sentiments on this score may have been a reflection of the debts he and other Virginia planters owed to British tobacco consignment merchants. He pointed out in 1786 that "long experience has proved to us that there never was an instance of a man's getting out of debt who was once in the hands of a tobacco merchant, and bound to consign his tobacco to him. It is the most delusive of all snares."[30] Yet the marketing of tobacco was Virginia's path to prosperity, just as New England looked to fisheries for its future. The answer then lay in devising new terms of trade and new partners.

These considerations were not new to Jefferson; he brought them with him from Philadelphia in 1784. His aim in France was to make a virtue out of a necessity by accepting the permanence of a commercial economy and facilitating the transfer of commerce from hostile Britain to putatively friendly France.

Jefferson's interest in physiocracy was much like his interest in other liberal philosophies encountered in France—namely, in the support the bearers of these philosophies would give to American concerns. He was constantly aware that the United States had to depend upon the favor of men of influence for any political or economic aid that France would grant. If, in the minds of Lafayette and his friends, the United States had achieved something about which French philosophers of the last generation had only fantasized, then he would do everything he could to promote this belief in order to exploit their influence on the Crown. He also knew that if these friends were to press America's cause at Versailles, it would be dangerous for them to learn of defects in the American system. His nation had to be worthy of their support. Jefferson took a justifiable pride in demonstrating the kind of society the French reformers would find through examination of his own accomplishments. His framing of Virginia's Statutes of Religious Freedom was an example of America's loyalty to the principles of freedom. He publicized wherever possible U.S. institutions to which Frenchmen might look with envy: a representative government, absence of a hereditary aristocracy, and equality of opportunity for all citizens.

## Coping with the Constitutional Convention

As the French turned to the reform of their government in 1787, Jefferson recognized the particular importance of the American example in this reformation. He feared that American prestige among reformers would suffer seriously if stories of deviation from their idealistic images of the New World drifted back to France at the very moment when they were presumably taking steps to adopt an American model for their country. Not incidentally, his efforts to use these friendships to expand economic ties between the two countries would also suffer just as it seemed that their influence at Versailles was becoming predominant. Consequently, Jefferson's earlier exasperation over the weakness of executive authority was muted as he warned against repression in America. His language became more extravagant as the tempo of the incipient French Revolution rose and as frightening news of Shays' Rebellion against the Massachusetts establishment crossed the ocean. Daniel Shays, a Massachusetts debtor farmer and Revolutionary War veteran, led a protest in 1786 against creditor-dominated courts. The state militia, supported by wealthy Boston merchants, suppressed it but failed to deal with the conditions that inspired it. Jefferson's reactions were schizophrenic: on the one hand, he feared for the future of American institutions at the hands of mobs and demagogues; on the other, he understood the reasons for the farmer's rebellion against an unresponsive oligarchy in Boston. Above all, he worried about his country's losing the respect of his French admirers if America appeared to be curtailing the liberties of its citizens.

It was in this context that he wrote to Abigail Adams in February 1787 that "the spirit of resistance to government is so valuable on certain occasions, that I wish it to be always kept alive. It will often be exercised when wrong, but better so than not to be exercised at all. I like a little rebellion now and then. It is like a storm in the Atmosphere."[31] This was not the judgment of his correspondent. She had informed him that "ignorant, wrestless desperadoes, without conscience or principals, have led a deluded multitude to follow their standard, under pretence of grievences which have no existance but in their immaginations."[32] Madison and Washington were equally severe in condemning Shays' Rebellion. For Madison the rebellion was not a glorious demonstration of man's love of freedom but a symptom of the government's inability to cope with anarchical forces.

It was not that Jefferson failed to understand the dangers that Shays posed to the stability of the Confederation. He had spoken and written frequently about the need for a stronger government to confront a hostile world, and applauded the calling of the Constitutional Convention in Philadelphia in 1787. At the same time, he worried that the movement toward a more powerful government in America could take a dangerous turn if that government appeared to rest on the suppression of liberties. In other words, if America moved toward a despotism that Jefferson had found so deplorable in Europe, the price for restoration of order might be too high. As the meetings of the Constitutional Convention proceeded behind closed doors, he was all the more concerned that America not retreat from its libertarian model. Such a step backward not only would damage his country's image with French political reformers, but it also could undermine the support those influential figures would give to American commercial interests.

Jefferson's concerns about the direction reforms in the Confederation might take arose from more than his strategies at Versailles. The disorders in Massachusetts evoked unhappy analogies with the situations in France, Poland, and Holland. The arbitrary government of the French monarchy, the impotence of the Polish kings, and the capriciousness of the aggressive Stadtholder in the Netherlands were constant reminders that American liberties were as vulnerable as they were precious. It was not vanity about his standing with Lafayette or Chastellux that most influenced his judgment, nor was it the difficulties of winning France as a counterbalance to British power that most deeply affected him. Jefferson's major reservations about the Constitution involved the possibility of America's losing the vital distinctions between the Old and New Worlds in the name of law and order.

The volatile status of the new nation in the 1780s had presented as many problems as opportunities for Jefferson when he cited the worthiness of the American experiment to friends in high places.

He worked tirelessly to encourage their advocacy at Versailles. But there were drawbacks. Appreciating America from afar, too many French intellectuals attributed a perfectibility of human conduct in that country that they would not expect from Europe. Jefferson was concerned that exaggerated expectations would lead to disillusionment and consequent disaffection with the new nation. He had reason to be concerned. Many European friends found Americans too conservative when momentum for change was rapidly developing in France. The Marquis de Condorcet observed limitations growing out of America's blessings; because Americans had never suffered from the abuses of aristocracy, they could not fully appreciate the radical solutions that France needed.

The notion of perfectibility permeated French liberal thinking about America, and ultimately about France's own future. It was reflected in Jefferson's correspondence and became one of the problems he had to contend with in winning and maintaining his ties with such important political philosophers as Condorcet, Morellet, Du Pont, and Chastellux. Economist Pierre-Samuel Du Pont de Nemours congratulated Jefferson in the fall of 1787 over the new Constitution that perfected the application of Reason to government. The Virginian was forced to respond as vaguely as he could that the American way proved the validity of Du Pont's thesis. But he was uneasy both with Du Pont's certitudes and with his own responses.

Jefferson already was sensitized to criticisms from Frenchmen who expected too much from the United States. Just the year before he had been caught up in an embarrassing quarrel between two intellectuals—Brissot de Warville and Chastellux—over the true state of affairs in America. When Chastellux accused the Quakers of indifference to the public welfare during the American Revolution, Brissot accused him of slandering America by implying the existence of imperfections in its society. Believing that Chastellux's accusations were probably too mild rather than too harsh, Jefferson tried to offset Brissot's angry reaction by urging other friends to lower their expectations when they visited America. He had learned from his experiences with French friends that while their admiration for the New World might be fervent, their understanding often was shallow.

Jefferson's difficulties in placating his friends in France were compounded by his ambivalent views on Shays' Rebellion. From one angle of observation, Lafayette expressed his indignation that Massachusetts farmers would rebel against their own government when they should have known that Britain and monarchy were their real enemy. Yet Jefferson sensed that the rebellion would provide too easy an excuse for selfish interests to revamp the Confederation into a monarchy or despotism. These fears intensified when the Constitutional Convention met. Having heard and read of reactionary sentiment in America, he asked William Stephens Smith, Adams's son-in-law, "Where does this anarchy exist? Where did it ever exist, except in the single instance of Massachusets? And can history produce an instance of a rebellion so honourably conducted? I say nothing of its motives. They were founded in ignorance, not wickedness. God forbid we should be 20 years without such a rebellion."[33]

The foregoing exclamations are another example of Jefferson's use of hyperbole that could haunt him in the future. To foreign correspondents his tone was calmer but the message much the same. The insurrection was not altogether unreasonable, originating as it did among "the imprudent number of those who have involved themselves in debt beyond their abilities to pay." The idea of "returning to anything like their ancient government never entered their heads." Besides, this single rebellion showed the infrequency of such outbreaks in America. Writing to David Hartley, Franklin's British friend in the peace negotiations, Jefferson calculated that "an insurrection in one of 13 states in the course of 11. years that they have subsisted amounts to one in any particular state in 143 years."[34] He assured the influential Milanese nobleman Francis dal Verme that "those commotions have been entirely quieted."[35]

The conjunction of Shays' Rebellion with the calling of the Constitutional Convention was not lost on Jefferson or on his American correspondents. While he comforted himself with the knowledge that the Convention's delegates were wise and good and well-meaning, he worried that they might react to anarchy by experimenting with monarchy. His conservative Virginia friend Edward Carrington and South Carolina historian David Ramsey warned of despotism or monarchy in the event of failure in Philadelphia. The secrecy of the proceedings in Philadelphia further worried Jefferson, and only after Madison explained matters to him was he reassured on this issue.

He expressed little of his internal agitation to Europeans, telling dal Verme, for example, that "time and trial had discovered defects in our federal constitution. A new essay, made in the midst of flames of war could not be perfect." The men meeting in Philadelphia were there to strengthen Congress with "exclusive sovereignty in every matter relative to foreign nations" and "to devise some peaceable means whereby Congress may enforce their decisions."[36] He assured dal Verme that with such men as General Washington presiding and with Benjamin Franklin in attendance, there should be no doubt about the outcome.

So he told Europeans. This optimistic version of events in Philadelphia was not in evidence when he corresponded with Americans. To his fellow countrymen he warned about the dangers of excessive change, citing the horrors of Europe as evidence. Using a bestiary image he often favored, he railed "against hereditary magistrates," as he wished to have "republics besiege the throne of heaven with eternal prayers to extirpate from creation this class of human lions, tygers, and mammouts called kings."[37] Perhaps only minor repairs would be sufficient to fix the Confederation. While he repeated pro forma his familiar advice to Washington about unifying the states where foreign affairs was concerned, but preserving them as separate entities on domestic matters, the main thrust of his letter was that "with all it's defects, the inconveniences resulting from [the Articles of Confederation] are so light in comparison with those existing in every other government on earth, that our citizens may be considered as in the happiest political situation which exists."[38]

Ironically, it was Washington who was part of the problem. On the assumption that he would be the first president of a stronger union, Jefferson anticipated that the "perpetual re-eligibility of the president" would make the office hereditary, given the general's popularity. Lafayette tried to calm his fears with the comforting comment that "I know him too well not to think he will find the danger, and less the authority Before he Goes over." Jefferson was less confident than his French friend, not because he suspected Washington of such designs but because "our jealousy is put to sleep by the unlimited confidence we all repose in the person to whom we all look as our president. After him inferior characters may perhaps succeed and awaken us to the danger which his merit has led us into."[39]

Jefferson failed to win his case on presidential tenure. He had a more serious concern to face—namely, the securing of a bill of rights that the framers of the Constitution had omitted. His interest in this cause reflected his European experience. First, the absence of fundamental individual rights could mean their abrogation in the future by an administration less sensitive than the new federal government. Jefferson had only to look around him in France to see the consequences of a system that did not honor the rights of its citizens. Beyond this consideration was the need to keep the respect of his French friends, who had admired the bills of rights found in the state constitutions, and who would look askance at a federal constitution that dispensed with them and at the same time prescribed an unlimited tenure for a powerful chief magistrate. Such a constitution would be evidence of America's backsliding, of its unfitness to serve as an exemplar for a new France at a time when the French reformers were hoping to secure a declaration of rights. This disillusionment in turn could adversely affect Jefferson's influence at the Court of Versailles.

To his European colleagues he gave as positive a spin as he could to the new Constitution by offering a confident prognosis for change whenever he had the opportunity. To French Foreign Minister the Comte de Moustier he admitted some shortcomings in the document but envisioned changes for the better in the immediate future. To Baron von Geismar he promised an addition of a declaration of rights. And his private doubts about General Washington notwithstanding, he could assure Europeans that his election as first president would be the final note of reassurance about America's fidelity to republican principles. The importance of the Constitution to European liberals was not a figment of a solipsistic American imagination: European interest in the events at Philadelphia was intense. Lafayette even wrote to General Henry Knox that he and Jefferson were debating the merits of the Constitution as if they were themselves present at the Convention.

## Influencing French Commercial Policy

Jefferson's careful manipulation of the meanings of Shays' Rebellion in Massachusetts and the Constitutional Convention in Philadelphia took place in the midst of his negotiations with Vergennes and, after the latter's death in 1787, with the Comte de Montmorin, over opening French markets to American products. If he was to be successful, the advocacy of his friends among the enlightened nobility was vital. What he preached to the French was not just the mutual economic advantages of unregulated trade but the opportunities that trade would provide for dealing with a common enemy, Great Britain. This was not the free exchange of goods in a physiocratic sense, although this was still the ideal that the American minister continued to profess. But if Americans could be weaned away from their traditional dependence upon British consignment merchants, and Frenchmen could be attuned to the benefits of replacing the British as the suppliers of manufactures to the United States, both nations would profit and Britain would suffer.

His was not an easy task. France provided a classic case of a mercantilist state, with a rigidly controlled centralized economy. The articles that Jefferson had in mind were among the most tightly controlled—tobacco in the hands of the monopolistic Farmers-General, to whom the Crown had "farmed out" the collection of indirect taxes, and whale oil barred by high duties from consumers in France. As a Virginia planter it was hardly surprising that his energies would be directed primarily toward breaking the grip of the Farmers-General. Removing the French middleman had the double goal of increasing Virginian prosperity and freeing Americans from the British middleman.

Jefferson himself was burdened with debts to English and Scottish merchants, inherited from his father-in-law's estate. While he agreed that Virginia courts be opened to the claims of British creditors as long as no interest was demanded for the war years, he had a chance to sublimate his resentment at his and his fellow countrymen's subordination to the power of the consignment merchant by his hopes for a new economic relationship with France. In a letter to a sympathetic friend he vented his feelings against the British merchant who initially extends credit liberally, and "then begins to give him less for his tobacco and ends with giving what he pleases for it, which is always so little that let the demands of the customer for necessaries be reduced ever so low in order to get himself out of debt, the merchant lowers his price in the same proportion so as always to keep such a balance against his customer as will oblige him to continue his consignment of tobacco."[40]

A more liberal French economic policy could serve the nation as well as the Virginia planter. But Jefferson needed all the help he could get from his well-placed friends. His own arguments were eloquent as he tried to convince Montmorin that abolishing the tobacco monopoly "will form a memorable epoch in the commerce of the two nations. It will establish at once a great basis of exchange, serving like a point of union to draw to it other members of our commerce."[41] Release from the "shackles" of the Farmers-General would also help Americans pay their debts to France. These arguments, however, would have been undercut by the three-year contract between the Farmers-General and financier Robert Morris for the exclusive supply of American tobacco. Given the power of these entrenched interests, it was a tribute to Jefferson's ability to cultivate influential members at Versailles that he was able have a committee appointed to study American trade practices, which broke the Morris monopoly and opened the way in 1787 for major concessions to American commerce.

Virginia tobacco was not the only beneficiary of Jefferson's intervention. Whale oil, a major concern of the minister after a visit in 1784 to New England port towns impoverished by British policy, would enter France in American vessels with only modest duties, according to an *arrêt* of December 29, 1787. That same ruling allowed rice and naval stores, vital to the economies of the Carolinas and Georgia, to be exported to France under similarly favorable conditions. The whale oil concessions, however, coincided with Britain's glut of the market with its own products as it took advantage of the Anglo-French commercial treaty of 1786, and triggered a reaction from French competitors. The initial result was an *arrêt* in 1788 that closed the French market to all foreign whale oil. A new round of lobbying emphasizing both the unfairness of the law and its ultimate service to Britain won over Montmorin, and the ban was lifted before the year ended. Jefferson reported to Jay "that this branch of commerce, after so threatening an appearance, will be on a better footing than ever, as enjoying jointly with the French oil, a monopoly of their markets."[42]

The year 1788 was the apex of Jefferson's diplomatic efforts. Not only did he succeed (with the help of his French allies) in bending, if not subverting, French regulations, but he also resolved America's discomfort with the consular convention that Franklin had signed with France in 1784. While it was important for the United States to have such a convention, both for the symbol of sovereignty it represented and for its service to American merchants and seamen abroad, Jay in particular regarded the convention as potentially compromising U.S. sovereignty. It would grant to French consuls an excessive power over their nationals in the United States. Additionally, the agreement called for the consuls to present their credentials to individual states, thereby undercutting the authority of the central government.

Consequently, Congress instructed Jefferson to seek revisions that would minimize the elements of extraterritoriality in the original convention. Whatever annoyance the French felt about the changes Congress wanted was allayed by the tact Jefferson displayed in gaining most of America's objectives in the revised convention of 1788. Jay would have preferred a time limit of ten years for the duration of the treaty, but the twelve-year limit was satisfactory. More important, as Jefferson reported, was the deletion of clauses in the convention of 1784 "cloathing Consuls with the privileges of the law of Nations." After 1788 consuls would be "expressly subjected, in their persons & property, to the laws of the land."[43]

The consular convention of 1788 was an example of Jefferson's statecraft at its best. But most scholars' attention has been spent on the putative failure of his major efforts to open France to American tobacco, whale oil, and rice. Certainly, there was something quixotic about his plan to have the French ally reorder its economy to serve the United States. It might have been in France's interest as well to replace Britain as America's supplier of manufactures and credit, but Jefferson should have been in a position to recognize how improbable it was for that sclerotic economy to follow his advice. Certainly, his victory over the Farmers-General was ephemeral, and his success with whale oil could be just a temporary breakthrough. Not only was the volume of the Virginia tobacco trade no further advanced in 1789 than it had been in 1784, but he also had to recognize the resentment of French merchants witnessing American ships carrying tobacco to France and then returning from Britain with the manufactured goods Jefferson had hoped France would supply. And, as historian Doron Ben-Atar suggests, Virginia planters might have been better off dealing with the Morris monopoly, which paid them in cash, instead of accepting the credit that made them dependent on British consignment merchants.[44]

The verdict of failure would be too harsh. It is unlikely that a nation tottering on the edge of revolution could have reordered its economy to satisfy the United States. The American Revolution seemed to have drained the last bit of energy from its political system. France was unable to pursue its own interests, let alone the interests of its American ally. Jefferson always recognized that he was criticizing a system that taxed a productive middle class while exempting an unproductive but wealthy nobility and clergy, and that permitted itself to remain dependent upon hostile Britain for vital products while looking with distrust at recommendations for a more open economy that might relieve France from financial distress.

France's foreign policy was as confused as its economic policy. Vergennes's grand design to establish a new Anglo-French entente against the eastern powers led to the commercial treaty of 1786 that poured British goods into France. So while the French wanted the United States to be strong enough to serve as a foil to Britain, they wanted the new nation to be dependent upon their own country for economic and political support. Versailles would rather forego payments of America's wartime debts than accept payment from too strong and independent a central government. Such ambivalence was as self-defeating as its position on economic policy. Had France loosened its commercial regulations in favor of American trade, as Jefferson advocated, it would have gained a far tighter control over American commerce and even over American politics.

Even though reformers did make a dent in French mercantilism, the merchant class could not accept the immediate results of the partial reforms Jefferson's friends had effected. Inured by habit and prejudice to the ways of mercantilism, members of the merchant class saw in free trade only the opportunity for Britain to inundate France with foreign manufactured goods that would undersell their products. They were not able to distinguish between the uncompromising free-trade principles of the physiocrats and the enlightened nationalism of Lafayette, which sought commercial privileges for the United States as a weapon against British interests. They may have yielded on tobacco and whale oil, but it was done reluctantly with no appreciation of long-run strategic purposes. Instead, they witnessed short-run losses that lent urgency to their campaign to keep American ships and products out of the French West Indies.

In retrospect, the American minister won as much success as any diplomatist could have hoped for in the dying days of the Ancien Régime. If he remained optimistic, it was in expectation that the revolution in the making in 1789 would bring his acolytes to power. He believed that his voice was heard among the moderate royalists and moderate republicans who used his home as a common meeting ground to debate the new order that was coming to France.

As he observed the rapid changes taking place in his last days in Paris, he could be excused for enthusiasm for the French Revolution. Much of the charge of Francophilia that would lead political enemies in the next decade to accuse him of subordinating American interests to those of the French republic stemmed from the excitement of rapid changes in 1789. In the year before, he had urged caution, concerned that the newly energized Estates-General would be satisfied with periodic meetings as well as the exclusive right of taxation. If they "are prudent," he observed in December 1788, "they will not aim at more than this at first, lest they should shock the dispositions of the court, and even alarm the public mind, which must be left to open itself by degrees to successive improvements."[45] Six months later he was ready to accept the Estates-General as a full-blown legislature, and by August 1789 he had no problem with plans for a constitution that would limit the king's power over foreign relations.

Was he influenced by the currents of the day? Undoubtedly. But his hopes for France had not changed. The ultimate object of his advices was the creation of a constitutional monarchy modeled after Britain's but purged of British flaws. His vision was hardly radical. When the new National Assembly proclaimed its Declaration of the Rights of Man and its plan for a liberal regime in August 1789, he noted that the American government "has professedly been their model, in which such changes are made as a difference of circumstances rendered necessary and some others neither necessary nor advantageous, but into which men will ever run, when versed in theory and new in the practice of government, when acquainted with man only as they see him in their books and not in the world."[46] But what gave Jefferson confidence were the leaders he assumed would take control of affairs; there would be mistakes, he thought, but if the American model remained in place, both France and the United States would benefit. In this context he could yield once again to an outburst of hyperbole in regarding the French Revolution as a transcendental phenomenon beyond human control that would overcome all obstacles, including its association with "mobs and murderers." They were merely "the rags in which religion robes the true god."[47]

The foregoing sentiments, expressed to Thomas Paine in October 1789 as Jefferson was leaving Europe, did not signify abandonment of his earlier reservations. Nor did they indicate any abandonment of advantages the United States might extract from events in France. Just a month before, he seemed willing to exploit the initial weaknesses that would accompany a revolutionary upheaval while he waited to exploit the future strength of a reformed France. With some complacency he expected famine and financial bankruptcy to yield to America the opening of West Indian ports and even the supplying of starving Paris with salted provisions to be admitted duty-free. In brief, Jefferson's doubts as well as his enthusiasms derived from the service he hoped that France would give to American interests. With the future of his own country uppermost in his mind, the newly appointed secretary of state could look back with some pride in his achievements and could look ahead with some confidence that the people and policies he had cultivated as minister to France would bolster America's position in the world. France, regenerated by reform and led by friends of America, could be a major factor in the continuing struggle for independence from British economic control.

## Notes

1. Chevalier de la Luzerne to Comte de Vergennes, May 17, 1774, in Mary Giunta and J. Dane Hartgrove, eds., *The Emerging Nation: A Documentary History of the Foreign Relations of the United States under the Articles of Confederation, 1780–1789*, 3 vols. (Washington, DC: National Historical Publications and Records Commission, 1996), 2:370–71.

2. TJ to William Temple Franklin, May 7, 1786, in Julian P. Boyd, ed., *The Papers of Thomas Jefferson*, 24+ vols. (Princeton: Princeton University Press, 1950), 9:467 (hereafter cited as Boyd).

3. TJ to Madison, May 8, 1784, ibid, 7:233; "Report on Letters from the American Ministers in Europe," December 20, 1783, ibid., 6:394.

4. TJ to Monroe, November 11, 1784, ibid., 7:509.

5. TJ to Washington, December 10, 1784, ibid., 566.

6. TJ to Madison, March 18, 1785, ibid., 8:40.

7. Adams to Jay, April 13, 1785, Giunta and Hartgrove, *The Emerging Nation*, 2:606.

8. Ibid.

9. TJ to Abigail Adams, September 25, 1785, Boyd, 8:548–49.

10. "An Interlude at Dolly's Chophouse," ibid., 9:350–52.

11. TJ to John Page, May 4, 1786, ibid., 445.

12. Ibid., 446.

13. TJ to Monroe, May 10, 1786, ibid., 500–501.

14. TJ to G. K. van Hogendorp, October 13, 1785, ibid, 8:633.

15. TJ to Monroe, November 11, 1784, ibid., 7:511–12.

16. TJ to William Carmichael, May 5, 1786, ibid., 9:448.

17. "Proposed Convention against the Barbary States," ibid., 10:567.

18. Lafayette to TJ, October 23, 1786, ibid., 486.

19. Reginald C. Stuart, *The Half-Way Pacifist: Thomas Jefferson's View of War* (Toronto: University of Toronto Press, 1978).

20. TJ to Jay, September 26, 1785, Boyd, 10:406.

21. TJ, "Opinion on Fiscal Policy," August 26, 1790, ibid., 17:425.

22. TJ to Jay, March 12, 1789, ibid., 14:645.

23. TJ to Jay, October 11, 1785, ibid., 8:608.

24. Jay to TJ, July 14, 1786, ibid., 10:135.

25. TJ to Benjamin Vaughan, July 2, 1787, ibid., 11:533; Adams to Francis Van der Kemp, February 23, 1815, quoted in Edward Handler, *America and Europe: The Political Thought of John Adams* (Cambridge, MA: Harvard University Press, 1964), 115.

26. TJ to Adams, September 27, 1787, Boyd, 12:189.

27. TJ to Jay, August 14, 1785, ibid., 8:373–74.

28. TJ to Jay, March 12, 1786, ibid., 9:326.

29. TJ to Francis Hopkinson, August 14, 1786, ibid., 250.

30. TJ to Lucy Ludwell Paradise, August 27, 1786, ibid., 10:304–5.

31. TJ to Abigail Adams, February 22, 1787, ibid., 11:174.

32. Abigail Adams to TJ, January 29, 1787, ibid., 86.

33. TJ to William Stephens Smith, November 13, 1787, ibid., 12:356.

34. TJ to David Hartley, July 2, 1787, ibid., 11:526.

35. TJ to Francis dal Verme, August 15, 1787, ibid., 12:43.

36. Ibid., 42–43.

37. TJ to David Humphreys, August 14, 1787, ibid., 33.

38. TJ to Washington, August 14, 1787, ibid., 36.

39. Lafayette to TJ, December 25, 1787, ibid., 460; TJ to Edward Carrington, May 27, 1788, ibid., 13:209.

40. TJ to Lucy Ludwell Paradise, August 27, 1786, ibid., 10:304–5.

41. TJ to Montmorin, July 23, 1787, ibid., 11:617.

42. TJ to Jay, November 19, 1788, ibid., 14:214.

43. TJ to Jay, November 14, 1788, Giunta and Hartgrove, *The Emerging Nation*, 3:858.

44. Doron S. Ben-Atar, *The Origins of Jeffersonian Commercial Policy and Diplomacy* (New York: St. Martin's Press, 1993), 81.

45. TJ to Washington, December 4, 1788, Boyd, 14:330.

46. TJ to Madison, August 28, 1789, ibid., 15:365.

47. TJ to Paine, October 14, 1789, ibid., 522.

# 4

## Secretary of State

### 1790–1793

A recent interpretation of Jefferson's statecraft dismissed his role in Europe as "in many respects quite traditional."[1] Robert Tucker and David Hendrickson did not find the Virginia statesman embracing the "empire of liberty" until he took office in New York, the federal capital, in 1790 and sharpened his conception of foreign relations by contrasting it with his rival, Alexander Hamilton. In other words, Jefferson in France followed the European practices of *raison d'état*, with its primacy of foreign over domestic policy and the needs of the state over those of individuals. Such was their reading of his search for alternative markets for American products and his courtship of influential French friends.

Jefferson's experience in the Old World, however, is open to other interpretations. A case may be made that he was the exemplar of the new diplomacy that would substitute statecraft for warfare, that would insulate the United States from the coils of monarchical Europe, and that would secure for Americans a life free of the corruption he found abroad. While he could be cited for Machiavellian maneuvers in order to manipulate a potential ally, he did not do so to entangle his country in its web. Three elements may be found in all his activities in the 1780s: 1) avoidance of foreign entanglements whenever possible, with Holland serving as a case study of the dangers of dependence; 2) recognition of the need to break the British economic stranglehold over America, and for this France would be the primary instrument; and 3) constant awareness of the importance of the West in ensuring American prosperity, and constant fear that any

European power, including France, would block America's westward movement. Although Spain was not a major player during
his tenure as minister in France, its potential threat to American
navigation of the Mississippi did not escape his attention.

Jefferson did not regard his appointment as secretary of state
in the new Washington administration as a reward for his services
as minister to France. Had he been given a choice, he would have
preferred to return to France to complete a mission that he expected
would be furthered by the revolutionary changes in that nation.
But he had no choice. There were only two other candidates with
credentials equal or superior to those of Jefferson—John Adams
and John Jay—and they already occupied key positions as vice
president of the United States and chief justice of the Supreme
Court, respectively. Arguably, the least appealing aspect of the
offer were the duties associated with the title. Unlike the title Jay
had held under the Confederation, secretary for foreign relations,
Jefferson would be secretary of state, which implied a host of domestic concerns that could leave foreign relations as a relatively
minor responsibility. Nevertheless, the president's invitation was
one he could not refuse. Such was the situation that he found himself in upon his arrival in Norfolk, Virginia, in November 1789.

Jefferson's reluctance to accept the honor was understandable.
His temperament was better suited to the Paris post, and he knew
it. In retrospect his reluctance seems all the more prescient in light
of the conflict that met him immediately and that ultimately consumed his position, causing him to resign in 1793. After years of
enjoying adulation as the exemplar of a society French liberals
wished for themselves, he encountered in New York an aristocratic
ruling class indulging in an Anglophilia that aped the aristocratic
customs of the British enemy and appeared to make a mockery of
the new nation's values. At the center of this circle was the influential young secretary of the treasury, Alexander Hamilton, who was
to personify for Jefferson what he most abhorred in government:
concentration of power in a central government, ostentatious cultivation of urban, mercantile, and financial elites, and promotion
of a foreign economic policy that valued a British connection over
one with France. Perhaps the most discomfiting factor in this scene
was the special favor the less distinguished rival enjoyed with President Washington.

Inevitably, the schism between Jefferson and Hamilton was
personal as well as ideological. The secretary of state, a lonely figure in a hostile Cabinet, could not but resent a secretary of the trea-

sury who surpassed him in power and prestige, although his junior in years and in political rank. Hamilton's ability to win the president's confidence, the success of his financial schemes, and his genius in administering them stimulated the formation of an opposition party, with Jefferson as nominal leader and with Madison and Monroe as his active aides. Jefferson sensed from the start that he could have the support of farmers, who disliked the Federalist mercantile aristocracy, and of the public attracted by the French Revolution. These people would be the natural allies for Americans who looked to France for support against putative plots of the republic's enemies. Rather than serving as a patronizing supporter of that country's revolution, he was to champion its efforts for the inspiration it offered to Americans struggling to retain the freedoms won by their own revolution against the presumed machinations of Anglophiles and monarchists.

## The Consensus of 1790

While the secretary of state often found himself at dinner parties given in his honor "for the most part, the only advocate on the republican side"[2] of politics, the common ground on which the Washington administration stood concealed most of the fissures that were to mark the president's second term in office. There was a consensus broad enough in 1790 to encompass all members of the Cabinet and most of Congress as well. Irrespective of personality conflicts and future ideological affiliations, the leaders of the government all agreed that the Confederation had failed to support a viable American foreign policy. They looked upon the reconstituted Federal Union as an opportunity to extract vital concessions from Europe that had been unattainable in the past —concessions ranging from the relocation of national boundary lines to expansion of trade.

In this context, Washington was the spokesman for the nation. Those factions for whom he did not speak had retired in confusion from the national scene. The Jeffersonians for the most part were not drawn from the anti-Federalists who stood with the Confederation. Given the wide consensus among Federalists over the acceptance of the Constitution at the onset of his administration, the president was unprepared for the fierce differences over the national mandate that developed in subsequent years. His mind, never quick, could neither comprehend fully the protean nature of the

Cabinet struggle nor accept its implications for American politics. Unwittingly, Washington contributed to Jefferson's problems by his own bent for foreign and military affairs. Hamilton, on the other hand, owed much of his freedom of operation to the president's lack of expertise in financial matters. Moreover, the vast range of Hamilton's activities, including consular affairs, provided the secretary of the treasury with a measure of influence with the president and Congress that would have aroused the animosity of any secretary of state, especially one who was his senior in age, distinction, and service to his country. The absentee Virginian, fresh from his laurels in France, had reasons other than political ones to build an opposition to Hamilton. He was jealous of the younger man's authority in the new government.

Nevertheless, the transfer of personal distaste for each other's manners and mannerisms to distaste for their ideas and policies was neither automatic nor immediate. Although hindsight reveals wide philosophical gaps from the outset, it often overlooks the instances when the two secretaries acted in concert under an imperfect Constitution that they both recognized to be the best possible instrument of government available in 1790. Each man had suppressed his misgivings about the shortcomings of the Constitution, Hamilton because the document was excessively susceptible to democratic manipulation, Jefferson because of its silence on a bill of rights. But both statesmen were united on the need for a central government strong enough to compel the respect of Europe.

All Jefferson's experiences in France had confirmed the importance of such an authority if British power were to be successfully resisted. Debts had to be paid, reciprocal agreements had to be fulfilled, navigation laws had to be enforced. The Confederation could not manage those tasks. Hamilton in New York had other reasons for objecting to the weaknesses of the Confederation, but none of them related to any special service he wished to confer on Great Britain. As a worshiper of order, he regarded as intolerable the incipient chaos in a government that could not pay its debts and that could not enforce its ordinances. He was a prime mover in the campaign to call a convention to restructure the governance of the United States. All told, he identified a dozen defects in the Articles of Confederation, all of them growing out of the limitations imposed upon executive power. Obviously, the Jeffersonian objectives of a French counterweight to British dominance did not inform Hamilton's activities, but the nation's ability to prevent a state— Connecticut, for example—from levying heavier duties on imports from Massachusetts than from Great Britain had the blessing of both men.

Hamilton's praise of British monarchy as the model for the Constitution's framers was not the measure of his final view of the Federal Union. He could accept the document without king or aristocracy just as Jefferson was able to live with a president eligible for indefinite reelection. The secretary of the treasury's concern for energetic government was directed against future rebellions of the Shays' variety, an objective hardly shared by his Cabinet colleague. But, as Hamilton pointed out clearly in Number 24 of *The Federalist*, his objective was also to have a government capable of coping with the dangers imperial Britain and imperial Spain might pose for America, separately or "in future concert." Jefferson would have no difficulty in associating himself with the author of these views. Similarly, there was a harmony in 1790 that blended the Hamilton who looked forward to a close American connection with the British mercantile system and the Jefferson who sought a French factor to break that very link. The latter was not seeking a dependent role for the United States; his vision, repeatedly articulated during his ministry in Paris, was to exploit the French ally for the advancement of American trade. And the former, with all his admiration for the British way of commerce, sought not merely present profit for America in a special relationship with Britain but also envisioned a future in which an American industrial economy would rival and prevail over its British competitor.

The secretary of state would also subscribe to the sentiments Hamilton expressed in Number 11 of *The Federalist* wherein he elaborated on the benefits of union that would confound "all the combinations of European jealousy to restrain our growth." Hamilton's paradigm in Number 11 of a domineering Europe pluming itself "as the Mistress of the World" was close to Jefferson's perceptions of Europe's pretensions of superiority over America. Jefferson had used almost the same language to rebuff the ideas of the Comte de Buffon and philosophe Guillaume-Thomas-François Raynal when he was in France: "Men admired as profound philosophers, have, in direct terms, attributed to her inhabitants a physical superiority, and have gravely asserted that all animals, and with them the human species, degenerate in America. . . . It belongs to us to vindicate the honor of the human race, and to teach that assuming brother, moderation. Union will enable us to do it."

If Jefferson and Hamilton shared anger over the pseudoscientific slanders of European philosophers, they shared as fully in the

initial building of a fabric of government strong enough to imple-
ment the promise of the Constitution. The two men had not met
until Jefferson's return from France to assume his new office, and
the absence of immediate friction was due more to a common outlook on national problems than to Jefferson's notorious reluctance
to involve himself openly in any feud. The secretary of state could
even accept Treasury's personnel force of some seventy men in-
truding into his department by virtue of their functions in consular affairs as long as he could accept President Washington's
assurance that his office, with its small staff of five, was the more
important.

Jefferson appeared as ready as Hamilton to act on the principle
that the executive branch should have maximal independence, at
least in foreign affairs. In April 1790, shortly after assuming his
duties, he presented a memorandum on the limited role of the Senate in diplomatic appointments. His theme was that such a transaction was altogether executive and almost exclusively so, "except
as to such portions of it as are specially submitted to the Senate.
Exceptions are to be construed strictly."[3] As for the president's question about the propriety of consulting the Senate on which countries should be approached about diplomatic exchanges, Jefferson
asserted that there was no constitutional requirement for soliciting
such advice. He felt it impolitic to set a precedent. The Senate's
powers extended no further than the approval or disapproval of
the person nominated by the president. In displaying this loose
construction of presidential authority, the secretary of state put himself in a position indistinguishable from that of his conservative
predecessor, Chief Justice John Jay, whom Washington had con-
sulted on the same issue.

Given this attitude, Jefferson and Madison, now a leader in the
House of Representatives, were not hostile to the Hamiltonian program as they first understood it. The raising of revenue through a
tariff, the repaying of obligations through federal assumption of
the debts of the Continental Congress and the Congress of the Confederation, and the creation of a navigation system to promote
American shipping were not objectionable to the secretary of state.
The two Virginians welcomed the liquidation of the foreign debt.
Even Jefferson's negative views on assumption of state debts in
exchange for relocation of the federal capital on the Potomac River
were visible only after the events; he initially brokered the arrangements. While he may have had doubts about the implications of
many of Hamilton's proposals at the start of Washington's admin-

istration, he was able to admit that whatever differences prevailed, his opponents were nonetheless "good men and bold men, and sensible men."[4]

Nowhere were the similarities and differences over foreign policy more clearly expressed in the early years of the Washington administration than over the Nootka Sound crisis of 1790 between Spain and Great Britain. The Spanish navy had seized a British merchant ship off the coast of Vancouver Island for violating Spain's claim to sovereignty over the west coast of the American continent. This was an opportunity for William Pitt, the youthful prime minister, to use the incident to display British power by threatening war. For the United States the threat raised the prospect of a British march across American territory to reach the Pacific. Hamilton's present day critics, particularly the historian Julian Boyd, have noted that the Treasury secretary had weakened America's bargaining power with the British by assuring their agent that the United States would not support Spain's position in the Pacific Northwest.

Such disinformation stiffened Britain's resistance to concessions that the secretary of state hoped might be secured in return for permission for British troops to cross over American territory in the event of war with Spain. He envisioned garnering such advantages for the United States from the quarrels among European powers. Hamilton's private assurance to George Beckwith, Britain's confidential agent, undercut Jefferson's plans. Nevertheless, had Jefferson known Hamilton's dealings with Britain at this time, he might have understood the reasons for them no matter how vigorously he deplored his rival's actions. Unquestionably, Hamilton intruded on Jefferson's responsibility for foreign relations, and unquestionably Hamilton rendered an inappropriate service to Britain. But his motives were not yet ideological. He was worried that American attempts to exact a high price for Britain to send its troops across the Northwest Territory would antagonize a business partner on whom American prosperity was built. "By rendering New Orleans the emporium of products of the Western Country," he informed the president, "Britain would, at a period not very distant, have little occasion for supplies or provisions for their islands from their Atlantic States . . . [w]hence a great diminution of the motives to establish liberal terms of Commercial Intercourse with the United States collectively."[5] If this was Anglophilia, it was severely qualified by the secretary's calculations. Fear, not friendship, moved Hamilton.

It is worth noting that Jefferson did not adamantly oppose concessions to the British per se. His point simply was that concessions ought to be reciprocal. In their first Cabinet debate the two secretaries differed more on tactics than on ideology. Both men's outlooks projected ultimate U.S. independence of foreign influences as well as cultivation of a policy designed to win security and prosperity for the new nation. If the common ground on which they stood in 1790 collapsed under them by 1793, it was the course of European events more than incompatible philosophies that accounted for their divergence.

The French Revolution fashioned new meanings for France and Britain in the minds of the two secretaries, indeed in the minds of a considerable part of the country. Hamilton increasingly found in Great Britain the model of the good society, the font of America's commercial growth, and the protector against French imperialism. His Anglophilic tendencies had been evident in the 1780s, but they were deepened and widened by the challenge of the French Revolution. For Jefferson, France became even more than ever the counterweight to British commercial power as the bellwether of republicanism in a hostile monarchical world. The Anglo-French war in 1793 pushed the country and the two statesmen into actions which neither had anticipated in 1790.

Indeed, by the end of 1793, Jefferson and Madison, each working on the other's fears, had discovered in Hamilton's program a divergence from the common good and in his person an arrogance that annoyed them at every turn. Funding of debts appeared to be a device to enrich speculators at the expense of the agrarian South; the blunting of Madison's efforts to construct a navigation system appeared to be the product of a dangerous attraction to monarchical Britain. Yet it is questionable if the conclusions of conspiracy implied in Hamilton's behavior were fully articulated during Washington's first administration, even though the foundations for them were being laid. It was not just the intellectual opacity of President Washington that accounted for his failure to perceive irreconcilable differences among his Cabinet members. If they existed in his perception, they related to means, not objectives. For the president in his first years in office, the consensus of 1790 over America's relations with the outside world persisted. And most of the evidence that suggested otherwise belongs to a later stage of the Hamilton-Jefferson rivalry.

There was nothing conspiratorial about the initial Hamiltonian policies that Jefferson encountered as secretary of state. The secretary of the treasury was quite open about his objectives—namely, to provide strong underpinnings for a centralized government. It was a government that Jefferson himself had wanted for the Confederation in August 1787, or at least half of what he wanted. The Federal Union could fulfill the wish he expressed in 1787 "to see our states made one as to all foreign, and several as to all domestic matters."[6] But even on domestic matters the distance between him and Hamilton seemed small.

In December 1787, Jefferson expressed his appreciation to Madison for the powers of taxation that would be given to the federal legislature to free it from the interference of state assemblies. For his part, Hamilton laid down in Number 11 of *The Federalist* a principle Jefferson had advocated for years: the power to "oblige foreign countries to bid against each other, for the privileges of our market. . . . Suppose, for instance, we had a government in America, capable of excluding Great Britain (with whom we have at present no treaty of commerce) from all our ports. . . . Would it not enable us to negotiate, with the fairest prospect of success, for commercial privileges of the most valuable and extensive kind, in the dominions of that kingdom?" Admission into the ports of the British West Indies could be one of the rewards of such a commercial policy, as specifically mentioned in this paper. Small wonder that Madison and Hamilton could combine their talents in support of the Constitution in 1787. Jefferson had every right to anticipate fulfillment of these expectations when he took his seat in the Cabinet.

That they went unrealized was prefigured in Madison's failure to win during the first session of Congress in July 1789 passage of a tonnage bill that would have discriminated against ships of nations without a commercial treaty with the United States. The bill failed because of fears of British retribution against planters and shippers dependent on British credit or accustomed to British channels of trade. Additionally, the new Treasury Department was concerned about the loss of revenue collected on British tonnage and imports.

## Breakdown of Consensus

Jefferson detected Hamilton's influence in the inability of Congress to pass a navigation law in either 1789 or in 1790 that would favor America's friends and punish its enemies. He found in his Cabinet colleague not only hostility to the expanding French Revolution but also a full-blown plan for an American polity that took Great

Britain as a partner, at least until the U.S. economy had grown to maturity. Jefferson also experienced frustration over his difficulty in responding to the protests of the French chargé d'affaires, who claimed that Congress had discriminated against France by placing its commerce on the same plane as Britain's. Despite Jefferson's sympathy for the French position, he feared that a tonnage exemption for France would have to be extended to all countries with which the United States had made a treaty of amity and commerce. His solution to grant the concession to France alone on the strength of the special favors the king had granted to American commerce in 1787 and 1788 was opposed by Hamilton as a dangerous precedent and as an unfriendly gesture toward Britain.

The exchange of ideas by the two secretaries about a discriminatory tonnage act reflected Jefferson's disadvantage in his differences with Hamilton. The secretary of state admitted to opposing the French construction of the treaty even as he felt it "essential to cook up some favor which may ensure continuance of the good dispositions they have toward us." Hamilton dismissed both Jefferson and the French complaint with his "conjecture that the communications of the Chargé des affaires of France are . . . expedients to improve a moment, in which it is perceived questions concerning navigation are to be discussed [rather] than the effects of serious instructions from his Court."[7]

By 1791, Hamilton had emerged as Jefferson's nemesis on every possible occasion. Despite the convergence in their long-range aspirations for the United States, the secretary of the treasury increasingly became the contemporary enemy of Jefferson's vision for America. For Hamilton, Britain was the source of American prosperity, its major market, its most reliable supplier of manufactures, and its source of credit. In the long run he anticipated problems with Britain as a competitor, but only after the United States had achieved equality as an industrial power. In the short run the French Revolution had added an element of danger as it attracted the allegiance of an American agrarian majority potentially hostile to the interests of the urban mercantile class, which required amicable relations with Britain.

The Jeffersonian vision for America encompassed a broader picture. While commerce would play a large role, it was to serve a larger segment of the population. Throughout 1790, Hamilton had outmaneuvered him at every turn. Recognizing the need to repay debts to European creditors, a cause that took so much of his time in France, Jefferson could have accepted Hamilton's funding program, but only one part of Hamilton's fiscal policy fitted each man's conception of the nation's obligations—namely, the discharge of the foreign debt to secure America's credit abroad. The federal government's assumption of the domestic debt as well as of state debts was another matter.

Jefferson and Madison recognized the justice of repaying domestic creditors, but their concern was with the original creditors, those former soldiers, farmers, and small merchants who had sold their shares of the Confederation's promissory notes to speculators at a fraction of their face value. When Hamilton rejected the idea of separating the original from the current holders of the public debt as ruinous to the public credit, he did not add that such action on behalf of the disadvantaged would undermine his plans for winning the allegiance of the wealthy and powerful. Madison's efforts to pay the original holders in full failed in the Senate.

Assessing Hamilton's funding plans, Jefferson concluded that "immense sums were thus filched from the poor and ignorant, and fortunes accumulated by those who had themselves been poor enough before. Men thus enriched by the dexterity of a leader, would follow of course the chief who was leading them to fortune, and become the zealous instruments of all his enterprises."[8] This clear condemnation was written years later. Had he been as aware of Hamilton's schemes as the foregoing statements suggest, he would not have acceded to the compromise that traded the federal assumption of state debts for the creation of a new capital on the Potomac.

Yet his charge of being duped by Hamilton into accepting the exchange of funding for assumption of state debts, which would benefit the northern states, was overblown. There seemed to be advantages at the time for a seat of government located at Georgetown on the Potomac that would serve the agrarian South. Two years later he claimed to understand that Hamilton's system "flowed from principles adverse to liberty." He realized that he was "made a tool for forwarding his [Hamilton's] schemes, not then sufficiently understood by me; and of all the errors of my political life, this has occasioned me the deepest regret."[9] While his assertion of ignorance about the political currents in New York is open to question, there is little doubt that he recognized a national interest as well as a parochial benefit in supporting the assumption of state debts. He was uncomfortable with the bargain, as he admitted to Monroe in June 1790, "but in the present instance I see the necessity of yielding for this time . . . to the cries of creditors in certain parts of the union, for the sake of union, and to save us from the greatest of all calamities, the total extinction of our credit in Europe."[10]

Whatever his mild reservations may have been in 1790 or his strong condemnation a generation later, he was persuaded early in his tenure as secretary of state that Hamilton's Treasury was following a different path from his own department. France and its revolution were factors that led to Jefferson's concern about American reactions almost from the moment he returned to the United States. Information about the momentous events in that country was filtered through the notoriously prejudiced British press, and Jefferson attempted to convince John Fenno, publisher of the influential *Gazette of the United States,* to make his journal a counterbalance to the anti-French propaganda emanating from London. For a time Jefferson succeeded, with the help of his authority to designate the newspapers that would print federal statutes. But Hamilton's Treasury Department, with more personnel and a broader reach, converted Fenno into a partisan of the Anglophilic Federalists. To replace Fenno, Jefferson sought a writer who could rebut the Federalist press of Philadelphia. With the help of Madison, he persuaded the poet-editor Philip Freneau, a Princeton classmate of Madison, to begin publishing the *National Gazette* in 1791 and to accept a post as translating clerk in the Department of State.

The secretary of state's hope was that the fires of political controversy stirred up by his friends in the press and Congress would advance the cause of the agrarian majority and frustrate the opponents of the French Revolution without involving him personally in the struggle. Writing articles and engaging in polemical debates were not only distasteful to him but also politically unnecessary as long as he could command the services of allies and subordinates. Symbolically, travels with Madison to Lake George and Saratoga fitted Jefferson's persona. A political alliance with northern opponents of Hamilton could be consummated under the guise of a botanical expedition.

Jefferson was never successful in concealing his hand in the controversies of his time. He failed to take into account the responsibilities of leadership that held him accountable for his every word and that exposed him to the attacks of enemies. Innocently—or at least unwillingly—Jefferson was hurled into the midst of the quarrel over the Anglophilic and putatively monarchical proclivities of the Hamiltonians by his praise of Thomas Paine's broadside, *The Rights of Man.* The secretary of state incited his opponents with a general condemnation of "political heresies" that had appeared in the United States.

Paine's fiery pamphlet, written in answer to Edmund Burke's strictures on the French Revolution, had elicited intense attack in Federalist journals. Sharpest of all was one by "Publicola," whose style was so similar to the well-known "Davila" (John Adams's pseudonym) that Jefferson immediately and mistakenly identified the author with the vice president; he was not aware that "Publicola" was actually John Quincy Adams.

It was with John Adams in mind that Jefferson provided the editor of the American edition of the pamphlet with a testimonial assailing the critics of Paine's defense of the French Revolution. Given his distaste for open controversy, he was probably sincere in denying foreknowledge of the publication of his note and the public attention it would receive. The sentiments expressed were his, but he seems to have intended them for private circulation and not as an open apologia for Paine's tract. No matter how angry he was with his old friend Adams's "apostacy to hereditary monarchy," he had no wish to expose himself to the type of abuse an ad hominem attack would inspire. He explained to President Washington that he was "afraid that the indiscretion of a printer has committed me with my friend Mr. Adams, for whom, as one of the most honest and disinterested men alive, I have a cordial esteem, increased by long habits of concurrence in opinion in the days of his republicanism; and even since his apostacy to hereditary monarchy and nobility, though we differ, we differ as friends do."[11]

Adams was not appeased even after a letter from his old friend tried to set matters straight, particularly when Jefferson tried to blame "Publicola" (whose identity was still unknown to him) for the misunderstanding between the two men. The vice president, always thin-skinned, believed that his were the "political heresies" that Jefferson excoriated. In this instance, Adams was correct. Jefferson, always unwilling to lose a friend, lost Adams for a generation. While Adams was never a Hamiltonian, the French Revolution pushed the vice president into the Federalist camp faster than it did the president himself.

Despite his awareness of political ineffectiveness in domestic affairs in the Hamilton-dominated Cabinet, the secretary of state hoped to pursue agendas in foreign relations that he had conceived in his service as a member of the Continental Congress and developed during his ministry to France. The infrastructure of the

Department of State, small as it was, provided little support. Nor did his ministers abroad compensate for the limited resources of the department. In 1791 they were either ineffective, as in the case of William Carmichael in Spain, or lacking authority, as in the case of his former secretary William Short, whom he had left behind in Paris as chargé d'affaires. In the critical London post there was a vacuum that was filled in part by the lively presence of Gouverneur Morris as an informal agent. These obstacles did not prevent Jefferson from promoting his long-standing objectives for America's foreign relations, particularly regarding forcing Britain through commercial retaliation to surrender the posts in the Northwest Territory and to open its ports to American commerce, building a firm economic and political partnership with France to free the nation from Britain's stranglehold, and promoting westward expansion through pressure on Spain.

## The Mississippi Question

Progress was made in all of these areas, and yet none came to fruition during his tenure in office. Relations with Spain should have been the most productive, if only because that nation was the weakest of the three European powers affecting the future of the United States. Jefferson's recognition of Spain's position in America was manifest in his concern that the use of the Mississippi was in danger of being abandoned in the course of Jay's negotiations with the Spanish minister, Diego de Gardoqui, in 1787. His immediate fear was not that the West would be lost, but that westerners would take matters into their own hands, seize the Mississippi, and separate themselves from the East. However, if the United States waited a generation before supporting the West, the West would be lost, and its loss would be the consequence of both American and Spanish weakness. Navigation of the Mississippi was "the only bone of contention which can arise between Spain and us for ages," he told Carmichael in 1787. "It is a pity it could not be settled amicably. When we consider that the Missisipi is the only issue to the ocean for five eighths of the territory of the U.S. and how fast that territory peoples, the ultimate event cannot be mistaken."[12] It was obvious that Jefferson had no doubt that the Mississippi would fall into American hands. He worried less about the Spanish than he did about the temper of the westerners.

Such was the confidence that he brought with him to the State Department in 1790. Therefore, when war between Britain and Spain over Nootka Sound appeared imminent, Jefferson perceived an opportunity to hasten Spain's concessions on the Mississippi. He was not above threatening Spain with an Anglo-American alliance unless the river and an entrepôt at New Orleans were made available to the United States. As he explained to Carmichael in outlining policy toward the Mississippi question, the United States had a right to the navigation of the Mississippi, by nature as well as by law. The secretary of state subsequently developed a doctrine of natural right to the navigation of the Mississippi, appealing to the authority of Emmerich de Vattel as he claimed that obstructions to river navigation were acts of force, at best. A nation that had access to the upper waters of a river had a natural right to the lower waters. "What sentiment," he asked, "is written in deeper characters than that the Ocean is free to all men, and their Rivers to all their inhabitants."[13] In brief, Jefferson was claiming that even if Spain controlled both shores of the river mouth, it had no right to exclude American traffic from the upper waters.

What gave urgency to the secretary's importunities in 1790 was concern that Britain would seize the west bank of the Mississippi along with New Orleans itself. Jefferson's preference was to use this crisis to force Spain to cede all territory east of the river in return for an American guarantee of its possessions west of the river. "In fine," according to his policy, "for a narrow slip of barren, detached, and expensive country, Spain secures the rest of her territory, and makes an Ally, where she might have a dangerous enemy."[14] Anticipation of a war between Britain and Spain over the Nootka question, Jefferson predicted, would bring France into the conflict as Spain's ally, which in turn would permit America's friends in Paris to bring pressure on Madrid to grant American demands.

The end of the war crisis did not end Jefferson's hopes for Spanish concessions in the West. Nor did it shake the secretary's optimism about the nation's ability to profit from the conflicts of Europe without having to surrender its own neutrality. Ultimately, Pinckney's Treaty recognizing the Mississippi as the western boundary of the United States vindicated Jefferson, as the shifting currents in the European balance of power persuaded Spain to concede to the United States the right of deposit of westerners' goods in New Orleans. But Thomas Pinckney's signature at San Lorenzo was appended in October 1795 after Jefferson left office. In the short run the European alliance system turned against Jefferson's diplomacy. The most that Spain would allow in 1791 was a resumption of negotiations with the United States that had been in abeyance since Gardoqui's failure to conclude an agreement with John Jay in 1786. France had appeared willing to support the American position even to the point of its foreign minister presenting a memorandum on the subject. William Short, then minister to The Hague, joined Carmichael, the chargé d'affaires at Madrid, as joint commissioners to conduct the negotiations.

The war in Europe undercut Jefferson's Spanish policy in 1793. Negotiations languished. The French Revolution had moved on from the reforms of the monarchy, which had kept alive the Bourbon Family Compact, to a republic that executed the king. Spain was as frightened of the consequences of the aggressive new regime in France as any monarchy in Europe, and consequently joined Britain in the First Coalition against republican France.

Instead of a French connection that could serve the United States in its relations with Spain, Jefferson had to face an Anglo-Spanish alliance linking the two nations that bordered the United States. Spain no longer had to be concerned with a British attack from Canada or a hostile Anglo-American combination. It could resist American importunities with some confidence, particularly as it negotiated treaties with Indian tribes that brought the Creeks together with the Cherokees, Choctaws, and Chickasaws into a pro-Spanish confederation. Spanish authorities in 1793 openly furnished arms and ammunition to the treaty tribes, who in turn served as a buffer in the disputed territory along the Yazoo River protecting Louisiana and Florida from American encroachment. What was particularly disturbing to Jefferson was Spain's undercutting of an American peace treaty with the Creeks in 1790 in which their chief, Alexander McGillivray, would have received an annual salary and a commission as a brigadier general in the United States Army. The Spanish governor of Louisiana lured McGillivray away from his commitments by doubling the pension the United States had offered.

This success emboldened the Spanish to fortify posts in the disputed territory as well as to renew intrigues with Kentucky dissidents such as Brigadier General James Wilkinson, who had worked for Spain during the Confederation period. When Jefferson protested, the Spanish agents in Philadelphia denied that Spain was stirring up the southwestern tribes and suggested that the negotiations then supposedly in progress in Madrid would resolve the question of both the boundary line and Indian relations.

Jefferson agreed to the proposition without realizing that Spain, confident in its new alliance with Britain, had no intention of even compromising with the United States. There was sufficient evidence of further Spanish intrigues with the southwestern Indians to lead the secretary of state to assume that the Spanish agents aimed at pushing the United States into war. As Jefferson pointed out to Carmichael and Short, "If Spain chooses to consider our self-defense against savage butchery as a cause of war to her, we must meet her also in war, with regret, but without fear; and we shall be happier to the last moment, to repair with her, to the tribunal of peace and reason."[15]

Jefferson's ambivalence about potential war with Spain was mirrored by an equal ambivalence about relations with Native American "nations." On the one hand, he wrote off Indians as savages who were incited by Britain or Spain to prey on American westerners, hardly deserving of equal standing under international law. On the other hand, as the *Notes on Virginia* revealed, he recognized their virtues and sought their ultimate assimilation into American society. While recognizing the necessity of defeating the Indians, particularly in the Northwest, he was opposed to seizure of their lands. Nevertheless, he advocated pre-empting enough lands to prevent other nations from taking possession. If war was necessary, he hoped for a quick victory, and then reconciliation. He did not want to see Indian depredations used as an excuse to raise troops or increase public debt.

His optimism over prospects for peace with Indians and concessions from Spain was overtaken by events in Europe in 1793. Jefferson had correctly anticipated war in Europe; he was mistaken that war would quickly serve America's case against Spain. In the longer run, turmoil in Europe did bring the Spanish to "the tribunal of peace and reason," but not until Jefferson had left office. Pinckney's Treaty of 1795, however, was a direct consequence of another shift in the European balance of power, following Spain's departure from its British connection and its consequent fear once again of an Anglo-American combination against its territories in North America. The victorious armies of the French Revolution had intimidated Spain into making a separate peace with the French republic. The result was its acceptance of American boundary claims and the right of deposit at New Orleans. It was a Federalist secretary of state and a Federalist diplomat who benefited politically from what Samuel Flagg Bemis has called "America's advantage from Europe's distress," but it was a clear fulfillment of Jefferson's vision and strategy.

## The Anglo-Federalist Connection

Frustrating as Jefferson's negotiations with Spain had been, he was not burdened with two obstacles that stood in the way of successful dealings with Great Britain—namely, the superior power of Britain and the influence of Hamilton on its behalf. With Spain there was a recognition of its basic weakness and an expectation of its eventual surrender to American demands. No such outcome was assured with Britain. The secretary of state was well aware of Britain's strategic advantages in the Northwest posts, its specious but effective arguments on the basis of the peace treaty of 1783, and its advantageous position with the Indians of the Northwest.

Their situation with respect to Anglo-American commerce was even stronger. Jefferson's introduction to the state of foreign affairs coincided with Hamilton's subversion of Madison's 1790 tariff and tonnage bill that had passed in the House but failed in the Senate, where Hamilton's influence prevailed. Madison's proposals were so watered down that there was discrimination in favor of American shipping but no special discrimination among foreign shippers. Britain was the beneficiary of this policy. For Jefferson and Madison the only way of forcing Britain to open up its ports to American shipping was to retaliate against its vessels and commerce by new navigation laws.

No other discriminatory measures succeeded during Jefferson's tenure in office. Gouverneur Morris, Washington's former aide-de-camp, had been the president's special agent in London examining Britain's intentions toward the new Federal Union. But if navigation laws could not be passed, what was Morris to use as his weapons to effect change in British thinking toward the United States? Hamilton's program would restructure the American economy along commercial and ultimately manufacturing lines, requiring close cooperation with that paragon of sound economy and expanding credit, Great Britain. That nation would buy American raw materials, extend loans to promising American business ventures, and by the volume of Anglo-American commerce promote the fortunes of shippers. In the long run, America would create an economic base that would outbid British competitors in manufactures, but in the short run, British goodwill was paramount as a prerequisite for the building of American power. By deferring to the British economy and accepting the unequal treatment of American commerce, Hamilton expected to persuade the British to relinquish the posts in the Northwest and to arrange a more equitable commercial agreement with the United States.

To prevent the Jeffersonians from undermining his program with their prejudice against British policy, Hamilton confided in Major George Beckwith, formerly an aide of Lord Dorchester, Governor-General of Canada and subsequently a British agent in New York and Philadelphia. Hamilton kept Beckwith informed of the prospects of new Congressional attempts in early 1791 to prohibit the importation of goods or products of a country that refused to accept American goods in American bottoms, as was the case in the British West Indies. Beckwith in turn communicated privately to Hamilton a warning from Foreign Minister George Grenville that if discrimination against their shipping should materialize, the British would respond vigorously. To Hamilton this warning threatened potential damage to America's credit as well as denial of access to British ports, and consequently destruction of the basis of his nation's prosperity. The secretary of the treasury was intimidated, and he responded undiplomatically that Congress would pass no discriminatory law against Britain.

Beckwith conveyed this intelligence to Grenville, and Whitehall's foreknowledge of America's internal politics and of Hamilton's Anglophilic influence closed whatever possibilities Gouverneur Morris might have had in London to bend British policies. Even when Grenville's information was erroneous or distorted—since Hamilton frequently attributed to the president views he did not have—the effect was the same. Britain was encouraged to hold the line on its occupation of Northwest posts, on its continued barring of American ships from its West Indian ports, and on its support for Indian hostilities against Americans in the Northwest Territory.

Morris, a tart-tongued conservative, was no kept man of the British aristocracy. He knew the president's mind, which was quite different in 1791 from Hamilton's, and occasionally used ambiguously threatening language to make his point in terms Washington and Jefferson would approve. Failing to make headway on the matter of a commercial treaty, Morris turned to an area that should have alarmed the British: American military action in the Northwest. Morris asserted that when the time and circumstances were ripe, the United States would exercise its rights and evict Britain from its illegal occupation of American territory. In 1790, Morris's veiled intimidation did not penetrate British sangfroid because Hamilton had already informed Beckwith that the expeditionary force sent against the Indians in the spring of 1790 was not intended for action against British posts.

Morris's frustration became the raw material for one of two reports that the secretary of state released early in 1791. Both were designed to feed the nation's Anglophobia and to further Jefferson's vision of an America freed from the grip of Britain's economic power. They allusively emphasized the virtues of a French connection by contrasting it with a stark portrayal of Britain's arrogant exploitation of America's economy. His elaborate explication of the state of the whale oil and codfish industries—extending the themes of the treatise he had written in 1788—described the unfair commercial competition between the United States and Great Britain in which the fisheries provided only one major example. The British, according to Jefferson's "Report on American Fisheries," were "mounting their navigation on the ruin of ours."[16] The report argued that to redress the balance created by British practices, the United States must either offer bounties to its fishermen or compel the British to lift their prohibitive duty on American whale oil. Failure to secure relief could destroy the nation's maritime industry. The means should be commercial retaliation against the country that damaged American interests, and commercial favors for Britain's adversary, France.

Jefferson's report on the failure of the Morris mission to London was more inflammatory. It had been prepared two months earlier, but its delivery had been delayed by Hamilton's objections to its tone of reproach to Britain. When finally delivered at the same time as the report on fisheries, it incited Congressional emotions against British behavior in a manner the other reports could not achieve. Hamilton did his best to defuse emotions by discrediting Morris, claiming that his failure was the result of his undiplomatic and provocative consorting with the French ambassador to London and of his indiscreet language in his communications with Whitehall. The president, however, shared Jefferson's view that the fault was Britain's, hence the release of a report that indicted the British in the guise of a description of Morris's problems in London. From the correspondence with Morris, Jefferson concluded that Britain had no intention of surrendering the Northwest posts, let alone admitting American ships into British West Indian ports. British ministers, he reported, "do not mean to submit their present advantages in commerce to the risk which might attend a discussion of them, whereon some reciprocity could not fail to be demanded."[17] Only if the United States would make an entangling alliance with Britain that would undermine the Franco-American treaty of 1778 would the British consent to a commercial treaty. In these circumstances there was no basis for further negotiation.

From the perspective of the secretary of state there was no more propitious time for Congress to pass retaliatory measures against Britain than in the winter of 1791. Madison's navigation laws should overcome Hamiltonian opposition at last. Jefferson's hopes for change were high enough to permit him to instruct ministers abroad about the usefulness of Madison's proposals as a model for other nations to adopt. The envoys were to emphasize reciprocity in their talks, a principle that British arrogance rejected. Should all the commercial nations of the world band together, they could force Britain to grant equity to every state. "This act is perfectly innocent as to other nations," he assured them, "and if adopted by other nations would inevitably defeat [Britain's] navigation act and reduce their power on the sea within safer limits."[18] In effect, the secretary of state was asking for a peacetime equivalent of the League of Armed Neutrals in conformity with the spirit of the Plan of 1776. Yet the idea was neither utopian nor altruistic. It seemed to Jefferson to be the quickest way to free America from British domination. It was also one more invitation to France to move into the vacuum that would be left by throwing off British domination of the American economy.

Even as he dispatched these advices to American ministers in Europe, Jefferson recognized that he had suffered defeat again at Hamilton's hands. Federalist Congressmen managed to postpone voting on a new navigation bill by asking the secretary of state for still another report on the state of American commerce. Hamilton's ascendancy in the making of foreign policy appeared pervasive long before the end of Washington's first administration. He moved steadily and with increasing assurance into foreign affairs, with notable influence on diplomatic appointments. To France went Gouverneur Morris, who may have annoyed Hamilton during his London mission, but whose aristocratic sensibilities made him more hostile to French republicans than he had been to the Court of St. James's. Morris went to France without the blessings of the secretary of state and with the belief that Hamilton had been responsible for his appointment. To England went Thomas Pinckney, a

Charleston Federalist whom Jefferson had never met and of whose appointment he had no prior notice. If one were to categorize diplomatists as Anglophiles or Francophiles, or as Hamiltonians or Jeffersonians, there should be no hesitation about the proper allegiance of the ministers to Great Britain and to France in 1791.

The one important by-product of the threat of a navigation system was the dispatch of George Hammond as British minister to the United States. The appointment did little to further Jefferson's policies. Hammond immediately took up the same comfortable and confidential relationship with the secretary of the treasury that his unofficial predecessor Beckwith had enjoyed. Expectation of this appointment had been Hamilton's ace in the sleeve to combat Madison's program. Presumably, rumors about the impending British decision stayed the hand of enough Congressmen to defuse Jefferson and Madison's campaign against Britain. In reality, the intention to send an official minister had antedated Jefferson's Anglophobic reports. The most that legitimately may be claimed was that American unrest in Congress advanced Hammond's travel schedule; the original decision to send an envoy reflected the fears engendered during the Nootka Sound crisis.

The dominant feature in the Hammond mission was not British fear of the Francophiles in Philadelphia but rather a sense that there was no need to worry over America's policy toward Britain. Hamilton had seen to this. Hammond's instructions allowed no treaty to be contracted; he was merely to dally with American leaders. He had no authority to settle issues of the Northwest posts or admission of American ships into British West Indian ports. The views he could express were largely concerned with the construction of an Indian barrier state similar in language and spirit to the British and Spanish schemes of the 1780s. Even Hamilton reacted negatively to this outrage.

Hamilton bore a responsibility, however, for the patronizing tone this twenty-seven-year-old diplomat adopted in dealing with the seasoned secretary of state. Jefferson quickly recognized that the British minister had no power to negotiate a commercial treaty, or any other kind of treaty. Still, the secretary was willing to discuss all the outstanding questions between the two countries— debts, boundaries, and posts. Hammond proceeded to marshal what he considered damning evidence of America's failure to fulfill the obligations of the peace treaty. The British had a case, particularly with the states' failure to repay debts to British creditors and restore confiscated Loyalist property. By contrasting British violations on such issues as evacuating Northwest posts with the federal government's efforts to respond to treaty obligations, Jefferson undercut Hammond's arguments. But nothing came of these talks beyond Hamilton's assurance that Jefferson's language did not represent the views of the president. Thus coached by his Federalist friends, the British minister stayed away from the secretary of state, dismissing him in much the same way that the Hamiltonians were doing in 1792.

While Jefferson's relations with Britain became tangled in the coils of France's incendiary actions in 1793, the secretary had not lost faith in popular resentment against British intransigence over a commercial treaty and over its involvement with Indian hostilities in the West. His long-delayed report on discrimination against American commerce that had been postponed in 1791 in anticipation of Hammond's arrival was released in 1793. There was little new in the secretary's condemnation. He mentioned cases of discrimination by other European powers, but the behavior of other nations, particularly France, was milder than Britain's, and their actions were susceptible to mutually satisfactory negotiation, again unlike Britain's. Jefferson's decision to resign from the Washington Cabinet was essentially a by-product of his inability to succeed in achieving a navigation law that would protect American interests from British control.

Given the variety and complexity of his frustrations as the Cabinet official in charge of foreign relations, Jefferson's willingness to remain in office beyond Washington's first administration is a matter worth considering. The primary reason lay in all probability in his perceptions of the president's role in the secretary of state's contest with the secretary of the treasury. It was not until the summer of 1792 that Washington became aware of the depth of the personal friction between the two men, and it is doubtful that he ever fully grasped the philosophical differences separating them. Refusing as long as he could to recognize factional divisions in his administration, he decided to keep the Cabinet intact as he began his second administration. But why did Jefferson remain as long as he did? Did he hope that another year in Philadelphia would bring the successes that eluded him in the first administration? Or did he assume that the president was not a committed Anglophile, monarchist, or Hamiltonian, and hence open to Jeffersonian persuasion?

## The French Alternative

If Jefferson responded positively to the latter question, his reaction was not a measure of his naiveté. Prior to the wars of the French Revolution, Washington showed considerable sympathy for France, if only because his disciple Lafayette was one of its leaders. When the president did follow Hamilton's guidance in the early years of his administration, it was often for the same reasons that moved Jefferson: the New Yorker's policies offered solutions to pressing financial claims, promoted the conception of a strong executive authority, and promised a stable government capable of winning Europe's respect. Moreover, Jefferson's specific objectives of settling border controversies with Spain and Britain and negotiating a new commercial treaty with France were programs to which the president subscribed. While the subtleties of Jefferson's vision of America may have escaped the president, his reaction to British impudence was not lost on the secretary of state. Washington's temper would not have tolerated the trespasses of Beckwith or Hammond had he known of their illicit connections with their American confidants. In view of these perceptions, Jefferson's appeal to Washington to accept re-election was a signal of his genuine belief that only Washington could save the nation from its internal enemies.

The course of the French Revolution and its impact on the United States changed Jefferson's perceptions of Washington after 1792. They would also change his views on France. In his first two years in office his treatment of France was based on a conviction that the revolutionary changes in that country were progressing at a steady pace. The fundamental assumption of stability there gave the secretary of state freedom to criticize the revolutionary government more sharply than he had ever spoken about the Ancien Régime. For Jefferson, the revolutionary regime of the National Assembly had none of the excuses of the old government for thwarting his objectives. The men who made the revolution in 1789 were his friends, and so it should have followed as a matter of course that an enlightened France would open all its colonies to American commerce and free American citizens from the restrictions imposed in prerevolutionary days.

When the desired results were not immediately forthcoming, Jefferson suggested to his former protégé William Short that he apply some pressure in his capacity as chargé d'affaires to focus the attention of the National Assembly on the needs of the United States. Inasmuch as France had a stake in the outcome of the new American loan then being negotiated in Amsterdam (half was destined for immediate payment to France), Short could mention that a favorable disposition of America's commercial problems in the West Indies would expedite the payment of the American debt: "You will of course find excuses for not paying the money which is ready and put under your orders, till you see that the moment has arrived when the emotions it may excite, may give a decisive cast to the demands of the colonies."[19] Jefferson was counting on pressure from French colonists to make his scheme work. No matter how Francophilic the secretary might sound when he compared France with Britain, his Machiavellian advice to Short was not that of a Francophile.

Jefferson had supported another measure that attracted even greater French attention. He encouraged the Congressional appointments of Sylvanus Bourne and Fulwar Skipwith to American consulships at Saint-Domingue and Martinique, respectively. Antoine de la Forest, the French consul in New York, immediately challenged the action on the ground that the appointments contradicted his government's commercial regulations. The Foreign Ministry expanded this view into the general proposition that no nation ever allows foreign trade with its colonies. Despite this French bluster, Jefferson cited the consular convention of 1788 for his authority to appoint consuls and refused to recall Bourne or Skipwith. Ultimately, the French government permitted the consuls to remain in the colonies provided they carried no official title. They could be designated "commercial agents."

France's delay in acceding to what the secretary of state considered to be a natural right—free trade everywhere—had deeper roots than the bureaucratic inefficiency of an inexperienced regime. The reformed monarchy of 1791 proved just as reluctant as the old monarchy to permit this breach of the colonial monopoly. Within a year of Jefferson's becoming secretary, it imposed extra duties on all foreign ships carrying commerce to mainland France. Chargé d'affaires Short objected to this decree, warning Foreign Minister Montmorin that these duties would have a harmful effect on Franco-American relations. Jefferson's reaction was sharper. France's actions seemed to him to be the height of stupidity and ingratitude, considering his plans for a prominent French role in America's economic life: "such an act of hostility against our navigation . . . was not to have been expected from the friendship of that Nation."[20]

This provocation, more than any other, forced Jefferson to realize that the brave new world of the French Revolution was not as new as it first seemed. The philosophy of mercantilism, with its jealous protectiveness toward colonies, still dominated French economic councils. The secretary was annoyed at France's inability to appreciate America's needs in those islands, or for that matter the needs of the colonies themselves. Impress upon our French friends, he advised Short, that their colonies might take joint action with the United States if the National Assembly does not see the light.

Jefferson derived little more satisfaction from his relations with France in 1792 and early 1793. He was doubtful of the attitude of the Chevalier de Ternant, the minister of the last Bourbon government, who seemed more comfortable with Hamilton than with the secretary of state. In April 1793, Jefferson presented once again his plan of offering to citizens of each country the privileges of natives in the ports of the other, which would have the effect of opening the West Indian trade to the United States, elevating France to a higher status than Britain's. There was some interest in Paris in the idea, but the tottering regime of the National Assembly was too feeble to advance the plan.

The basic difficulty between France and the United States was not distrust of Jefferson's intentions or the desirability of deepening the American connection. Rather, it was the revolutionary renascence of French mercantilism under the auspices of the National and Legislative Assemblies. Mercantilists had been among the most ardent supporters of revolution, seeking to advance their interests through a more efficient government. Lafayette was actually less effective against their power in the National Assembly than he had been in the old regime in the days when passions were less inflamed. Even the more farsighted mercantilists who had no intention of injuring American commerce wanted, as a matter of principle, to deprive American ships of the right to carry their own tobacco to France and to restrain American commerce from supplying its natural market in the West Indies.

## The Neutrality Proclamation

In the summer of 1792, Jefferson's complex of attitudes toward France underwent radical change. His earlier approval of the revolution, which he had vaguely identified with the limited monarchy of 1789, gave way to passionate acceptance of French republicanism. His cool objectivity toward points of conflict between French and American interests was replaced by an empathy with French needs in a spirit he had not shown before. The reasons for this transformation had little connection with the vagaries of domestic problems. Intensification of party conflict in the United States would not have accounted for the passion with which he now viewed the fortunes of the French Revolution. His battle with Hamilton had been joined, after all, before 1792 without curbing his criticism of the French regime.

The cause of change was external. War between revolutionary France and a European coalition of Prussia and Austria destroyed in one stroke Jefferson's assumptions about France's position as a counterbalance to Britain. No longer could he rely upon the existence of a stable government in Paris to prod or cajole its leaders into serving the role he had identified for them. The survival of the revolution was now at stake, and with it the security of American republicanism. Victory of the monarchical coalition would provide the "monocrats" of America with the inspiration and possibly the material means to establish a monarchy in the United States. As he informed Lafayette, then at the head of France's army, "While you are estimating the monster Aristocracy, and pulling out the teeth of its associate, Monarchy, a contrary tendency is discovered in some here. A sect has shown itself among us, who declare they espoused our new Constitution not as a good and sufficient thing in itself, but only as a step to an English constitution."[21] To avert this catastrophe the secretary of state seemed ready to follow any course the revolution might take to ensure its survival.

His new devotion was quickly put to a test. External invasion of France brought to the surface the internal war in the United States between monarchists and republicans, moderates and radicals, nationalists and internationalists. Jefferson, three thousand miles away from the scene, had only a hazy understanding of the nature of the conflict among the parties that had either emerged or changed since his departure from France in the fall of 1789. He had difficulty in distinguishing the federalist, relatively moderate Girondists, who wished to spread the revolution through war, from the radical, nationalist Jacobins, whose bloody battles were with the enemy within France. Referring to the Girondists, he noted: "Notwithstanding the very general abuse of the Jacobins, I begin to consider them as representing the true revolution-spirit of the whole nation."[22]

This was Jefferson writing in June 1792. Two months later the revolution took a new turn. Moderate and radical republicans joined the mob-dominated Paris Commune in deposing and imprisoning the king, in massacring suspected counterrevolutionaries, and in replacing the limited monarchy with a republic governed by a National Convention endowed with executive as well as legislative powers. This was a revolutionary event as profound as the fall of the Bastille in July 1789.

The diplomat in Paris three years earlier would have been horrified by this development. It seemed to be the fulfillment of all the warnings he had given to his French friends about the consequences of pushing reforms too fast. Many of his friends fell victim to the new regime as liberals who failed the radical tests of revolutionary purity. Among them was his closest ally and his personal link to the French Revolution, the Marquis de Lafayette, who fled into exile in August rather than face the guillotine in Paris. Yet the secretary of state welcomed the Girondist party that bore responsibility for the September massacres, and hailed its leaders as fellow republicans, the counterparts of the patriots of 1789. His fears of excess were apparently forgotten when William Short in Paris expressed his disgust over the new direction of the revolution. He disregarded Short's information and, seeking to restore his protégé's wavering faith in the French republic, burst out with perhaps the most celebrated of his hyperbolic statements: "The liberty of the whole earth was depending on the issue of the contest. . . . My own affections have been deeply wounded by some of the martyrs to this cause, but rather than it should have failed I would have seen half the earth desolated."[23]

These words were written on January 3, 1793, less than three weeks before Louis XVI was beheaded, an act that brought Britain into the European war against France. It led to an agonizing decision of the president on how to respond to a war in which the United States as France's ally might become involved. Given Jefferson's emotional state, there was no question about where he stood with respect both to the validity of the Franco-American alliance of 1778 and to which side he hoped would prevail. His emotions were further roiled by the opportunity Hamilton seized in using the death of the king as an opportunity to break the French connection, or at least to place Jefferson on the defensive in preparation for other assaults against the alliance.

The secretary of state won the first round as he ridiculed the Federalist contention that the destruction of the monarchy meant the end of the alliance. Rhetorically, he asked: "Who is the American who can say with truth that he would not have allied himself to France if she had been a republic?"[24] Such was his response to the president's question in April about the validity of the treaty with France. To Gouverneur Morris he asserted: "We surely cannot deny the right to any nation that right whereon our own government is founded, that everyone may govern itself according to whatever form it pleases, and change these forms at its own will."[25]

The secretary of the treasury seemed not only ready but anxious to deny precisely this right when he claimed that the original contracts had been made with Louis XVI and not with the usurpers who had murdered their sovereign and temporarily ruled France. The treaties, Hamilton advised, should be suspended until the air was cleared and the legitimate authorities were restored to power. How would the royal government react subsequently toward the American ally if it defeated the revolutionaries? The act of war was sufficient to absolve the United States from its obligations under the alliance, since that treaty stipulated assistance only in a defensive, not offensive, war.

How serious was Hamilton in making his case? The secretary of the treasury may have intentionally raised the temper of Jefferson and Madison so that subsequently he could—and did—make an ostensible concession on the matter of recognition in order to extract an advantage in other areas of Franco-American relations. Similarly, Hamilton's recommendation to reject Edmond Charles Genêt, Ternant's successor, until the results of the war in Europe were known was either frivolous or purposely provocative. After all, he had no trouble accepting Ternant, who represented republican France, before the execution of the king. Jefferson rose to the bait in challenging Hamilton.

Jefferson not only won over Washington on the question of recognizing republican France but also established a precedent that became a tradition in American diplomatic history—namely, that the government in control of a nation, able and willing to discharge its treaty obligations, would be recognized irrespective of its ideology. Yet there is a temptation to wonder if Jefferson would have come to a different conclusion if a republican France had been overthrown by a pro-British monarchy. Would his genuine revulsion at such a prospect have allowed him to grant legitimacy to a hostile monarchical France? Conceivably, the secretary of state might have taken the Hamiltonian position and established an ideological test of legitimacy, such as has been applied to the Soviet Union, China, and Cuba at various times in the twentieth century.

The heart of the controversy over Franco-American relations in 1793 lay in the form American neutrality should take toward the European war. This was the third and most crucial question raised by the president. Hamilton desired a neutrality that would minimize the aid the United States was expected to offer and hence lessen the impact of the alliance upon Great Britain. As with the other two questions, the president had tipped his hand before he raised the issue. Six days before he had presented his queries, he had written to both men of the need for a "strict neutrality" that would keep the United States out of the agonies of a foreign war.[26]

Jefferson's response to Washington's preference for neutrality displayed the limits of his devotion to the French cause. Supportive as he was, he was no more willing than Hamilton to accept an interpretation of the treaty of alliance that would obligate the United States to enter war on the side of its ally. When Washington proclaimed American neutrality in 1793, Jefferson agreed with its objective. War with Britain would invite financial bankruptcy and internal chaos, even without a possible British invasion. Jefferson had no interest in looking at the fine print in the text of the treaty to distance the United States from its ally. He tacitly accepted Hamilton's argument for legitimately evading the obligations of the alliance—namely, that France, not Britain, was the aggressor. The government of the Convention had declared war on Britain and Holland on February 1, 1793.

France was as silent on the military obligations of the treaty as Jefferson was. Its concern was with the benefits the other treaty of 1778, of amity and commerce, would bring to its war with Britain. There was no doubt about the secretary of state's wish to aid France's effort, but not at the expense of a war with Britain. The way out of his dilemma was to have the president couch a notice of neutrality that permitted maximum American economic aid to the French ally. The secretary of the treasury, on the other hand, wanted an announcement that would imply America's acceptance of Britain's restrictive interpretation of neutral rights. Hamilton's position prevailed.

With Madison's support, Jefferson then turned to a constitutional objection to proclaiming neutrality. An executive proclamation without approval of Congress would infringe on the constitutional power of the legislative branch to declare war. Rejecting this construction of the Constitution, the secretary of the treasury in his anonymous *Pacificus Papers* replied that the president could make such a proclamation by virtue of his powers as commander in chief when Congress was not in session. The most that the secretary of state could extract was the deletion of the term "neutrality" from the document that Attorney General Edmund Randolph issued on April 20.

Jefferson was unhappy with the outcome and sensitive to the bitter commentary of Madison, who condemned the proclamation as a shabby denunciation of America's psychic debt to France and a dangerous accretion of executive authority. Aroused by fears of creating an "English neutrality" and angered by Hamilton's anonymous blasts in print, Jefferson urged Madison to take up his pen and "cut him to pieces in the face of the public."[27] Under the name of "Helvidius," Madison followed Jefferson's advice. It was futile in the summer of 1793. The matter of Congressional powers was essentially irrelevant. The proclamation was already in effect, and it was bound to antagonize the French.

Jefferson's basic problem was his unwillingness to face up to the incompatibility of "neutrality" and "alliance," and this was Hamilton's advantage. The secretary of the treasury confronted the issue more clearly and candidly than his rival. He could afford to. Hamilton's aim, after all, was to distance the United States from France and push it toward Britain in any way he could. If he could not have the treaties suspended, he could make a case that Jefferson himself had to accept. His argument that France could not defend the United States if it were caught up in the French war against Britain was not lost on the Jeffersonians.

Jefferson was deluding himself in believing that he could advance a conception of neutral rights in this conflict that could serve the French cause. The opportunities for manipulating "neutrality" were all on Hamilton's side. The very use of the term itself in all but the official declaration was a source of comfort to Britain and of disturbance to France. And Jefferson knew this when he used the metaphor "disagreeable pill" to describe it. When he urged Morris to point out to the French that "we shall be more useful as neutrals than as parties by the protection which our flag will give to supplies of provision," he was applying sugar coating to the pill as well as expressing his own hopes for the future.[28] His idea of a "fair neutrality" would permit American ships to carry goods to France from the West Indies in accordance with the construction of neutral rights embodied in the treaty of amity and commerce. The disagreeable pill would be the acceptance of the restrictive British interpretation of neutral rights.

The Girondist leaders of France were too busy conducting their war to examine the nature of Jefferson's attitude toward their country. They had grandiose schemes for the liberation of the world from the grip of monarchy and assumed as a matter of course that their friend would welcome a role in this noble effort. There seemed to be no reason to warn Genêt that the secretary of state might not approve all the instructions given to him upon his departure from France. One major feature of Genêt's objectives was eminently satisfactory to Jefferson: a new treaty in which the commercial privileges of each country's citizens would be exchanged between the allies. Such an agreement would have opened the French West Indies to American ships, a proposal the secretary of state had made to Genêt's predecessor unsuccessfully in 1791. An embattled France had changed its mind about such concessions. Other objectives, such as arming French privateers in American ports and stirring insurrection in British and Spanish territories, seemed to the Girondist leadership equally calculated to win the fraternal sympathy and support of the secretary of state.

Jefferson's first impressions of the attractive young French minister blurred the problems inherent in his instructions and, for that matter, in Genêt's personality. As Genêt traveled slowly from Charleston over a four-week triumphal tour to Philadelphia he was greeted by Francophile crowds with praises that would have turned the heads of men older and wiser than the thirty-year-old romantic revolutionary. Elated by Genêt's apparent popularity, Jefferson encouraged the minister to believe that he agreed to France's objectives in every particular. He was relieved that the French ally did not ask for America's entry into the war or even its defense of the West Indies. All Genêt seemed to want was Jefferson's own version of a "fair neutrality" that would benefit from full freedom of commerce between the two countries under a liberal interpretation of neutral rights. "In short he offers everything, and asks nothing," Jefferson wrote to Madison.[29]

In his relief over France's apparent graciousness in overlooking Hamilton's, and even Washington's, embarrassing doubts about the role of the United States, Jefferson initially excused the vanity and impetuosity in Genêt's behavior. Indeed, he contributed to the Frenchman's general euphoria by making derogatory comments in private about Federalists. Genêt later claimed that Jefferson's comments on the president's lack of power to make a proclamation of neutrality inspired his self-defeating attack on Washington. But this contretemps came in the summer; in May the two men saw the proclamation as serving the interests of both countries. For France, neutrality was preferable to U.S. participation in the war if American ships could carry provisions to the homeland. A neutral America serving France's economic needs would be of much more use than a belligerent America whose ships would be subject to British seizure and whose armies would require French subvention and probable rescue. The record of the Continental forces in the American Revolution could not have stirred sentiment in France for mobilization of an American army to help the French revolutionary cause.

In fact, the terms of Genêt's instructions made a mockery of Jefferson's interpretations. Rather than asking nothing and giving everything, Genêt's instructions did demand American defense of the French West Indies but not until that support became a part of a revised treaty between the two countries. Nor was Jefferson aware of the dangers inherent in the Convention's instructions to Genêt "to take all measures comportable with his position to plant the principles of liberty and independence in Louisiana and the other provinces adjacent to the United States."[30] While this was not an explicit invitation to push Americans into violating a European power's domain, it exposed an imperial vision that would have brought the two allies into collision had it been realized.

The secretary of state never comprehended the threat of France's expansive ambitions in 1793 in the way he recognized Napoleon Bonaparte's a decade later or, for that matter, the Bourbons' a decade earlier. He even contributed his mite to France's plans by supplying André Michaux, the distinguished botanist, with a letter of introduction to Governor Isaac C. Shelby of Kentucky. Even though the French scientist had a genuine assignment from the American Philosophical Society in Philadelphia to engage in research on trans-Mississippi flora, his mission was primarily political. Jefferson knew that Michaux intended to commission Americans for an expedition against Spanish Louisiana to establish an independent state west of the Mississippi under French protection. Although the secretary warned against any enlistment of Americans within U.S. borders, he confided to the French minister that he did not "care what insurrections should be excited in Louisiana," beyond America's sovereignty.[31] Jefferson displayed his lack of care by failing to warn Kentuckians about Michaux's purposes.

For the moment, Jefferson had lost his composure in the excitement aroused by Genêt's arrival. Conceivably, had he restrained the impressionable young Frenchman and informed him of the limits Americans would place on the services they would render

France, he might have spared the minister some of the errors he committed. In his early interviews with Genêt, Jefferson had given him the impression that the people, if not the government, would approve his every action. It was a mistaken impression. While Jefferson was as anxious as Genêt to have Britain accept the liberal principles of neutral rights, particularly that of free ships carrying free goods, he had no intention of going to war to make Britain accept free passage of French provisions en route to France on American ships. France, not Britain, was bound to accept this interpretation of neutral rights under the treaty of amity and commerce. He had to admit to Genêt "that, by the general law of nations, the goods of a friend found in the vessel of an enemy are free, and the goods of an enemy found in the vessel of a friend are lawful prize."[32]

The primary cause of a break between Genêt and Jefferson centered on matters of commissioning and equipping privateers in American ports, of recruiting American seamen on American soil for French service, and especially of utilizing French consulates as admiralty prize courts for disposing of British merchantmen. Genêt ultimately commissioned twelve privateers, which subsequently captured more than eighty enemy vessels whose cargoes were condemned and sold by French consuls in the United States. All these actions were performed under the color of the Franco-American treaty as interpreted by the French minister.

Jefferson could not accept this concept of American neutrality. Despite occasional indiscretions in his communications with Genêt, the secretary of state was increasingly uncomfortable with the aggressive spirit behind the minister's policy. Genêt's assertion that the treaty conferred on France the right to arm privateers in American ports or to commission officers in the United States was not part of Jefferson's understanding of the 1778 Treaty of Amity and Commerce. Article 22 obligated the United States to close its ports to British prizes and to the servicing of British privateers in wartime, but it did not confer on France privileges it denied to France's enemy. All the treaty allowed was the opening of American ports to French ships and their prizes, a conventional permission that was found in the Anglo-French treaty of 1786. Fitting out privateers or setting up prize courts was of a different order, and Jefferson made clear to Genêt his own views on this matter so directly that Genêt later mused that the secretary of state's communications needed only Hammond's signature to identify them as British documents.

Even before the arrival of Genêt in Philadelphia, Jefferson had been disturbed by the threats to neutrality contained in his disposing of prizes and equipping privateers in American ports: "Shall we permit her to sell them? The treaty does not say we shall, and it says we shall not permit the like to England. Shall we permit France to fit our privateers here? The treaty does not say we shall, and it says we shall not permit the like to England."[33] Thus at the very time that he was most receptive to Genêt's ideas, Jefferson was looking for a means of denying to France an important source of revenue in its pursuance of the war, and of nullifying a vital weapon against British sea power. As much as any mistake of Genêt's, the secretary's insistence on something less than a pro-French neutrality opened the way for Hamilton's Anglophilic program.

The French minister eased Hamilton's way by the folly of his brash assault on the president. Of all the cases in which Genêt challenged the administration, the example of the *Little Democrat* incident was the most serious. Knowing and discounting the prohibitions of Washington's Neutrality Proclamation in 1793, Genêt permitted the prize ship (formerly *Little Sarah*) to be outfitted in Philadelphia as a privateer in July 1793. Asked by Pennsylvania's Governor Thomas Mifflin to keep the vessel in port, he not only refused to comply with the request but also denounced Washington and threatened to appeal for public support over the president's head. Although Jefferson recognized the danger of British reprisals, he still opposed Hamilton's recommendation that force be used to prevent the ship's departure. Jefferson maintained that having borne so many injuries from Britain over the years, Americans should not "rise at a feather against their friends and benefactors. I would not gratify the combination of kings with the spectacle of the only two republics on earth destroying each other for two cannon; nor would I, for infinitely greater cause, add this country to that combination, turn the scale of contest, and let it be from our hands that the hopes of men received their last stab."[34]

This burst of rhetoric notwithstanding, Jefferson turned his back on Genêt. The vessel left Philadelphia unhindered, Jefferson lost face, and Hamilton increased his personal influence over the government. The secretary understood the damage Genêt had done to the Franco-American alliance. Hamilton did not make Jefferson's position easier for him when he spread Governor Mifflin's story about Genêt's threats against Washington. No one then exceeded the secretary of state in the vigor of his denunciation of the French minister or subscribed more wholeheartedly to the cry for

his recall. "Never in my opinion, was so calamitous an appointment made, as that of the present Minister of France here," as he
told Madison. "Finding at length that the man was absolutely in-
corrigible, I saw the necessity of quitting a wreck which could not
but sink all who should cling to it."[35]

## Retirement

The last six months of Jefferson's tenure as secretary of state reflected the depression that his encounter with Genêt generated.
Conceivably, his disillusionment with France was exacerbated by
an unacknowedged recognition that he had played a part in feed-
ing Genêt's illusions. The Anglo-French war should have been the
occasion for advancing all the goals he had conceived over the past
generation. While avoiding participation in the war, the United
States could have provided economic aid to an ally whose battles
against European monarchy and British imperialism were increasingly America's own battles against the Federalist counterpart. He
left office in December 1793 with a sense of failure. Genêt was recalled by the Jacobin successor to the Girondist government and
wisely chose to remain in the United States rather than face a guillotine in Paris. But it was too late to help the Jeffersonians. The
secretary of state had failed to win from the British a modern interpretation of the rights of neutrals. Britain continued to confiscate
French goods on American ships. Jefferson also had to witness the
British broadening their definition of contraband and intensifying
the impressment of American seamen as well as their stiffening their
hold on posts in the Northwest and encouraging Indians in their
attacks on American citizens in those territories. The victor appeared to be Hamilton, who seemed willing to link the success of
his own financial system to that of his unofficial British ally.

Dispirited though Jefferson was in his last months in office,
monarchism in the person of Hamilton had not yet triumphed in
the United States, and Great Britain's policies had not yet destroyed
American independence. In fact, the damage done to Franco-
American relations was largely undone by Britain's conduct of the
war. New provocative British Orders in Council in June made
American grains subject to British seizure and antagonized Hamiltonian merchants. It also deflected anger that Genêt's behavior had
generated in the country. It led to understanding, at least, for the
Girondist application of an embargo against American ships carrying provisions to England.

Most important, British behavior put Hamilton on the defensive, forcing him to protest British seizure of American grain as contraband. The resulting turmoil produced Jefferson's last hurrah or, as biographer Merrill Peterson put it, his own "farewell address" in the form of a fifth draft of his deferred report to Congress on commercial policy.[36] In this action he had the support of President Washington. British arrogance pushed Genêt's insolence into the background. The contents of the report were familiar. It railed against British control of American commerce, which inflicted losses on agriculture as well as on ships and their crews. By contrast, France, which had been almost as restrictive in its relations with American merchants, had been working toward liberalizing international trade. He urged, as he had done for years in many different forums, punishing those countries that discriminated against the United States and rewarding those that opened their doors.

Jefferson returned to Monticello discomfited by his experience in Washington's administration. There were few specific triumphs to buoy him. The Hamiltonian miasma that hovered over Philadelphia at the beginning of his tenure had thickened over the years. While Washington fitfully supported Jefferson, the secretary of state felt isolated in an administration where the influence of an Anglophile elite was increasingly dominant. None of Jefferson's aspirations came to fruition. The western empire of liberty was still blocked by hostile Indians aided by Britain in the northwest and Spain in the southwest. The opportunity to move the Spanish out of the Mississippi area never materialized as the Nootka Sound crisis evaporated and as a short-lived Anglo-Spanish alliance emboldened Spanish resistance. British power over the American economy was stronger than ever in 1793, after repeated failures to punish Britain with navigation laws. Britain's war with France yielded increasing insults to American sovereignty on the high seas as well as increasing damage to American property. Even worse, hopes for a French connection to replace Britain as an economic partner failed under the republic as well as under the monarchy, even as friends of France worried about the survival of the revolutions of both countries.

Yet the image of a failed statesman would be as exaggerated as the familiar charge of Jefferson as a captive of the French Revolution. His penchant for extravagant language, reflecting frustrations and passions of the moment, could obscure the positions of the diplomatist whose objectives were never as distant from Hamilton's as critics and partisans would insist. His tactics were not those of an ideologue. His pressure for control of the Mississippi or his support for the French war against Britain was never carried to extremes. His objective, like that of Hamilton, was an America that ultimately would be independent of Europe. His behavior toward Genêt was the exception, not the rule. He was not prepared to have the country enter the European conflict, no matter how engaged his emotions were. On balance, Jefferson displayed a sangfroid toward his French ally greater than his rival showed toward Britain. Even if in the short run Hamilton's Anglophilic policies were more useful to the nation, Jefferson's concern for British dominance, shared by Madison, was a factor in mitigating British arrogance and bringing about the Jay mission in the following year. Whatever his failures in office, he consistently pursued freedom from the restrictions of the Old World and opportunity for westward advance in the New World. These goals guided him throughout his tenure in Washington's administration.

## Notes

1. Robert W. Tucker and David C. Hendrickson, *Empire of Liberty: The Statecraft of Thomas Jefferson* (New York: Oxford University Press, 1990), ix.

2. TJ, "The Anas," in Andrew A. Lipscomb and Albert E. Bergh, eds., *The Writings of Thomas Jefferson*, 20 vols. (Washington, DC: Thomas Jefferson Memorial Association, 1903–04), 1:270–71 (hereafter cited as Lipscomb and Bergh).

3. "Jefferson's Opinion on the Powers of the Senate Respecting Diplomatic Appointments," April 24, 1790, in Julian P. Boyd, ed., *The Papers of Thomas Jefferson*, 24+ vols. (Princeton: Princeton University Press, 1950), 16:379 (hereafter cited as Boyd).

4. TJ to Edward Rutledge, July 4, 1790, ibid., 601.

5. Hamilton to Washington, September 15, 1790, in Harold C. Syrett and Jacob C. Cooke, eds., *The Papers of Alexander Hamilton*, 26 vols. (New York: Columbia University Press, 1961–1979), 7:46–47.

6. TJ to Joseph Jones, August 4, 1787, Boyd, 12:34.

7. TJ to Hamilton, January 13, 1791; Hamilton to TJ, January 13, 1791, ibid., 18:563–64.

8. TJ, "Anas," Lipscomb and Bergh, 1:272–73.

9. TJ to Washington, September 9, 1792, John Catanzariti [successor to Cullen] et al., eds., *Papers of Thomas Jefferson*, 24:352–53.

10. TJ to Monroe, June 20, 1790, Boyd, 16:537.

11. TJ to Washington, May 8, 1791, ibid., 20:291.

12. TJ to William Carmichael, September 25, 1787, ibid., 12:173.

13. TJ on Negotiations with Spain, Charles C. Cullen [successor to Boyd], ed., *Papers of Thomas Jefferson*, 23:301.

14. Secretary of State to William Carmichael, enclosing "Outline of Policy on the Mississippi Question," August 2, 1790, Boyd, 17:116.

15. TJ to William Short and William Carmichael, June 30, 1793, Catanzariti, 26:411.

16. TJ, "Report on American Fisheries," February 1, 1791, Boyd, 19: 218.

17. "Report of Secretary of State," December 15, 1790, ibid., 18:302.

18. TJ to William Short, March 15, 1791, ibid., 19:571.

19. TJ to Short, August 26, 1790, ibid., 17:434.

20. TJ to Short, July 28, 1791, ibid., 20:687.

21. TJ to Lafayette, June 16, 1792, Catanzariti, 24:85.

22. TJ to Madison, June 29, 1792, ibid., 134.

23. TJ to Short, January 3, 1793, ibid., 25:14.

24. "Notes for Opinion on the Treaty of Alliance with France," April 28, 1793, ibid., 617.

25. TJ to Morris, March 12, 1793, ibid., 367.

26. Washington to TJ and Hamilton, April 12, 1793, ibid., 541.

27. TJ to Madison, July 7, 1793, ibid., 26:444.

28. TJ to Morris, April 20, 1793, ibid., 25:576.

29. TJ to Madison, May 29, 1793, ibid., 26:62.

30. Frederick Jackson Turner, ed., "Correspondence of French Ministers to the United States, 1791–1797," *Annual Report* of the American Historical Association, 1903 (Washington, DC, 1904), 1:201.

31. TJ, "Anas," Lipscomb and Bergh, 1:362.

32. TJ to Genêt, July 24, 1793, Catanzariti, 26:557–58.

33. TJ to Madison, April 28, 1793, ibid., 25:619.

34. TJ to Washington, July 8, 1793, "Dissenting Opinion on 'Little Sarah,' " ibid., 26:450–51.

35. TJ to Madison, August 11, 1793, ibid., 652.

36. Merrill D. Peterson, "Thomas Jefferson and Commercial Policy, 1783–1793," *William and Mary Quarterly* 22 (October 1965): 609.

# 5

## In Opposition

### 1794–1800

It is tempting to write off Jefferson's retirement to Monticello in 1794 in terms of Arnold Toynbee's "withdrawal and return," as if this were merely a temporary withdrawal to prepare himself for a victorious return. In retirement he would "realize powers within himself," as Toynbee claimed for Saint Paul and Mohammed, "which might have remained dormant if he had not been released for the time being from his social toils and trammels."[1] There was an aura of predestination in the lives of spiritual leaders that could be applied to the American statesman. Jefferson had suffered rebuffs and seeming failure in his mission as leader that would make a return to Monticello an opportunity to reflect on the state of the nation and on the role he might play in the future. Two years later he was on center stage once again as the Republican candidate against Washington's Federalist successor, John Adams. It was a stage he was not to leave until the end of two terms as president in 1809.

### Amid the Lucerne and Potatoes

Yet there is no reason to question the pleasure he took in cultivating his estate at Monticello as a genuine escape from the burdens of office. Nor are there grounds to suspect that he was consciously planning for an early return. He had property of over 10,000 acres to busy himself with, an occupation made all the more urgent because of his long absences from Virginia. Crop rotation, tree planting, and the beginnings of nail manufacture all consumed his time. As he wrote to John Adams, "I return to farming with an ardor which I scarcely knew in my youth and which has got the better entirely of my love of study. Instead of writing 10 or 12 letters a day, which I have been in the habit of doing as a thing of course, I put off answering letters, farmer-like, till a rainy day, & then find it sometimes postponed by other necessary occupations."[2] There was no doubt about his reducing the volume of letters, or of his absorption in the agrarian life. A week later in one of the letters he did write, he outlined detailed plans for rotating crops and noted how he was helping a neighbor with seeds brought from France. He removed himself from the issues of the day as he contemplated "the tranquil growth of my lucerne [alfalfa] & potatoes." This thought led him to express pride in the fact that "I do not take a single newspaper, nor read one a month; & and [*sic*] I feel myself infinitely the happier for it."[3]

Despite these professions there is some reason to question the totality of his absorption in domestic matters. In the letter to John Adams cited above, he could not restrain himself from observing that Americans were "groaning under the insults of Gr Britain." And after informing Tench Coxe about his complete withdrawal from affairs of state, he confessed his anger over the invasion of France by foreign tyrants and hoped that the "wrath of the people of Europe" would "bring at length kings, nobles, & priests to the scaffolds which they have been so long deluging with human blood."[4] Granted that these emotions did not signify a return to political combat, they did suggest that his mind and body were not wholly devoted to lucerne and potatoes. He may not have subscribed to newspapers, or even read any in this period, but he had no need to do so. Jefferson had a host of friends to keep him abreast of events in Philadelphia and abroad. Interspersed with the information he supplied to friends about his experiences with new agricultural techniques were reports of his Virginia neighbors' passionate resentment of Britain's behavior. Nor did he confine his observations to the local scene; he expressed his concern about America's problems with the West Indies and with the European belligerents in far more vehement terms than he had as secretary of state.

These contradictions may be more apparent than real, if they are to be interpreted as a species of hypocrisy. Did he conceal his hopes of returning to national office by masking it in expressions of pleasure in the bucolic life as well as of satisfaction in renouncing the "little spice of ambition which I had in my younger days"?[5]

It is more likely that he was perfectly sincere in retreating to Monticello. The years in Philadelphia had been increasingly difficult, particularly in the last six months of his service as secretary of state. The psychic cost of losing the contest with Hamilton was high, and the failure of an immediate reaction to his final efforts to punish Britain made retirement all the more welcome. Always sensitive to personal criticism, Jefferson preferred to encourage his friends and disciples to carry on the good fight from the sidelines.

Even as he felt exhausted by the struggles in the Cabinet and by his loss of confidence in the president's impartiality, he had some reason to anticipate vindication of his policies. As he wrote his daughter just a week before leaving office, the exposure of British crimes against America in the Northwest Territory, on the high seas, and in the Mediterranean would inspire Congress to pass retaliatory commercial measures against Britain. Leaving Philadelphia when he did was the right psychological moment to dissociate himself from the increasingly unpopular policies of the Washington administration. A happy outcome would be the repudiation of the Hamilton financial system, with its Anglophile ties and its corruption of the nation's values. But these expectations did not cast him in a Machiavellian, or even a Svengalian, mode; he would have been happy enough for Madison and Congress to carry the burden. They would heed his advice certainly, but not necessarily to prepare him for a triumphant return as their leader.

Jefferson's role as a civilian Cincinnatus permanently removed from the fray might have been realized if Madison's resolutions of January 3, 1794, had been accepted in Congress. Madison once again tried to have high taxes imposed on products of those countries without treaties with the United States. These resolutions essentially were those of 1791, with an additional tariff designed to settle losses suffered by Americans in the course of the Franco-British war. The retired secretary of state had counted on the national revulsion against the British Orders in Council of November 1793 to overcome the Federalist objections that had prevented retaliation in the past. This action had authorized the seizure of all American vessels carrying provisions to the French West Indies. Hundreds of American ships were confiscated. The Order even violated the stringent interpretations of neutral rights Britain had forced on neutral powers. The rule of 1756, for example, which denied access to ports in wartime that were closed in peacetime, should not have applied to an American trade with the West Indies that had antedated the Anglo-French war.

This Order in Council might have been taken as a *casus belli* even by Federalists. Indeed, Federalist Congressmen took the lead in initiating a short-term embargo on trade with Great Britain, authorizing the building of frigates and displaying a belligerency that seemingly surpassed that of the Republicans. Actually, all the leaders shied away from the prospect of war. Characteristically, Jefferson expressed his anxiety to "give the world still another useful lesson, by showing to them other modes of punishing injuries than by war, which is as much a punishment to the punisher as to the sufferer."[6] Adams's concern was over the cost of a war, and Hamilton's was over the damage it would do to his conception of America's future. The alternative to Madison's sanctions was the Federalist dispatch of John Jay, now chief justice of the United States, on a special mission to London in a last effort to reach an agreement on all the points of friction between the two countries. To the Republicans it looked like another trick to postpone appropriate punitive action against Britain, particularly when it was rumored that the Anglophile Hamilton himself was to be the messenger. Such was the story communicated to Monticello. Jefferson responded with anger and disgust; he was convinced that the object of the mission was to place "the aristocracy of this country under the patronage" of Great Britain and asserted that "a more degrading measure could not have been proposed."[7]

## Impact of Jay's Treaty

The Jay treaty that followed later in 1794 confirmed Jefferson's worst fears—namely, that Jay, as Hamilton's tool, sold out American interests for the sake of securing trade with Britain on British terms. Despite his instructions, Jay was unable to gain access for American ships to the British West Indies, or cessation of the practice of impressment, or a loose interpretation of contraband. He gave away to the British the privilege of bringing prizes captured from France into the United States; this directly contradicted the French treaty. While the Jay treaty stipulated that nothing in that document would affect obligations already binding on the signatory powers, the contents made a mockery of the Franco-American treaties. Small wonder that there were violent demonstrations in every major city against the pact, and it barely passed the Senate after the president reluctantly submitted it. Even Hamilton was distressed by its vulnerability. But it was Hamilton whose assurance to British Minister Hammond that the United States would not join another French-inspired League of Armed Neutrality that stiffened Lord Grenville's negotiating position, even if it may not have been the critical factor in the negotiations.

Once the initial shock had subsided, the Federalists recognized the positive aspects of the treaty. It secured for the United States what Hamilton had felt were the minimal conditions for a rapprochement: the evacuation of British posts in the Northwest; and indemnification for spoliations committed under the Order in Council of June 8, 1793, which authorized the seizure of American ships carrying provisions to French ports. In fact, the treaty did far more. It avoided war with Britain and deepened a mutually beneficial relationship between American merchants and shippers with their British creditors and consumers. As an unexpected consequence, Jay's Treaty opened the way for Minister Thomas Pinckney in Madrid to extract from the Spanish government the right of deposit in New Orleans of goods floated down the Mississippi by Kentuckians and Tennesseans for transshipment abroad. Spain's defection from its alliance with Britain had aroused Spanish fears in 1795 that the Jay treaty may have had secret protocols involving an Anglo-American assault on Louisiana.

These foregoing benefits were hardly appreciated, or even recognized, by the Republican opposition. Rather, Jay's Treaty was final proof of Hamilton's domination of the Washington administration. Jefferson saw the treaty as "an execrable thing. . . . I trust the popular branch of our legislature will disapprove of it, and thus rid us of this infamous act, which is really nothing more than a treaty of alliance between England & the Anglomen of this country against the legislature & the people of the United States."[8] The Jay treaty fueled Jefferson's efforts to have his friends in Congress undo the damage that Jay, Hamilton, and Washington had done. Indeed, much of his anger was now directed against the president. He could not understand how Washington could have accepted the treaty unless he was wholly under the control of Hamilton and the "monocrats."

Jefferson in retirement seemed to have lost the sense of perspective that had served him well as secretary of state. In the past he had given in to flights of fancy on occasion, but the occasions were rare and the consequences slight. But from his perch in Monticello he wrote letters so indiscreet that their contents created considerable embarrassment. It was as if the enemy of the nation was centered in Philadelphia rather than in London. (The federal capital, at New York from 1785 through 1790, was again at Philadelphia from 1790 through 1800.) And if he recognized clearly for the most part the role France should play in American foreign policy, that clarity was muddled after Washington submitted the Jay treaty to the Senate.

Part of his problem was the colorful language he employed to pour out his feelings. It was very much in evidence in three letters written to close friends, the contents of which should have been kept in confidence. His anger at Washington's putative betrayal was best expressed in a letter he wrote to an Italian friend and former neighbor in Virginia, Philip Mazzei, then living in Florence. Railing against the "Anglican, monarchical, & aristocratical party" that was destroying the republic Mazzei had known, he claimed that "it would give you a fever were I to name to you the apostates who have gone over to these heresies, men who were Samsons in the field & Solomons in the Council, but who have had their heads shorn by the harlot England."[9] Mazzei was so excited by this letter that he had it translated into Italian and published in a Florence newspaper. From there it was picked up and translated from Italian to French for the Paris *Moniteur*, and ultimately back into English for American newspapers a year later. Despite the bowdlerization that took place in the course of translations, the substance remained intact. The Samsons and Solomons were one man, George Washington, the object of Jefferson's attack.

The Jay treaty was also indirectly responsible for another embarrassment, Jefferson's endorsement of Monroe's apologia for his activities as minister to France. Federalists had charged Monroe with deluding France into believing that the treaty dealt with settlement of wartime debts rather than acceptance of British interpretations of neutral rights. Timothy Pickering, secretary of state in the Adams administration, laid as much blame for hostile French reaction as he could on Monroe's Francophilic behavior in Paris in 1794 and 1795. Monroe, in turn, felt betrayed by the Federalists and mounted a monumental tome of vindication 407 pages long, with a 66-page introduction explaining how Federalist failure to respect French sensibilities undercut his position as minister. Had a different policy been followed, he asserted, both a humiliating treaty and a break with France would have been avoided. His accusation centered on Washington. While Madison recognized the futility of the effort, Jefferson, now vice president, rallied around his friend. He described Monroe's intemperate attack against Washington as "masterly by all those who are not opposed in principle, and it is deemed unanswerable."[10] Whatever the merits of Monroe's activities in France, Jefferson identified his friend's fate as victim with his own. Advocacy of the French cause was far less in evidence than a visceral dislike of the common enemies of the time—the Federalists at home and the British abroad.

These epistolary outbursts, embarrassing as they were, were mild in comparison with the sentiments in his letter to Virginia Congressman William Branch Giles concerning France's campaigns against the European monarchical coalition. Jefferson was so pleased with the prospect of French armies liberating Britain that he was tempted, he said, to leave his "clover for a while" to dine with General Charles Pichegru in London, where he could join his French friends in hailing "the dawn of liberty and republicanism in that island."[11] At least this suggestion did not receive public attention, unlike the sentiments in the other letters.

This may have been the apex of Jefferson's flights from reality, in some ways more fanciful than his preferring half the earth depopulated to the defeat of the French Revolution. Some of the most vivid images were "pedagogical in purpose," as Dumas Malone has suggested, particularly when he was writing to his disciples.[12] Cautious in his public statements, Jefferson would blow off steam in private communications with his friends. But to defend, even to glory in, the occupation of England by France seems to go beyond venting repressed feelings among intimates or misusing hyperbole for instructional purposes. It could be interpreted as a serious misunderstanding of the balance of power, an error he would not have made in office, or a temporary aberration caused by an exaggerated fear of enemies at home and abroad.

## The Vice Presidency

The Anglo-French war inevitably was the centerpiece of the presidential election of 1796. It was not surprising that Republicans such as Monroe and Jefferson identified France as the injured party in Jay's Treaty and empathized with the sense of betrayal that France communicated by formalizing its seizure of American ships carrying goods to the enemy's country. Self-righteously, the French government protested that the 1778 Franco-American Treaty of Amity and Commerce had obliged France to respect British goods on American vessels, while Jay's Treaty unfairly allowed Britain to seize French goods on neutral ships. Such was their justification for following the British pattern of confiscating American vessels. It was in the context of an easing of Anglo-American tensions as a result of Jay's Treaty and of incipient conflict with France that Madison and other close friends persuaded Jefferson to seek the presidency.

There are many plausible reasons to account for Jefferson's reluctance to become a candidate. His gracious deference to Adams as his senior and hence the more appropriate candidate was arguably less persuasive than his concern that he would be tainted by a new Francophobia in America that would permanently doom his hopes for a French counterweight against Britain. More credible was a genuine revulsion against the process of achieving the presidency. There was no pattern of party nomination to guide him, assuming he was anxious to seek the position. His declared preference for the presidency was Madison, as leader of the Jeffersonian faction in Congress. If Jefferson agreed to stand for the office, it was because his friends had convinced him that there was no alternative leader to carry the banner of the people against the entrenched interests of the Anglophiles, aristocrats, and financial speculators.

Jefferson failed to win the election in 1796. John Adams had the advantage of not only being Washington's logical heir as vice president but also the beneficiary of the fruits of Jay's Treaty, including the freeing of the Northwest Territory from the British and their Indian allies. Adams also benefited from the 1795 Pinckney's Treaty that opened the Mississippi Valley to Americans. Jefferson, by contrast, had to contend with France's interference in his behalf. Pierre Adet, its minister in Philadelphia in 1796, used the threat of breaking relations with the United States to intimidate the electorate. While Adet's actions certainly aroused public antagonism toward the French, his interference was not the critical factor in winning the presidency for Adams.

Under the Constitution prior to the Twelfth Amendment, Jefferson's election as vice president was simply the consequence of his receiving fewer electoral votes than President Adams. The new vice president's perception of France posed a problem he did not recognize at the time. He accepted by his silence France's overt actions. Would he have done so had he been more aware of the events in that country between 1794 and 1796? Just as he had been unable to distinguish between the more moderate Girondists, with their aim of liberating as much of the world as they could from the old regimes, from the radical Jacobins who were primarily concerned with the internal revolution in France, so he had difficulty in recognizing the foreign policy objectives of the successor regime, the Directory. That government, more conservative than the Jacobins in social and political terms, had transformed the liberation ideology of Girondist idealists into an imperialism reminiscent of the Bourbons but more dynamic and more dangerous to the established order. The United States would have a place in the new order, but only as a satellite of an imperial France. Ultimately, Louisiana would be restored with all the implications such restoration would have for the United States. In the meantime, the Directory looked upon the United States in 1795 as a participant in a war against Britain whose outcome was still uncertain. Toward this end, Minister Adet sought to ensure the victory of a Francophile president.

But the French were deluding themselves if they genuinely believed that the Republicans in general and Jefferson in particular would serve as satellites to French overlords. Adet in Philadelphia followed his instructions to break relations with the United States, but he was acute enough to recognize that President Adams would not be a captive of the Hamiltonians, and certainly not of Hamilton himself. The retired secretary of the treasury might control Adams's Cabinet from his law office in New York, but he had little influence over the new president. More surprising was Adet's recognition that Jefferson would not be a reliable acolyte. Although he knew that the vice president continued to admire the French Revolution, "he may not be wholly devoted to our interests. Mr. Jefferson likes us because he detests England; he seeks to draw near to us because he fears us less than Great Britain; but he might change his opinion of us tomorrow, if tomorrow Britain should cease to inspire his fears."[13]

Adet was correct in the long run when he identified Jefferson as an "American, and as such he cannot be sincerely our friend. An American is the born enemy of all the European peoples."[14] Before the end of Adams's term, Jefferson had turned against France without, however, embracing Britain in its place. If the French minister's predictions were not immediately realized, it was partly because of Jefferson's lingering dependence upon an unrealistic conception of the France of 1797. Although the new vice president realized that France made a mistake in rejecting Charles Cotesworth Pinckney as American minister (in conjunction with the withdrawal of its own minister from the United States), he could excuse the act on the grounds that Jay's Treaty had made France the injured party in Franco-American relations. After a brief political honeymoon with Adams, Jefferson blamed France's truculence on the eagerness of his own government to precipitate a war between the two countries. Feeling isolated by his enemies in Philadelphia, the vice president still had hopes that France could serve his party as Britain had served the Federalists in the past.

Maintaining this illusion required ignorance of the Directory's ambitions. Although the Girondists had specific plans for the conquest of Louisiana as far back as 1792, their plan was to emancipate the territory, to the advantage of its residents as well as of France. The Directory, on the other hand, frankly wanted Louisiana returned as part of a new empire, and wanted to exploit as many Francophile leaders as it could to achieve its objectives. Jefferson initially considered the Directory to be a restoration of the Revolution that had been distorted by the brutality of the Terror. Such doubts as he had about the events that had devoured so many of his friends were stilled by the guillotining in July 1794 of Robespierre, the personification of the errors of the Revolution.

In the early years of his vice presidency, Jefferson could attribute the fate of Lafayette, Mme. de Tessé, and other victims of the Revolution to the extremists. He was never able to untangle the twisted course of events that led from a reformed monarchy in 1791 to an aggressive Directory five years later that combined the trappings of the Revolution with the imperial ambitions of the Ancien Régime. His friends, including James Monroe from his new post in Paris, failed to enlighten him. Nor did the intellectuals who had survived the Terror inform him of the nature of the Directory even when they knew of the aims of its foreign policy. One of them, Constantin, Comte de Volney, visited Monticello in this period and enjoyed the hospitality of its proprietor as a fellow scholar and fellow republican. At the same time, Volney acted as an informal agent of Charles Maurice de Talleyrand, the Directory's foreign minister, examining possibilities for French colonization on the American continent. Although Volney subsequently advised Talleyrand that French plans for Louisiana would antagonize Americans, he did not confide the Directory's designs to his American friend. Even close associates who had suffered from the Revolution, such as Lafayette, then languishing in an Austrian prison, could not bring themselves to condemn the regime. As Lafayette told Thomas Pinckney, the cause of liberty required the defeat of France's foreign enemies even though the nation itself was governed by tyrants.

Granted that the silence of his correspondents helped to perpetuate Jefferson's misperceptions of the French government, there were political factors on the domestic scene that kept alive his fear of monarchy at home and hence the need for an ally abroad. He overlooked Adams's honest efforts to mend the strained relations with France as well as Hamilton's more calculating wish to avoid war with France at this time. What seemed fixed in the vice president's mind was Adams's call for a military buildup in 1797 after news reached America of the Directory's rejection of Charles Cotesworth Pinckney as minister, and of the escalating depredations against American commerce that followed. Jefferson's anxiety paralleled that of his friends in Congress when a new mission to France —with John Marshall and Elbridge Gerry joining Pinckney—failed to settle the friction between the two nations. If only the United States had followed his advice to employ a navigation system that would have forced both parties to respect American freedom of the seas, the threat of war with France would have been avoided and the prospect of equality with Britain would have been achieved. While his views in 1797 suggest some cooling toward the French ally, he could appreciate, as he told Madison in June, the French military victories under Bonaparte, which could bankrupt England and cause that country's fleet to mutiny. Volney was his authority for suggesting that "France will not make peace with England because it is such an opportunity for sinking her as she never had & may not have again."[15] France's successes helped to compensate for the Anglophilia that characterized the Federalist ascendancy.

## Toward Morfontaine

There was not much occasion, however, for complacency. In 1798, President Adams released the XYZ dispatches, which unleashed an undeclared naval war against France in response to the demands of Talleyrand's agents—X, Y, and Z—for an American loan to his government and a bribe for himself before France would agree to negotiate with Ministers Pinckney, Marshall, and Gerry. The result was the mobilization of an army under Hamilton and the passage of alien, naturalization, and sedition acts, presumably to save the country from French immigrants and Republican traitors. Jefferson's estrangement from Adams was now complete.

The vice president was upset with France's folly in striking at the United States, but he was also convinced that Britain was the primary offender. "A just and rational censure ought to be expressed on [the French]. . . . It is at the same time true, that their enemies set the first example of violating neutral rights, & continue them to this day; insomuch that it is declared on all hands . . . that the British spoliations have considerably exceeded the French during the last 6 months. Yet not a word of these things is said officially to the legislature." Moreover, France's behavior was no cause for war. "Every one who ever read a book on the law of nations knows, that it is an unquestionable right in every power to refuse to receive any minister who is personally disagreeable."[16] As for the humiliating treatment of the American commissioners, he saw the XYZ affair as "a dish cooked up by Marshall where the swindlers are made to appear as the French government."[17] The policies of his domestic enemies obviously modified his resentment against those of his foreign allies.

In the campaign for war against the Directory the treaties of 1778 inevitably became the object of special attack. France, after all, opened the way by its refusal to receive an American minister, but it did not denounce the treaty of alliance. Under Hamilton's guidance, the Federalists managed to unilaterally void the alliance in preparation, as the Republicans believed, for a formal declaration of war, and with it an alliance with Britain and suppression of Jeffersonian dissent. From the floor of Congress, the Jeffersonians worked to save the treaties. Albert Gallatin, their leader from Pennsylvania, admitted France's violations of the Treaty of Alliance and Commerce but claimed that the alliance itself was not affected by French seizures of American ships and sailors. If the Federalists had asked for the abrogation of the commercial treaty, he could have understood the argument, although he felt that Jay's Treaty deserved equal treatment.

The Federalists prevailed against the Jeffersonian opposition. The alliance was unilaterally declared void. The vice president himself could do little but witness what he feared was a step-by-step movement toward full-scale war with France, an open alliance with Britain, and a destruction of liberty in America. Jefferson was formally mute in his office of vice president.

In the rapid course of events following the revelations of the XYZ affair, Jefferson's opposition to Federalist plans was no longer based on a Revolution-driven Francophilia. While no specific information was available about France's imperial intentions in America, the treatment of European satellite nations did not go unnoticed among Jeffersonians. The Directory's ambitions in Louisiana may not have been fully clear, but Madison had no hesitation about speculating on the threat of an angry France conspiring with the Spanish to disturb navigation on the Mississippi. Jefferson gloomily predicted that there will be "new neighbors in Louisiana (probably the present French armies when disbanded)," who would add to the "enemies on that side where we were most vulnerable."[18] These fears were raised before the XYZ imbroglio and subsequent conflict with France, and obviously were not over the survival of the French republic; rather, it was the American republic whose survival was at stake. Although the Jeffersonians could admit justification for France's reaction to Federalist policies, they were worried about the revenge the victorious Directory would exact on all Americans.

If neither full-scale war with France nor triumph of the Anglophile monocrats developed from the ominous actions of the Directory and the Federalists in 1798, it was due to external and internal events over which the Jeffersonians had no control. What Jefferson himself later called the "chapter of accidents" that served America in times of need benefited him and his partisans.[19] The external action was Talleyrand's initiative in recognizing the unfortunate effect the XYZ affair would have on France's plans for Louisiana. Given that there was no advantage for the Directory in a war with the United States, the French foreign minister took steps to defuse tensions. He began by informing the few influential Americans still in France that French privateers operating in the West Indies would cease molesting American vessels, and then went on to tell the American consul general in Paris that the Directory would raise the embargo on American vessels in French ports and release imprisoned seamen.

It is understandable that the Federalists doubted the sincerity of Talleyrand's pronouncements. The minister who mistreated the American commissioners was not an authority to be trusted. Moreover, Federalist leaders had no immediate interest in reducing tensions; the XYZ insults had damaged the status of Republicans and made possible the 1798 alien and sedition acts that would further reduce their political power. The alien and naturalization laws were targeted at Frenchmen in the United States, all presumably Jeffersonian sympathizers. By deporting subversive aliens and passing a rigorous sedition law directed against disloyal American Jacobins, the Federalists hoped to do irreparable damage to their political opponents. Beyond this consideration was Hamilton's hope to use the undeclared war with France to collaborate with Britain on an attack against the common enemy, France's Spanish satellite in Louisiana and the Floridas. The retired secretary of the treasury, anticipating command of the American armies under the nominal leadership of General Washington, had a special purpose in keeping the Franco-American imbroglio alive.

Such were the sentiments of the Hamiltonian Federalists in and out of Adams's Cabinet, but they were not shared by the president. Once his anger over the XYZ affair had cooled, he was prepared to listen to reports, including those from his son, John Quincy Adams, then minister to Prussia, that Talleyrand was sincere in his efforts to repair the damage he had caused. For his part, Adams saw as clearly as Jefferson the misfortune war would bring to the United States, and he understood better than his vice president the folly of permitting the nation to fall into the orbit of any foreign power. Adams never succumbed to the Federalist Anglophilia. He wanted a peace that respected the dignity of the United States. Accordingly, he announced the appointment of a new minister to France to follow up Talleyrand's overtures.

The president's action shocked the Hamiltonians in his Cabinet. They, along with Hamilton himself, never wanted Adams in office; their preference in 1796 had been Thomas Pinckney. With the appointment of William Vans Murray, Adams had confirmed the wisdom of their skepticism. Although the Hamiltonians managed to increase the number of negotiators to three—the same number that had failed two years before—with the hope of sabotaging its chances for success, they were unable to stop the mission itself.

Partly because of his political isolation in Philadelphia, it took some time before the vice president recognized that there was a serious break between Adams and his Cabinet. Jefferson initially dismissed the mission as a Federalist ruse to sidetrack a rapprochement with France, and he was convinced of it when the president added two more identifiable Federalists to the mission. The arrangement was, he feared, a plot to parry "the overtures of France under the guise of a dignified acceptance of them."[20] His suspicions were inspired not by a renewed faith in France but by a deepening distrust of the Federalist administration. In a letter to Thomas Lomax in March 1799, he was as censorious as any Francophobe in denouncing the "atrocious proceedings of France" that could give the Federalists a pretext for destroying the American republic. He clearly anticipated the sentiments of his Inaugural Address as president two years later when he advocated "abjuring all political connection with every foreign power," asserting that "commerce with all nations, alliance with none, should be our motto."[21]

This was a major reversal of position from the leader of the party that rejected a unilateral termination of the alliance. It was given special substance by news of the coup d'état on November 9, 1799, that overthrew the Directory and established a three-man Consulate under Napoleon Bonaparte, the thirty-year-old general whose exploits in Italy and Egypt had been admired by Jefferson. This upheaval was a shock to the sensibilities of a man who now had to confront the reality of the Revolution's demise. Even if Bonaparte's autocracy was no more a betrayal of the republican spirit than the Directory's oligarchy had been, its appearance was more difficult to disguise.

As soon as the character of Bonaparte's regime became clear, the vice president examined the political capacities of the French people, a subject he really had not examined for ten years. In 1800 he noted that the French lacked the "habit of self-government," and that a military dictatorship might be the most suitable form of government for a people without the political traditions of Americans.[22] Such was not the case for the United States even though Jefferson linked Hamilton with Bonaparte as dangerous men on horseback.

When it became clear to the Jeffersonians that the break between Adams and the Hamiltonians was serious and that the president intended to have the mission of Pinckney, Marshall, and Gerry restore relations with France, they expressed no interest in undoing the Congressional abrogation of the alliance. Nor was Bonaparte interested. In assessing the commissioners' skills, however, he believed he could manipulate the Americans into serving French interests. If they wanted to end the alliance, the price would be moral support, if not membership, in a new anti-British league of armed neutrals he was planning after the defeat of the Austrians. Only incidentally did he refer to any indemnities France might have paid for depredations against American commerce. And, according to the Treaty of Morfontaine that terminated the alliance, France's obligations would be liquidated if the United States failed to deny British privateers and prizes the use of American ports after seven years. But after keeping the American negotiators in limbo through the first half of 1800, Bonaparte did agree to end the twenty-two-year-old alliance.

When Adams's peace commissioners signed the new agreement with France, there was not a single protest from Jefferson, nor from his colleagues, nor from the Republican press. By 1800, Jefferson had won the presidency, largely because of the division among the Federalists over Adams's reelection but also because Jefferson the presidential candidate deemphasized his former sympathies for France. The new president's estrangement was deeper than

Bonapartism and older than the most recent coup. Suspicions of its intentions in Louisiana, resentment over its commercial policies in the Caribbean, and fear of entanglement in its imperial projects had characterized Jefferson's attitudes toward France throughout the decade, and indeed from the moment the alliance had been made. While his Francophilia in the course of the French Revolution was genuine, his friendship with that country was more often based on fears of British designs on American independence and on the dangerous Anglophilia of Britain's Federalist allies. Although British malevolence was to remain more dangerous in Jefferson's mind than its French counterpart, the old dream of a French economic partner to replace Britain died along with the notion of France as a republican ally against European monarchism. Neither would be revived in the future even though he still nourished hopes of using that nation as a counterpoise to Britain.

The election of 1800 was marked by even more bitterness than had prevailed in 1796. Republican anger over the 1798 alien and sedition laws was manifested in the Kentucky Resolutions of 1798, written in secret by Jefferson and designed to strike at a central government that seemingly usurped the rights of states. Because of a perceived threat to his own freedom, the vice president had the resolutions denouncing the usurpation of states' rights by Congress issued from the Kentucky state legislature through the agency of his friend, John Breckenridge. The Hamiltonians recognized that the divisions within their own party created by Adams's French policies might give victory to Jefferson over Adams and over the Federalists' favorite, Charles C. Pinckney. Consequently, they heaped abuse on the vice president as a danger to the morality of the nation. Given these circumstances, it is not surprising that Jefferson's election would be called the "revolution of 1800." Power was passed peacefully from one political party to another, and from one vision of American society to a very different one.

Or so it seemed. From another perspective there was continuity rather than revolution in the results of the election. The person responsible for selecting his political enemy was none other than Alexander Hamilton, who urged his followers to support Jefferson in place of Aaron Burr, a leader in New York's Tammany Hall and a nominal Republican. Hamilton characterized Jefferson as wrongheaded, but in Burr he saw a man without principles who professed a willingness to accept Federalism in exchange for the presidency. While neither Hamilton nor Adams had been converted into

Jeffersonian Republicans, there was more to link them in 1800 than there was to separate them.

Without accepting the desirability of a British connection or the virtues of a commercial society, Jefferson shared with his adversaries the awareness that America had to maintain its independence from all foreign powers, that its future lay in continental expansion, and that the economic ties with Britain fashioned since Jay's Treaty could not be broken. Equally significant was Jefferson's clearly stated acceptance of the end of the Franco-American alliance when he asked in his Inaugural Address for "Peace, commerce, and honest friendship with all nations, entangling alliances with none."[23] If he called the Treaty of Morfontaine "a bungling negotiation," it was because it failed to win compensation for damages France committed against American shipping, and because the British might retaliate against the United States.[24] From this angle of observation the election might reflect the "consensus of 1800" as well as the "revolution of 1800." Without giving Adams the credit he deserved, both Hamilton and Jefferson agreed that Morfontaine served the national interest.

## Notes

1. Arnold Toynbee, *A Study of History* (New York: Oxford University Press, 1947), 217.

2. TJ to John Adams, April 25, 1794, in Paul Leicester Ford, ed., *The Works of Thomas Jefferson*, 12 vols. (New York: G. P. Putnam's Sons, 1904–05), 8:144–45 (hereafter cited as Ford).

3. TJ to Tench Coxe, May 1, 1794, ibid., 147.

4. Ibid.

5. TJ to James Madison, April 27, 1795, ibid., 170.

6. TJ to Tench Coxe, May 1, 1794, ibid., 148.

7. TJ to Monroe, April 24, 1794, ibid., 143–44.

8. TJ to Edward Rutledge, November 30, 1795, ibid., 200.

9. TJ to Philip Mazzei, April 24, 1796, ibid., 238.

10. TJ to Madison, January 3, 1798, ibid., 357.

11. TJ to Giles, April 27, 1795, ibid., 172.

12. Dumas Malone, *Jefferson and the Order of Liberty* (Boston: Little, Brown, and Co., 1962), 16.

13. Adet to Minister of Foreign Affairs, December 31, 1796, in Frederick Jackson Turner, ed., "Correspondence of the French Ministers to the United States, 1791–1797," *Annual Report* of the American Historical Association, 1903 (Washington, DC, 1904), 982–83.

14. Ibid.

15. TJ to Madison, June 15, 1797, Ford, 8:307.

16. TJ to Edmund Pendleton, February 14, 1799, ibid., 9:48–49.

17. TJ to Edmund Pendleton, January 29, 1799, ibid., 27.

18. TJ to Thomas Pinckney, May 29, 1797, ibid., 8:293.

19. TJ to Thomas Leiper, August 21, 1807, ibid., 10:483–84.

20. TJ to Thomas M. Randolph, February 26, 1799, Jefferson Papers, reel 21, Library of Congress, Washington, DC.

21. TJ to Thomas Lomax, March 12, 1799, Ford, 9:64.

22. TJ to John Breckenridge, January 29, 1800, ibid., 106–7.

23. First Inaugural Address, March 4, 1801, ibid., 197.

24. TJ to Madison, December 19, 1800, ibid., 159.

# 6

## Toward an Empire of Liberty

### 1801–1805

President Jefferson entered office unencumbered by the weight of the French Revolution that had been such a burden on Republican foreign policy since his return from Paris. His Inaugural Address projected a spirit of reconciliation with his political opponents that gave meaning to the comforting phrase, "We are all Republicans—we are all Federalists."[1] A recent biographer, Joseph Ellis, has offered a new gloss on that famous declaration, noting that in the handwritten version of his speech the party labels were not capitalized and represented "more a political platitude than an ideological concession."[2] In this context, Jefferson was not blurring distinctions between two divided factions but only observing the common ground of a republican government linked by a federal bond that all Americans could share. There was nothing in this phrase that would inhibit the president from pursuing a course that would undo Federalist policies ranging from Anglophilia and a strong military to actions that enhanced the powers of the urban elite.

Jefferson's record in his first term in office certainly lends some credence to this view. His support of agrarian interests in reducing the price of western land, his allowing the alien and sedition laws to lapse, and his severe reductions in appropriations for the armed services were obvious reversals of Federalist policies. But in the important area of foreign relations he affirmed from the beginning of his administration a continuity with Federalism. Indeed, his positions repudiated subtexts of his diatribes against the Hamiltonians. More consistent with his past attitudes, if not more significant in his Inaugural

Address, was his judgment that no matter how much independence he would allow the states, in the matter of foreign relations they must be united. This was his view from Paris as a delegate of the Confederation, and it remained his view in 1798 even as he was ready to have Kentucky nullify the alien and sedition acts of the federal Congress. Unlike his statement on Republicans and Federalists, there is no ambiguity in language that stipulated "entangling alliances with none."

Although Jefferson's aversion to entangling alliances applied in full measure to France, it did not exclude an equally long-standing hope of exploiting French power—economic, political, or military—to redress the imbalance with Britain. In this respect his emphasis on continuity with Federalist policy can be misleading. If he kept the Federalist minister to London, Rufus King, in office, it was not a signal that Anglophilia would replace Francophilia. Rather, it was a hardheaded calculation that King's cordial relations with the British ministry would resolve outstanding debts dating from the Revolution. Similarly, his professions to Edward Thornton, the British chargé d'affaires in Washington, that his hostility was "only for electioneering purposes" should be weighed against his assertion in the same interview that British seizures of property and sailors were "two sources of dissension and irritation without the removal of which it was not possible to preserve harmony."[3] Jefferson's spirit was that of a nationalist, and defense of nationhood required, as it did during his years as secretary of state, a defense of America's commercial rights.

His evenhanded approach was soon to be tested when he recognized that France was about to occupy Louisiana. At this juncture, France was for the moment the more dangerous adversary if it moved into what Jefferson had regarded as ultimately the American West. This was not a new perception. As minister in Paris he had expressed concerns about French exploratory expeditions; as secretary of state his designs on Spanish America were clearly seen in his advice during the Nootka Sound crisis; and as vice president his unhappiness over the Federalist war with France was compounded by his fear that France's retribution would include barring American westward advance. The Michaux incident in 1793 and his apparent support of a French invasion of Britain in 1795 were aberrations. But his seeming willingness to counter the potential French occupation of New Orleans by "marrying ourselves to the British fleet and nation" was not an aberration.[4] Unlike his outbursts against the British, this was a ploy the president was using to encourage his minister in Paris to prevent both events from happening.

## War with Tripoli

The president's posture of keeping his distance from both super-powers was a constant during his first administration. When Britain resumed its menacing role of earlier years, Jefferson once again turned to France for a counterweight in his second administration. But at the outset of his presidency his policy toward the Barbary powers was a challenge not only to the corsairs preying on American shipping in the Mediterranean but also to the British and French alike who profited from America's troubles with Algiers and Tripoli. Jefferson's militant response to the Barbary menace was a reprise of a sentiment he had held during his ministry in France—namely, a wish to punish the offender with force rather than to continue payments of tribute to the pirate regimes. In the 1780s he had to accept John Adams's logic that the weak American government lacked the strength to strike back and could barely afford the payments that kept the Algerines at bay, let alone build a navy to deal with the raiders. But now as president of a stronger union he had an opportunity to put just such a policy into effect.

Jefferson's efforts to reduce the military budgets that had characterized the Hamiltonian ascendancy in the 1790s were an accurate reflection of his dislike of war. Nor should there be any doubt about his preference for economic coercion as its substitute, as expressed in his dealings with the Napoleonic Wars. But there was always the element of national interest. For Jefferson it was the protection of American rights on the seas, of the commerce that was the lifeblood of prosperity in his presidential years. If he could wage a war with Algiers or Tripoli at little cost, it would send a message to the world that America should be respected. The Barbary city-states seemed to offer the occasion to put this idea to the test.

When Tripoli increased its attacks on American shipping in the spring of 1801 and then declared war on the United States, Jefferson dispatched the navy to the Mediterranean. The pasha of Tripoli had acted out of pique, irritated that the United States was paying less tribute to him than to the Dey of Algiers. Continuing the practice of tribute, Jefferson claimed, would be "money thrown away," since "there is no end to the demand of these powers, nor any security in their promises."[5] The alternative to military action would have been to abandon the Mediterranean and thereby damage not only America's commerce but also its standing in the world. Tripoli's decision permitted the president to take an initiative that was unavailable to the Confederation in 1786 and too ambitious for the nominally more aggressive Federalist administration a decade later.

It is somewhat ironic that it was a Republican president distrustful of a military establishment who was able to use a navy enhanced during the Adams administration to strike a blow for the American economy as well as for freedom of the seas. Jefferson had the advantage during his first term of a respite in the Anglo-French wars and of an enemy that he felt could be defeated with limited resources. He distinguished between a domestic program centered on executive restraint and Congressional leadership and a foreign affairs agenda in which the president was the prime mover. Presidential initiative was all that was necessary to conduct a small-scale naval war in the Mediterranean, not a formal declaration by, or even consultation with, Congress.

The "Mediterranean Fund" established by Secretary of the Treasury Albert Gallatin consisted of special loans to cover expenses beyond the appropriations for the naval budget, and it enabled the chief executive to finance his war. Jefferson justified this "Federalist" conception of presidential authority through the responsibility he reserved for himself in dealing with foreign affairs. The three frigates constructed in the 1790s would serve to deliver the desired lesson to the four Barbary states without jeopardizing the smaller, more economical government he intended to achieve in Washington (now the federal capital). As Joseph Ellis eloquently observed, "the campaign against the Barbary pirates was perfect: It was a safe and limited projection of American power abroad, it displayed Jefferson's resolve as president, it produced convenient heroes to celebrate, and it cost very little. It was, if you will, the ideal miniature war for Jefferson's minimalist presidency."[6]

In fact, the conduct of the four-year war was not ideal. Even though the president was not troubled by constitutional constraints or by any pacifist considerations, the war lasted longer and was more expensive than anticipated. Morocco threatened to become involved. The American naval blockade had no immediate results beyond persuading Algiers and Tunis to abandon their intention of joining Tripoli. It required the action of Commodore Edward Preble, who bombarded Tripoli five times, to win the respect of the Barbary states; Morocco, which had joined Tripoli in an alliance, renewed its treaty with the United States. The war also produced heroes in the persons of Stephen Decatur, who sailed into Tripoli harbor to rescue American prisoners from the captured frigate *Philadelphia*, and William Eaton, former consul at Tunis, who mobilized a motley collection of American marines and Tripoli dissidents in 1805. In that year the beleaguered pasha of Tripoli sued for peace. But even this success was not untarnished. The United States agreed to pay a ransom when in all probability a direct assault on Tripoli could have forced that state into submission.

Despite the president's vacillation from time to time over the extent of force to be used and despite the inadequate leadership on the part of some of his naval officers, the Barbary wars did affirm Jefferson's sense of national pride and his determination to show the flag in a way that would impress Europe. The kingdoms of Sardinia and the Two Sicilies applauded the U.S. initiative and allowed American ships to refit in their ports. Sweden and Denmark, which also suffered from the Barbary pirates, offered some financial aid, although these smaller powers were not prepared to follow Jefferson into the kind of "Antipiratical Confederacy" that he had advocated twenty years before.

Jefferson seemed apologetic in his fifth annual message to Congress when he noted that the agreement to ransom American captives in Tripoli was based on an assumption that "in a government bottomed on the will of all, the life and liberty of every individual citizen become interesting to all."[7] Notwithstanding his stated position against surrender to the pirates, the president did arrange for tribute to be sent to Algiers, as he worried about taking on too many of the Barbary states. Before Tripoli sued for peace, he was ready to recall the ships from the Mediterranean but at the same time keep one frigate and two small vessels for a perpetual blockade. "Such a blockade," he claimed, "will cost us no more than a state of peace, and will save us from increased tributes, and the disgrace attached to them."[8]

There was no disgrace in the outcome of the Barbary wars, even if troubles in the Mediterranean continued for another decade. Jefferson was justified in suggesting "that there is reason to believe the example we have set, begins already to work on the dispositions of the powers of Europe to emancipate themselves from that degrading yoke. Should we produce such a revolution there, we shall be amply rewarded for what we have done."[9] And even if no such revolution took place, the president recognized that the exercise of force—at least against weaker adversaries—was more effective than either the payment of tribute or protracted diplomacy.

For this to be achieved a navy was necessary, but neither expensive nor larger ships would be required. The lesson of the Tripolitan War was that gunboats able to navigate in the shallow waters of the Mediterranean were more effective than large frigates.

His attraction to gunboats helped to resolve the contradiction between his (and Gallatin's) interest in reducing naval expenditures as a means of both cutting taxes and retiring the national debt and the need to develop a means of projecting American power on the high seas, particularly in the Mediterranean. His initial plan in 1801 was to close navy yards, sell naval vessels, and keep only three, rather than six, frigates in service. The Tripolitan War altered his naval policy, as Congress authorized construction or purchase of four warships (along with $50,000) suitable for the shallow waters of the North African coast. It did not escape the notice of the administration that gunboats would be useful in any operation on the Mississippi River, a theater that would have involved another weak power, Spain, which had suspended the right of deposit in 1802. While Jefferson's gunboats have been the object of ridicule since Henry Adams and Alfred Thayer Mahan disparaged them a century ago, a case may be made that the Jeffersonian navy, less expensive and less ambitious than the Federalist navy, would serve the same national purpose of projecting American power, if not on the high seas, at least in the inland seas. It is reasonable to conclude that Jefferson's gunboat policies were not a break with the Federalist past. When confronted with threats to American commerce in the Mediterranean or to American expansion in the West, the president's support for limited government gave way to a foreign policy that required greater, rather than lesser, executive authority.

## Louisiana and the French Idéologues

The Barbary wars were essentially a sideshow compared with other problems in Jefferson's foreign policy. Ultimately, the protection of American commerce, ships, and sailors from British and French depredations weighed more heavily in the shaping of relations with the outside world. The behavior of superpowers would obviously be of more significance than that of Tripoli or Algiers. But in his first term in office, obstacles on the part of foreign powers to American westward expansion occupied pride of place in the president's thinking. Like the Barbary challenge, a western empire had been on Jefferson's mind since the Revolution. Even during his most fervent reveries about France as a counterbalance to British malevolence he expressed concerns about a French expedition into western America. It was clear in the 1790s that an unintended consequence of the Federalist quasi-war with France could be the latter's occupation of Louisiana. Unlike Spain on the western frontier, a powerful France would represent a more immediate threat to American interests than Britain during the brief interval of peace between the two European powers.

The president also knew that waging war to preserve the vast territories west of the Mississippi for American settlement would have to be a last resort when confronting the Old World. Republican ideology alone would prevent the buildup of the military and naval establishment to cope with a major enemy. While the ideal of Reason replacing violence in resolving international problems was never lost from sight, Jefferson's caution was based on the practical problems of assessing the cost of an army and of mobilizing the public to support a retreat from the limited government the Republicans had sought. War would be avoided because he had better instruments to remove the French danger. The recourse to a British connection in the event that France occupied New Orleans was not a serious prospect; rather, it was a gambit in a diplomatic game he believed he could play—and win—with France. In the long run, Britain was still the greater danger to America's future, and France still the instrument to counter British malevolence.

News of Spain's retrocession of Louisiana to France developed from rumors emanating in London. British agents had learned of the results of the Treaty of San Ildefonso and gladly communicated them to the president through Rufus King. The details were not known, given the veil of secrecy Bonaparte had cast over the act, but they were not necessary to trigger a strong American reaction. The First Consul once again was a step ahead of his adversaries. Knowing that the United States would react negatively to France replacing Spain in North America, he instructed his representatives in Madrid to sign the secret Treaty of San Ildefonso on October 1, 1800, one day after the Treaty of Morfontaine terminating the Franco-American alliance had been concluded. Bonaparte thereby celebrated a reconciliation with the United States at the same time that he was issuing a new and more dangerous challenge than the Directory had posed.

The delicate matter of Louisiana did not inhibit Bonaparte for the moment, since he had no intention of revealing its transfer until French troops had occupied the territory. Another reason to delay the dissemination of the news was the impropriety—to put it mildly—of offering Spain the duchy of Parma until he had secured it from his war with Austria. After Britain had been defeated with New Orleans safely in French hands, there would be time enough to deal with American discontent. While Bonaparte astutely recognized that even a traditionally friendly Jefferson would not accept easily France's return to the American continent, he wanted to use the president's putatively Francophilic sensibilities to his advantage. The First Consul was well aware that Jefferson's acceptance of nomination in November 1801 to the Class of Moral and Political Science of the National Institute would bestow a presidential blessing upon France under the Consulate.

There was implicit contempt on the First Consul's part not only for American naiveté but also for the susceptibility of Jefferson and French intellectuals to his charms. Bonaparte appeared to many of the French friends of America as one of themselves—a liberal in politics, a student of science, an advocate of revolution through reform. He himself was a member of the National Institute and had shown favor during his years in Italy and Egypt to men of letters. Their illusions about this man on horseback did not fade immediately. Too many prominent friends of America became too closely identified with the Constitution that legitimized Bonaparte's seizure of power to make repudiation an easy matter. The Comte de Volney and philosopher Destutt de Tracy held seats in Bonaparte's Senate. Even those who could not accept the general as a republican considered him the heir of the Revolution, the only cure for the shortcomings of the Directory. Lafayette, who admitted that the First Consul had overthrown the republic, assured Jefferson in 1801 of Bonaparte's goodwill toward the United States. Lafayette himself was in debt to the dictator who brought him back to France, if not to office, after long years of prison and exile. These were the men whom Bonaparte expected to restrain Jefferson when he learned about France's plans for Louisiana.

Instead of worrying about Jefferson's discovery of his duplicity, Bonaparte sounded out the possibility of inducing the president to bring the United States into a new League of Armed Neutrality. He suspected that Jefferson's well-known ties with France in general and with its philosophers in particular could serve his purpose. The president's reputation as an ideologue suggested that he might be receptive to the proposals of Thomas Paine and Joel Barlow, two prominent Americans in Paris who were intimates of the intelligentsia. Either by coincidence or by direction of French officials they had chosen the week in which the Treaty of Morfontaine was signed to suggest to their old friend that the United States join with European powers to check British aggression on the high seas. If men such as Volney, Destutt de Tracy, Du Pont, and Lafayette as well as Barlow and Paine could succumb to Bonaparte's charms, their transatlantic colleague should be no more difficult to conquer.

Louis Pichon, the French chargé d'affaires and a old friend of America, was less certain about Jefferson, although the new president was particularly gracious in celebrating the restoration of Franco-American diplomatic relations. Jefferson's reservations about Bonaparte's dictatorship and France's ambitions generally had been largely confined to intimates. But Pichon was aware of considerations that restricted whatever Francophilic tendencies Jefferson still possessed. The president could not afford to expose himself to Federalist attacks by rallying to a new league of armed neutrals. The most that could be expected of him would be his blessings for France's success in its struggle with Britain. Pichon also knew that Jefferson would react as negatively as any Federalist to information that he possessed about France's secret treaty with Spain.

The French diplomat was accurate in his perceptions. As early as March 1801, Rufus King reported the news of a double disaster: the Spanish cession of Louisiana and the Floridas to France, and negotiations for a Franco-British peace that would enable Bonaparte to take possession of his new property. The president expressed his feelings clearly in May 1802 when he told Monroe that "we have great reason to fear that Spain is to cede Louisiana and the Floridas to France."[10] It was an unhappy prospect, filled with opportunities for violence in the event that the French attempted to build an empire in America. Even if they did not intend to violate U.S. territory, their probable interference with commerce on the Mississippi could drive the westerners to war. Coping with this situation involved challenges not only from Jefferson's Republican supporters but also from his Federalist enemies, who would taunt him for passivity or complicity if he failed to respond.

A declaration of war was hardly the answer. France was not Algiers. It was the most powerful nation in Europe under a shrewd and ambitious leader. Jefferson's administration, bent on reducing the military establishment and mindful of the dangers of building a military elite, sought a peaceful solution. Initially, Jefferson was willing to accept the fiction that Louisiana was still Spanish. If he did not have to recognize the existence of a transfer, he would not have to take any action until France was actually in possession of the territory. Writing to his young protégé Governor William C. Claiborne of the Mississippi Territory in July 1801, he urged him to keep an "amiable and even affectionate" relationship with the Spanish neighbor: "We consider her possession of the adjacent country as most favorable to her interests, & should see, with extreme pain any other nation substituted for them." That France was the "other nation" was never in doubt. But he had no solution for the moment beyond delay.[11] For this reason his message to Congress in the fall of 1801 contained no reference to the Louisiana problem.

The president was in denial—or pretended to be—as rumors about the retrocession of Louisiana flew about Washington. His communications concerning France in 1801 seemed to skirt the subject, concentrating instead on accepting Bonaparte's conditions for ratification of the Treaty of Morfontaine and accepting as well French envoys whom he regarded to be anti-republican if not anti-American. This attitude may have been part of a design to avoid looking for difficulties that he would not wish to find. In assuring Louis Pichon that he believed France's disclaimers about Louisiana, he was playing for time. There was always the possibility that some obstacle could arise to nullify the Franco-Spanish deal.

By 1802, Jefferson could no longer put the matter aside. His instrument of persuasion was classic diplomacy, hinting that a rupture between the two countries would take place once war was resumed in Europe. To prevent this situation the president suggested that France grant Americans favorable commercial concessions on the Mississippi. Jefferson, under pressure from western allies and Federalist adversaries, had decided to face the fact of French imperialism without waiting for the arrival of French troops in America to rouse him to action. This was a first step in a campaign to intimidate France to give up its ambitions in America. The price of American friendship, particularly in the context of a new round of warfare in Europe, would be more than commercial favors: France would have to surrender New Orleans, the Floridas, all the territory that Spain presumably had ceded in a treaty whose terms were still unknown to him. The alternative to a voluntary arrangement would be loss of this territory the moment the perennial troubles of Europe distracted the belligerents' attention from the New World. And in this circumstance, Bonaparte would find the United States in an alliance with France's enemy, Great Britain. Dramatically, Jefferson warned that "the day that France takes possession of N. Orleans, fixes the sentence which is to restrain her forever within her low-water mark." It was in this context that he wrote the often-quoted statement about Americans "marrying ourselves to the British fleet and nation."[12]

These words were in a letter to Robert R. Livingston, the American minister to France, for the beneficial effect the president hoped it would have on its bearer, Pierre-Samuel Du Pont de Nemours. Du Pont, Jefferson's friend of twenty years, was a distinguished physiocrat who was returning to Paris for what he thought would be only a brief stay. The president intended to use French friends of America to influence French policy, a mirror image of Bonaparte's strategy of using these same friends to influence American policy on France's behalf. Du Pont was fully apprised of the contents of the letter to Livingston. And lest the Livingston letter be insufficient, Jefferson sent a note to Du Pont asking him to impress upon his fellow countrymen the importance of ceding all French territory, not just New Orleans, to the United States. He warned him that failure to respond to American overtures would end in a war that would remove France from the ocean and push the United States into the arms of Britain. The president was reluctant to join Britain against a country that had served America in the past and could do so again. France's possession of Louisiana—"this speck which now appears as an almost invisible point in the horizon, is the embryo of a tornado which will burst on the countries on both sides of the Atlantic. . . . That it may yet be avoided is my sincere prayer; and if you can be the means of informing the wisdom of Bonaparte of all its consequences, you have deserved well of both countries."[13]

The unofficial emissary agreed to the assignment the president had asked of him, but not before his pride as a Frenchman had been appeased. The president's tactics, Du Pont thought, would antagonize rather than intimidate the French. It would be better for the United States to help them win back Canada in exchange for the surrender of Louisiana, for such a gesture would make the arrangement appear reciprocal. If this proposal was more than the United States could make, he then advised Jefferson to offer a reasonable price for the territory at issue in language that would not offend the First Consul.

Du Pont's response reflected the ambivalence of the French intelligentsia: a friendly concern for a country that was the hope of their youth, along with a patriotic impatience with lack of appreciation in the United States for France's problems. There was no record that Jefferson's craftily constructed instructions to Livingston and advice to Du Pont ever reached Bonaparte. Nothing in Livingston's dispatches indicates that the president's threat of making common cause with Britain was clearly communicated to the First Consul. If Jefferson failed to exploit his French connections in this critical instance, it may be noted that Bonaparte was no more successful than the president in utilizing the same connections to serve French interests.

But the spectacular success of the Louisiana Purchase rendered moot whether or not it was his warnings that induced Bonaparte to accede to American concerns. As far as Jefferson was concerned, his tactics had great potential for the future. Later in 1802, James Monroe unwittingly gave the president an opportunity to express fully his expectations in cultivating foreign friendships. While in Paris as a special envoy to Bonaparte, Monroe noticed that Jefferson's correspondence with certain influential Frenchmen had produced a good effect during his mission. He suggested, therefore, that relations with literary and philosophical personages be continued and nourished, especially when connected with the National Institute. He was convinced that it was the most powerful organization in France outside the executive circle itself.

If the president's reply to these observations was somewhat patronizing, it was not because he thought Monroe had misunderstood or overestimated the role of the intellectual in imperial France. He merely regarded the advice as gratuitous, since he had examined long before and had put into effect just such a project with respect to British as well as French intellectuals. Indeed, he had consciously made use of his relations with Lafayette and Du Pont, he pointed out, when he was minister to France. More recently he had been writing freely to men of the stature of Volney, Du Pont, and philospher Pierre-Jean-Georges Cabanis "on subjects of literature, and to a certain degree on politics, respecting however their personal opinions, and their situation so as not to compromit them were a letter intercepted." Most of his suggestions were of the kind that "would do us good if known to their governments, and, as probably as not, are communicated to them." Jefferson expressed pride in his ability to make "private friendships instrumental to the public good by inspiring a confidence which is denied to public, and official communications."[14] It was no coincidence that both Destutt de Tracy and Du Pont were elected to the American Philosophical Society during his presidency of that organization. In 1801, Bonaparte had Jefferson elected to France's counterpart, the National Institute, for the same reason that the president honored Destutt de Tracy and Du Pont.

## The Louisiana Purchase

In the interval between Monroe's letter in 1802 and Jefferson's response in 1804, Bonaparte, now First Consul for life, sold not only New Orleans but all of Louisiana and possibly parts of Florida to the United States. To follow up Du Pont's return to France the president dispatched Monroe as his special envoy to help Livingston win Louisiana. This was an act of desperation rather than confidence. The 1802 Treaty of Amiens between the two European rivals, no matter how tenuous, would free Bonaparte to complete his plans to occupy the recovered territory. At home, westerners were increasingly restless over the prospect of losing the right of deposit in New Orleans. As 1802 came to a close, word came to Washington that Spain had suspended the rights won in Pinckney's Treaty. Jefferson had to act, and did so. Ordering the building of new gunboats was a message to the French; expelling Indians across the Mississippi to generate new problems for the French was another; assistance to the Haitian revolutionaries was a third. All of these gestures, including his putative overtures to Britain, were in support of the peaceful persuasion his message to Livingston via Du Pont had indicated.

Jefferson seemed to succeed beyond his wildest expectations. New Orleans, for which he would pay $10 million, was offered to Monroe and Livingston, and much more—all of Louisiana for an additional $5 million. The president's statecraft had forced the French dictator to accept America's terms. Success also presented Jefferson with a dilemma. How could he fit the purchase of Louisiana into the construction of the Constitution that he and his party had maintained so vigorously during the Federalist years? The answer was to apply as loose a construction to that basic document as Hamilton had done with the National Bank in 1791. The appropriate measure would have been a constitutional amendment, but that would have taken too much time. Conceivably, Federalist opponents fearful of western territories that would reduce their influence in Congress and in the country would use this period to defeat an amendment. More seriously, the Jeffersonians were concerned that Bonaparte would change his mind if the treaty ceding Louisiana was delayed excessively. Such were the considerations that determined annexation by treaty.

That the president was aware that "the Constitution has made no provision for our holding foreign territory, still less for incorporating foreign nations into our Union" was obvious. But there was no alternative, he felt, to him or to Congress, whose members "I presume, will see their duty to their country in ratifying and paying for it, so as to secure a good which would otherwise probably be never again in their power." He likened the acquisition of Louisiana to "the case of a guardian, investing the money of his ward in purchasing an important adjacent territory; and saying to him when of age, I did this for your good; I pretend to no right to bind you: you may disavow me, and I must get out of the scrape as I can: I thought it my duty to risk myself for you."[15] Jefferson wrote these words in the expectation that the nation would not disavow the purchase. Indeed, he asserted that the transaction would strengthen the Constitution by more strongly marking out its lines. As historian Alexander DeConde expressed it, expansion into Louisiana "did not emerge suddenly, or haphazardly a full-blown success. It reflected a well-developed expansionist tradition and a conscious vision of the national future."[16]

Understandably, Jefferson gloried in his windfall. Bonaparte's offer advanced the time when Americans would move into the trans-Mississippi West, and the president could interpret his success as a product of shrewd statecraft. The French succumbed to the logic of the arguments he presented through Du Pont. The territory was ceded without war, by skillfully playing on the shifting balance of power in Europe. The president knew as well as the First Consul that the peace of Amiens was tenuous, and that a renewal of the Anglo-French conflict was only a matter of time, and a short time at that. Once war in Europe erupted again, it was obvious that Britain's control of the seas would make it difficult, if not impossible, for France to reoccupy Louisiana. Britain could sweep down from Canada to occupy the territory. In this context, selling Louisiana to the Americans was simply a question of prudence, if not necessity.

Was the transaction then a triumph of diplomacy, or of good fortune? It was both, with the latter deserving the larger share of the credit. Had Bonaparte been able to dispatch troops to New Orleans as he had planned, then formal announcement of the retrocession of the territory from Spain would have been made, which presumably would have placed France in a position to resist both American and British reactions to the action. In Bonaparte's scheme of things, Louisiana would have provided the granary for the French

West Indies in an empire linking Saint-Domingue to New Orleans. But before French forces could occupy New Orleans, they had to put down the long-simmering rebellion in Haiti, led by the charismatic black general, Toussaint L'Ouverture. Although Toussaint was captured and deported to France in 1802, the French were unable to suppress the Haitian rebels. Its army was decimated by the yellow fever that claimed its leader, Charles Victor-Emmanuel Leclerc, Bonaparte's close friend and brother-in-law. Still, had reinforcements arrived in time, Saint-Domingue conceivably might have been pacified and the occupation of New Orleans would have followed. But the fleet scheduled to depart for the West from the Netherlands was icebound in the port of Helvoet Sluys, one of the rare occasions when the harbor froze. By the time of the spring thaws in 1803 it was too late; war with Britain was on the horizon, and Louisiana was lost to France for the time being.

Whatever Jefferson's estimation of his statecraft may have been, it was not shared by Bonaparte, who proclaimed himself emperor in 1804. For him, American possession of Louisiana was a temporary arrangement designed to keep it out of the hands of the British enemy. Once Great Britain was conquered, the United States would be persuaded to return it to French sovereignty. Napoleon's contempt for American diplomacy was soon manifested both in the cavalier treatment his foreign minister, Talleyrand, accorded American claims on the Floridas and in his contemptuous dismissal of the neutral rights of the United States during Jefferson's second administration.

## The Haitian Dilemma

The president, flushed with the success of the Louisiana mission, was unaware of French calculations and might have been unconcerned had he known the details. Certainly, Napoleon's capacity for mischief would not have surprised him. After all, it was not until the First Consul actually offered the territory for sale that he admitted that France indeed had retrieved Louisiana from Spain. But Jefferson felt that despite all the craft and deception of the French, he had outmaneuvered them over Saint-Domingue. There he played a difficult game in wishing to aid the independence of that black republic without recognizing the regime. He wanted the new nation to embarrass and impede France's efforts to rebuild an empire, and yet he did not want to encourage the black leaders to the point of antagonizing his slaveholding supporters in the South.

Jefferson's position on Saint-Domingue highlighted the ambi-guities of his thoughts about blacks and slavery. He was as con-cerned as any other slaveholder about a linkage between the failed Gabriel slave conspiracy in 1800 in Virginia and a successful insur-rection of slaves and former slaves in the Caribbean. While he shared the fears of southerners about the presence of a black re-public near their shores, his reactions were not identical to those of other slaveholders. Twenty years earlier, he had made clear his con-demnation of the evils of slavery as well as his belief in the inabil-ity of white America to assimilate freed slaves; his solution had been—and continued to be—gradual emancipation and repatria-tion to Africa. In the short run he initially appeared to support a concert of concerned nations against the black regime of General Toussaint. But this instinctive impulse was tempered by opposi-tion to the Leclerc expedition when he recognized its implications for French control of Louisiana. He backed away from his promise to help the French blockade Saint-Domingue's ports, and in fact conducted a policy of neutrality that provided the insurrectionists with provisions and even arms and ammunition.

The death of Leclerc and resumption of war in Europe caused another abrupt change of policy. Once the French threat was re-moved, the threat of free blacks took center stage, particularly as Toussaint's successor, General Jean-Jacques Dessalines—who named the new republic Haiti in 1804—embarked on an expansion-ist program that included all of the island of Hispaniola. Anxious southerners envisioned the newly independent republic as a ha-ven for escaped slaves and an inspiration for slaves in the United States. Did Jefferson the Virginian then revert to an older role as, in the language of Paul Finkelman, "a self-indulgent and negrophobic Virginia planter"?[17] There is sufficient evidence in Jefferson's writ-ings and correspondence to give credibility to the charge of rac-ism. Yet it is doubtful if his behavior toward the slave revolution was governed by his prejudices. Unlike most slaveholders, he was not particularly fearful of the existence of a black state. In fact, he considered it as a possible "receptacle of the blacks transplanted into this hemisphere," as he observed to Monroe in 1801: "The pos-sibility that these exiles might stimulate & conduct vindictive or predatory descents on our coasts, & facilitate concert with their brethren here, looks to a state of things between that island & us not probable on a contemplation of our relative strength."[18] Here was an expression of a long-standing belief that the evil of slavery could be exorcised by removing freed slaves from America to Africa or, in this particular instance, to the West Indies.

If the president did not respond to Dessalines's efforts to cultivate close commercial and political ties with the United States, it was not because of his personal fears of a slave revolt in the South or of revulsion against the concept of an independent black nation. Rather, it was a political decision in response to public opinion in the South. There was nothing reflexive about it; he weighed southern reaction against that of northern merchants with commercial ties to Haiti, and found the former stronger. In principle, Jefferson was not opposed to a relationship that would make the United States a protector of a weak independent nation that would be free from French or British domination.

The president once again raised the idea of a consortium to neutralize the island, or at least to prevent the supply of arms to the republic. It failed to materialize. Instead, he tried, as his address to Congress in November 1804 suggested, to walk a fine line between northern merchants with commercial interests in Saint-Domingue and southern slaveholders wanting to keep as much distance as possible from the black republic. But the issue that determined the maintenance of a prohibition against selling arms to Saint-Domingue was France's insistence that the island was still its colony, even though in a state of rebellion. He did not want to antagonize Napoleon as long as France could be of service in defining the territory of Louisiana. If France would intercede with Spain over the Floridas, it would be worth deferring to French claims on Saint-Domingue. An embargo would be a small price to pay for the large prize envisioned by the president.

In this context, Jefferson's supposed distaste for black sovereignty was of less importance in defining policy than his interest in expanding the borders of Louisiana as far as possible. France was to be the instrument once again of advancing American interests. Although he recognized that the movement southward of the cotton frontier would ultimately force Madrid to yield Florida, he preferred to avoid conflict with Spain and use diplomacy to gain peaceful title to the territory. This strategy would involve accepting a prohibition of trade with any part of Haiti not in possession of France, a concession embodied in the Logan Act of 1806 that would appease both southern planters and the French emperor. The ban on trade remained in place through Jefferson's second administration, continuing under the Embargo Act of 1807 after the

Logan Act had expired. The president hoped that diplomatic success in the Floridas would compensate for the loss of northern trade with the island. This was a species of statecraft that rested on two assumptions: 1) that the nation at large shared the president's nationalist feelings about expanding Louisiana's boundaries as far as possible; and 2) that Napoleon's control of Spain would bring Florida into the American fold. The first assumption ultimately had more validity than the second.

## Seeking the Floridas

The prospects for exploiting French influence to expand the boundaries of Louisiana seemed favorable. Jefferson would consider West Florida as part of the Louisiana Purchase even if neither the French nor the Spanish accepted the connection. In a revealing March 1804 letter to William Dunbar, a Natchez planter and explorer, Jefferson noted that on his first visit to Monticello after receiving the treaty he investigated the "limits of Louisiana" from materials he had collected in Europe. "One single fact in it," he observed, "was taken from a publication in a newspaper, supposed to be written by Judge Bay, who had lived in West Florida. This asserted that the country from the Iberville to the Perdido was to this day called Louisiana, and part of the government of Louisiana." And as far as the president was concerned, "though the name and division of West Florida have been retained; and in strictness, that country is still called by that name; yet it is also called Louisiana in common parlance, and even in some authentic documents." Equally revealing was Jefferson's addendum that "the fact, however, is not of much importance."[19] What mattered was the opportunity the Louisiana Purchase offered to test the limits of expansion.

If Spain disputed this assertion, that nation's depredations against American commerce over the years were sufficient to overcome shaky legal claims. As early as August 1803, Jefferson asserted that "the ancient boundary of Louisiana" extended eastward to the Perdido River, between Mobile and Pensacola. While these claims would be the subject of negotiation with Spain, "as soon as she is at war, . . . we shall certainly obtain the Floridas, and all in good time."[20] Beyond West Florida lay the rest of Spain's possessions east of the Mississippi, and this too should fall to the United States by exercise of statecraft or of military pressure. Congress's passage of the Mobile Act of 1804, with its assumption that the territory west of the Perdido River was part of Louisiana, and thereby American, was just the first step in a process that would end in the United States controlling all of the Floridas. West Florida was not explicitly annexed by this act, but since Jefferson was empowered to erect a separate customs district in the territory, it was a distinction without much difference.

Although Jefferson had sent Monroe to Spain to secure that country's acceptance of his interpretation of Louisiana's borders, he anticipated and discounted Spanish objections. He was not disturbed by Spain's keen sense of injury over Napoleon's betrayal of his promise not to alienate the territory. He assumed that rising American power, along with the complacency of France, would soften Spanish resistance. He was mistaken. Spain was still under the illusion that the acquisition of Louisiana might disrupt the American union and relieve pressures on the Floridas.

The president remained under the spell of his brilliant success with France. If he could manipulate the great power, he should do even more with the lesser power. The new American governor of Louisiana, William Claiborne, repeatedly urged him to adopt the simple course of seizing West Florida and challenge the Spanish to dispute the action. But Jefferson had a more attractive, and more familiar, alternative: exploit the troubles of Europe to serve the advantage of America. Press France, the country that now held Spain as a satellite, to provide the solution without war or bloodshed. Jefferson believed that this strategy should yield results, especially since the United States had many unresolved claims against France, including claims for damages to American commerce by Spanish vessels operating under French orders. In Madrid, the French ambassador even appeared to take the initiative in supporting American boundary claims, invoking the invitation attributed to the French foreign minister that "you have made a noble bargain for yourselves, and I suppose you will make the most of it."[21] Then, too, there was the practical matter of money, which could be a decisive factor in favor of French mediation, according to Monroe's informants in Paris in 1804.

Jefferson's expectations did not materialize. Talleyrand's hostility to the United States, rarely repressed for long, combined with Napoleon's own schemes for a European continental empire to undo Jefferson's hopes of French intervention on America. In fact, Talleyrand made it clear before the end of 1804 that West Florida was not included in the Louisiana cession. General Louis Marie Turreau, the French minister in Washington, professed shock over America's aggressive behavior toward France's Spanish ally.

Jefferson was undisturbed. He assured Attorney General Levi Lincoln that "good humor and reason" would calm Spanish anger over the Mobile Act, which claimed the territory west of the Perdido. Once again, he had in mind playing the British card against Britain's adversaries in Europe. This mood was in no way shared by his intimates: Monroe, writing from Madrid, urged force in Florida despite the risk of war with all the European rivals; Madison, sharing Jefferson's methods but not his sangfroid, wanted to make no move that would threaten the status quo; and Gallatin, more annoyed than alarmed by the president's initiatives, doubted if the Floridas were worth the risks that would follow. It seemed to his advisers that the president was prepared to advocate some kind of alliance with Britain to achieve his objectives.

Jefferson's expectations embraced far more than the issue of West Florida, which the Mobile Act had resolved to his satisfaction. They involved Texas in the West, which under no stretch of imagination could be considered part of Louisiana, and opportunity for settlement as far west as the Sabine River. As for the rest of Florida, east of the Perdido River, Jefferson was willing to consider buying it for no more than $2 million. Moreover, Spain should be warned against strengthening its garrisons west of the Perdido or interrupting American navigation on any of the rivers: "If they will not give such an order instantly, they should be told that we have for peace sake only, forborne till they could have time to give such an order, but that as soon as we receive notice of their refusal to give the order we shall intermit the exercise of our right of navigating the Mobile."[22]

It was hardly surprising if Jefferson looked to Britain to help him inadvertently realize such an ambitious program. Jefferson's means, however, were less clear than his ends. Assuming that France's backing explained Spain's resistance to America's demands, he was prepared in 1805 to outmaneuver Napoleon much as he felt he had done in 1803. He would induce the emperor to acquiesce by making him believe that the United States was not averse to war or to a military connection with Britain. He asserted those sentiments to his Cabinet so vigorously that Madison, if not Napoleon, took them seriously. The secretary of state thought that it was reasonable to mention the possibility of increased friendship with Britain, but talking of a treaty and a provisional alliance was going too far.

The president quickly cleared up all doubts about his flirtation with the British. He was even a little annoyed that an old friend like Madison should have misunderstood his intentions. A treaty with Britain, he emphasized, would be provisional, effective only "on the event of our being engaged in war with either France or Spain during the present war in Europe." Such an eventuality was unlikely, but even if it were to come to pass, he would insist that Britain guarantee American possession of Louisiana and the Floridas as well as Spanish indemnification for damages inflicted in the Floridas.[23] This explanation mollified Madison, who knew as well as Jefferson that Britain would never fight a war to win territorial advantages for the United States without exacting reciprocation on terms unacceptable to the Americans. All that Jefferson wanted was speculation abroad that would push France and Spain into settling boundary and indemnity claims.

The president's bluff was never tested. Britain's war with Napoleon after 1805 became a war of attrition, with the United States as the primary victim. This turn of events dissolved whatever hopes Jefferson had of playing Britain against France to win the Floridas. But even without the changed circumstances there is no evidence that Jefferson ever wished to go beyond annoying France by posturing as a partner of Britain in some kind of entente, if not in a formal alliance. He placed greater faith in Napoleon's attack against Austria as an occasion to renew negotiations over Florida. In fact, he seemed to revert for the moment to the caution of Gallatin, who, during rumors of alliance and treaty with Britain, had urged suspension of all diplomatic efforts without abandoning any ground. Napoleon's engagement in what was expected to be a protracted Austrian campaign should have made the French more vulnerable to American pressure. The emperor's spectacular victory at Austerlitz in December 1805 dashed such hopes and, when combined with Admiral Horatio Nelson's equally spectacular naval victory at Trafalgar two months earlier, rendered British intervention even more unlikely than it had been before.

These setbacks did not deter the president from raising again the possibility of military action, even as its use was less credible in 1805 than it had been a few years earlier. But a combination of threats and blandishments applied to Spain was an option some of his advisers urged. His minister to France, John Armstrong, joined Monroe in recommending the occupation of Texas, and Robert Smith, former secretary of the navy, advised building battleships to carry out attacks against Spanish territory. Jefferson's annual message to Congress at the end of 1805 spoke of forceful action in Florida and the active defense of free citizens along the Mississippi.

But in a secret message he asked Congress for $2 million to purchase East Florida. He concealed this pacific move beneath a show of martial ardor to prevent Europeans from suspecting a change in tactics. To the historian Henry Adams, however, these efforts were pathetic. His attempt to outwit Talleyrand, the shrewdest actor on the European stage, "resembled an amateur imitating Talma and Garrick,"[24] the leading lights of the French and English theater.

This maneuver failed ignominiously, if only because the situation in Europe differed considerably from that of 1803. Even before the Two Millions Act was signed into law in February 1806, the war that Jefferson had welcomed as a means of softening Napoleon had ended. To European observers and Jefferson's enemies in America, as well as most historians today, his attempts to bend Europe's power to America's advantage looked ludicrous. Both Britain and France understood that his bellicosity was fraudulent, and that beneath his bravado was neither the will nor the ability to use force for his objectives east of the Perdido River. His clumsy attempts to play one European power against the other had only convinced the two major powers that American threats could be ignored. As for the third power, Spain, it believed its fragile grip on power in North America could survive, at least in the short run.

But Jefferson's failure was only in the short run. American settlers continued to move into East and West Florida, and in the War of 1812 Congress annexed West Florida, parcelling it out between Louisiana and the Territory of Mississippi. While Spain still held East Florida at the end of the war, its fate was soon to be sealed by its cession in 1819. In the long run, Jefferson's expectation that the Floridas—and the continent itself—were to be American was justified. And to certify the national consensus over a territory of particular concern to the South and West, it was a New England secretary of state, John Quincy Adams, who finally secured the Floridas from Spain.

## Westward the Course of Empire

Despite the attention Jefferson gave to the eastern limits of Louisiana, the Floridas were of less importance than the western borders of that territory. It was not just that they were not well defined. Rather, the uncertain boundaries in the West invited opportunities not only to extend the western limits of the new territory but also to use the demarcation as a starting point for further acquisitions of Spanish lands. Exploiting the issue of the Sabine River, which separated Texas from Louisiana, Americans following the president's policy demanded that the Spanish commandant in Texas withdraw all his troops from the eastern shore of the Sabine. When he refused to comply, 150 Americans moved into the disputed area. Both sides backed down from this confrontation, Spain because of its inherent weakness, the United States because of its distrust of Louisiana Creoles who might have joined with the Spanish. But turmoil in the West was never far below the surface. In the same year, 1806, discredited former vice president Aaron Burr was accused of plotting to raise an army to invade Texas and Mexico, and possibly detaching Louisiana as well from the Federal Union to establish an empire of his own. This scheme failed, but the idea of a military expedition composed of aggressive westerners was always alive in these years.

While Jefferson opposed any separatist plans (particularly when they involved figures as unsavory as Aaron Burr), his interest in the West was as active as any war hawk's. The difference was a caution based on presidential responsibilities, a hostile Federalist opposition, and a recognition that the future of the Continent would fall to the United States in time. The Louisiana Purchase was simply an opportunity to activate policies that had been on his mind since the Revolution. It did not matter that Spain stood in the way, or whether France or Britain had their own ambitions for western expansion. In December 1783, a month after he had taken his seat in Congress, he had learned of money being raised in Britain "for exploring the country from the Missisipi" to California: "They pretend it is only to promote knolege. I am afraid they have thoughts of colonising into that quarter." He tried but failed to lure George Rogers Clark into leading an expedition to head off a British initiative.[25] Two years later Jefferson, then minister in Paris, heard about a French expedition under Jean François de La Pérouse to search for the Northwest Passage, and once again his suspicions were aroused over France's intentions to colonize. But his chosen agent to counter these ambitions, John Ledyard, was unable to fulfill the mission.

Not until he was president did Jefferson find the explorers who would succeed where Clark and Ledyard failed. Meriwether Lewis and William Clark were commissioned to explore the new Louisiana Territory in 1803, and then into the Oregon country all the way to the Pacific Ocean. But the inspiration for this expedition did not come from France's return to Louisiana. As historian Stephen Ambrose observed, "It was not the French who got Jefferson to start another project for an exploring expedition across the West—the retrocession had nothing to do with it—but the British."[26] The particular Briton in this case was a Scot, Alexander Mackenzie, who while a fur trader in Montreal in the 1780s had crossed the continent to the Pacific coast but found his route unsuitable for commercial use. When Jefferson learned that an account of his travels had been published in London in 1801, his immediate reaction was to challenge this latest British effort to take over the western part of the continent. His intimate friend Meriwether Lewis was to be the instrument that would ensure this vast area for the United States. At the same time that he sent Monroe to Paris to buy New Orleans, he obtained passports for Lewis from both the British and French ministers in Washington. This was advisable since Spain presumably had ceded the Louisiana Territory to France, and British traders could be useful in facilitating the mission.

The Lewis and Clark expedition was an appropriate complement to the Louisiana Purchase, and elicited from Jefferson arguably more enthusiasm than the acquisition of the new territory itself. Preempting European occupation was not the only motive driving the president. As Donald Jackson observed, his directions to Lewis and his experienced colleague Clark symbolized the culmination of a lifetime of study and speculation about the West: "They barely conceal his excitement at realizing that at last he would have facts, not vague guesses, about the Stony Mountains, the river courses, the wild Indian tribes, the flora and fauna of untrodden places—perhaps even some evidence of the late, great creatures whose bones he loved to collect."[27] There was no doubt that these interests carried as much weight as the implication for foreign relations in his support of the expedition. A few months earlier he had noted that while Lewis was not a botanist, he was familiar with natural history and astronomy and could carry out the detailed instructions of the president. For the rugged experiences that lay ahead, Clark, the younger brother of George Rogers Clark and a veteran woodsman and surveyor, would be a valuable partner in the enterprise.

Jefferson's preoccupation with the scientific advances that exploration of the West would yield did not displace his sense of an American destiny that would create a continental empire of liberty. Behind his policies lay a recognition that a restless growing population would be a major force in realizing that destiny. The obstacles, particularly Britain and France, were formidable but manageable, as his successful statecraft in his first administration demonstrated. If Britain had not acceded to the American positions on impressment, at least it had allowed its ships to carry goods from the Spanish and French West Indies to Europe. And if Napoleon's France remained an uncertain entity, at least the president's diplomacy could turn French cupidity to America's advantage.

The immediate obstacle after Louisiana was acquired was relations with Indians, an issue that was both more easy and more difficult to resolve than relations with Europe. Jefferson's ambivalence toward Indians was reflected in his *Notes on Virginia*, and it had not changed over the years. He admired many of their qualities, convinced, as he told Chastellux in 1785, that "the proof of genius given by the Indians of N. America, place them on a level with Whites in the same uncultivated state."[28] He foresaw assimilation in the future, which he believed was impossible with blacks. But Indian progress toward equality depended upon what Marie-Jeanne Rossignol has called "civilization" by education, farming, and Christianity. That Indians might follow another path was not admissable. They could not be allowed to stand in the way of American expansion any more than any external power. American nationalism was defined as much by its treatment of Indians—and for that matter Haitians and even the Creoles of Louisiana—as by its rejection of the Old World.[29]

Jefferson's optimism about the future of Indian relations was accompanied by an assumption that in the present time, Indians would have to be prevented from obstructing the westward movement of settlers. Bargaining for Indian lands should be a peaceful process in which the Indian partner would be considered nominally as a sovereign nation. In reality American benevolence extended only to the point of dealing with Indians as children. Their alleged savagery must yield to civilization, and once treaties were made they would have to leave the land unless they adapted to American ways. As Bernard Sheehan observed, "Jefferson probably spent more time cultivating the art of commiserating with them than anyone else in the late eighteenth and early nineteenth century. He always employed a conciliatory tone, but it held a note of realistic necessity."[30]

Jefferson's vision of Indian relations was clearly articulated in the advice he offered in 1803 to William Henry Harrison, governor of the Indiana Territory: "Our system is to live in perpetual peace with the Indians, to cultivate an affectionate attachment which we can do for them within the bounds of reason, and by giving them effectual protection against the wrongs from our own people. The decrease of game rendering their subsistence by hunting insufficient, we wish to draw them to agriculture." But this benevolent goal was more a lure than an invitation to citizenship. The president went on to note that as farmers, Indians would fall into debt; and "when these debts get beyond what the individuals can pay, they become willing to lop them off by a cession of lands." While he suggested a choice of Indians becoming citizens, his expectations were that they would be removed beyond the Mississippi. In brief, he anticipated that the Louisiana Territory would be the new home of Indians as American settlers pressed westward. Jefferson concluded with the information that "the occupation of New Orleans, hourly expected, by the French, is already felt like a light breeze by the Indians. You know the sentiments they entertain of that nation; under the hope of their protection they will immediately stiffen against cessions of lands to us. We had better, therefore, do at once what can be done."[31] Such was the path of realism—and racism.

The cession of Louisiana permitted the president to put into action his plan of removing Indians peacefully, if possible, from lands by whatever means were available in anticipation of a westward surge of settlers. If Indians accepted the American civilizing mission, they would be incorporated into civilized society. If they persisted in their tribal ways, they would be encouraged by intimidation or blandishments to move across the Mississippi, thereby clearing the lands east of the river for peaceful settlement. The Indians, like the Europeans, were barriers to western expansionism. In acquiring Louisiana, Jefferson envisioned the breakdown of all barriers: the Indians through negotiations bolstered by the growing numbers of U.S. citizens in the West, the Europeans through negotiations advanced by the perennial internecine wars of the Old World.

The acquisition of Louisiana was the transforming experience in Jefferson's political life. It was, as Henry Adams admitted, "the greatest diplomatic success recorded in American history."[32] Doubling the size of the nation offered proof of the validity of his vision, and that of many of his close colleagues—namely, that the new American republic not only could create a continental empire, but also that empire would not be a mirror of the Old World's despotic monarchic empires with their exploitive mercantilist policies. The American empire would be different in every respect. The land acquired was in essence empty once Indian relations had been solved; the peoples would be free farmers with opportunities to organize themselves into political units on terms of equality with the older states. Historian Drew McCoy called Jefferson's "notion of a continuously expanding 'empire of liberty' in the Western Hemisphere . . . a bold intellectual stroke."[33] Instead of replicating the experience of Europe, it would preserve the republican character of America.

This concept of a special destiny for his country suggests a consistency in Jefferson's foreign policies that helps to explain the apparent inconsistencies in his political philosophy: the putative pacifist willing to employ force against the appropriate adversary; the Francophile ready to hint at a British alliance; the advocate of a self-reliant farmer seeking access to foreign markets; the proponent of limited government using a loose construction of the Constitution to secure Louisiana. Jefferson's "conscious vision of a national future," as Alexander DeConde expressed it, was not a product of political expediency, even as he sought to calm passions of aggressive westerners, prevent the breakup of the Union, and—not the least—to preserve his party in power.[34] Given the success of the president's statecraft in his first administration, it is hardly surprising that he would expand his expectations in his second term. He expected the setback over the Floridas to be overcome by new triumphs that lay ahead for himself and for his country.

## Notes

1. Inaugural Address, March 4, 1801, in Paul Leicester Ford, ed., *The Works of Thomas Jefferson*, 12 vols. (New York: G. P. Putnam's Sons, 1904–05), 9:365 (hereafter cited as Ford).

2. Joseph J. Ellis, *The American Sphinx: The Character of Thomas Jefferson* (New York: Alfred A. Knopf, 1997), 182.

3. Edward Thornton to Lord Grenville, March 7, 1801, No. 17, 16216, FO5/32, Public Record Office, Kew, London.

4. TJ to Robert R. Livingston, April 18, 1802, Ford, 9:365.

5. TJ to Wilson Cary Nicholas, June 11, 1801, ibid., 265.

6. Ellis, *The American Sphinx*, 204.

7. "Fifth Annual Message," in Andrew A. Lipscomb and Albert E. Bergh, eds., *The Writings of Thomas Jefferson*, 20 vols. (Washington, DC: Thomas Jefferson Memorial Association, 1903–04), 3:390 (hereafter cited as Lipscomb and Bergh).

8. TJ to John Tyler, March 29, 1805, ibid., 11:70.

9. Ibid.

10. TJ to Monroe, May 29, 1801, Ford, 9:263

11. TJ to Claiborne, July 13. 1801, ibid., 275.

12. TJ to Livingston, April 18, 1802, ibid., 365.

13. TJ to Du Pont de Nemours, April 14, 1802, Lipscomb and Bergh, 10:317–18

14. TJ to Monroe, January 8, 1804, Ford, 10.60–61.

15. TJ to John Breckenridge, August 12, 1803, Lipscomb and Bergh, 10:411.

16. Alexander DeConde, *This Affair of Louisiana* (New York: Charles Scribner's Sons, 1976), 249.

17. Paul Finkelman, "Jefferson and Slavery: 'Treason against the Hopes of the World'," in Peter S. Onuf, ed., *Jeffersonian Legacies* (Charlottesville: University Press of Virginia, 1993), 210.

18. TJ to Monroe, November 24, 1801, Ford, 9:318.

19. TJ to William Dunbar, March 13, 1804, Lipscomb and Bergh, 11: 20–21.

20. TJ to Breckenridge, August 12, 1803, ibid., 10:408.

21. Quoted in Henry Adams, *History of the United States of America in the Administration of Thomas Jefferson*, Books 1 and 2 (New York: Albert and Charles Boni, 1930), 2:44.

22. TJ to Madison, July 5, 1804, Ford, 10:91.

23. TJ to Madison, August 27, 1805, ibid., 172.

24. Adams, *History*, 3:115.

25. TJ to Clark, December 4, 1783, Boyd, 6:371.

26. Stephen S. Ambrose, *Undaunted Courage: Meriwether Lewis, Thomas Jefferson, and the Opening of the American West* (New York: Simon and Schuster, 1996), 73.

27. Donald Jackson, *Thomas Jefferson & the Stony Mountains: Exploring the West from Monticello* (Norman: University of Oklahoma Press, 1993), 139.

28. TJ to Chastellux, June 7, 1785, Boyd, 8:185.

29. Marie-Jeanne Rossignol, *Le ferment nationaliste: Aux origines de la politique extérieure des Etats-Unis, 1789–1812* (Paris: Belin, 1994), 279.

30. Bernard W. Sheehan, *Seeds of Extinction: Jeffersonian Philanthropy and the American Indian* (Chapel Hill: University of North Carolina Press, 1973), 152.

31. TJ to William Henry Harrison, February 27, 1803, Lipscomb and Bergh, 10:369, 370, 373.

32. Adams, *History*, 2:48.

33. Drew R. McCoy, *The Elusive Republic: Political Economy in Jeffersonian America* (Chapel Hill: University of North Carolina Press, 1980), 204.

34. DeConde, *This Affair of Louisiana*, 249.

# 7

## Between the Lions and the Tigers

### 1805–1809

Not long after Louisiana had fallen into his hands, Jefferson used a bestiary image to identify his country's position in a world seemingly controlled by superpowers: "Tremendous times in Europe! How mighty this battle of lions and tigers! With what sensations should the common herd of cattle look on it? With no partialities certainly. If they can so far worry one another as to destroy their power of tyrannizing, the one over the earth, the other the waters, the world may perhaps enjoy peace, till they recruit again."[1] Had his first term as president not been marked by such remarkable success, the term "common herd of cattle" might have suggested that Americans would be victims of the larger beasts. But in 1803 and, indeed, well into his second administration, Jefferson was confident that the United States not only would survive the strife in the world jungle but also would "fatten on the follies of the old [nations]," as he had written a dozen years earlier, by winning spoils from their wars.[2]

The president seemed justified in believing that he could manipulate the three powers with interests affecting the United States without damage to the nation's security. His experience as president proved that whatever dangers he might court in foreign relations would not stand in the way of an expanding America, growing in physical size, in population, and in economic power. While the term "manifest destiny" would not be in use for a generation, America's destiny was manifest to Jefferson, and he would use the authority of his office to see that the nation's destiny was manifest as well to the Old World. As he repeated the oath of office in 1805, he felt he had taken the measure of Britain, France, and Spain.

Britain was always the greatest threat, with its sea power and history of malevolence toward the United States. But its behavior had been moderated by its obvious dependence on American trade. Or so the president believed. Britain had accepted the "broken voyage" whereby American vessels could "Americanize" goods transported from the French or Spanish West Indies through a brief stop at an American port. There the foreign produce would be reshipped (after paying refundable duties to a French port) without interference by the British navy. By keeping a Federalist at the Court of St. James's in the person of Rufus King, Jefferson had signaled his own intention to treat Britain on the same terms as its French adversary. Although such thorny issues as impressment of sailors from American ships were in the background, Britain could be—and was—used as a counterpoise to France whenever such use was needed.

From the French perspective the treatment of Britain as its equal by the United States had led to a naval war a decade earlier when Jay's Treaty had erased distinctions between an ally and a mutual enemy. But France under the self-crowned Emperor Napoleon was no longer an ally, and as a potential neighbor west of the Mississippi it had been an obstacle to America's westward advancement. Yet Jefferson was able to detach Louisiana from the French and hoped to induce France to exploit its influence with Spain in behalf of America's sovereignty over West Florida. Whatever partiality the president had for France in the revolutionary past had long since disappeared. What remained was a sense that France was the less dangerous of the two great powers and could be expected to serve the United States as an occasional counterpoise to Britain, and simultaneously provide the United States a Florida settlement at the expense of Spain.

As always, Spain was the weakest of the Europeans in the Western Hemisphere, and so could be treated with threats of war, almost in the manner of the Barbary states. Spain in the previous decade had oscillated between being a client of France under the Bourbons, then of England in the First Coalition, and then again of France under the Revolution. A client once again, this time of imperial France, Spain was expected to yield, either by force or diplomacy, its control of Florida and as much of the western border of Louisiana as the United States could stretch. The initial failure of

Spain to respond to American pressures over West Florida was considered temporary; Madrid would succumb to the United States in the near future as it had done under Pinckney's Treaty in the recent past.

War on the Continent would surely bring to America advantages from Europe's distress. This was the means whereby the lions and the tigers would "so far worry one another as to destroy their power of tyrannizing" over the earth. Such were Jefferson's expectations as the Third Coalition mobilized against Britain. They were not to be met. Rather than the United States profiting from the struggle between the Colossus of the Land and the Leviathan of the Sea, the nation found itself the victim of both powers. The critical year was 1805, not 1803 when war between Britain and France resumed. In fact, the measures taken by the belligerents involved rights of neutrals, but initially they did not affect American prosperity or dampen Jefferson's hopes. Bonaparte took immediate steps in 1803 to close ports of Italy, the Netherlands, and Spain to Britain's commerce and then moved to interfere with its trade with the neutral Hanseatic ports of Hamburg and Bremen, Britain's customary entry into continental markets. In both ports he ordered seizure of British ships, goods, and sailors. In return, Britain declared a blockade of all French ports on the Channel and the North Sea and set out to capture any ship that challenged the blockade. Since much of American prosperity was based on trade with both Britain and the Continent, these should have been warning signs of trouble ahead for the American neutral.

The United States was able to ignore the implications of these measures in the early stages of the Third Coalition's war against Britain. American trade was still governed by Jay's Treaty with Britain and by the terms of the Treaty of Morfontaine with France. The British continued to abide by the *Polly* decision of 1800, allowing the United States to trade in noncontraband goods with enemy colonies as long as its ships did not sail directly to the enemy homeland. The re-exporting of these goods through a "broken voyage" to an American port remained in place. This situation satisfied the French, who could use the American neutral to circumvent capture on the high seas or blockade of their home ports.

This beneficial situation ended with the *Essex* decision in the spring of 1805, which abruptly reversed the *Polly* verdict. The case involved the seizure of an American ship carrying wine from Barcelona to Havana. Even though it briefly stopped in the United States under the "broken voyage" understanding, the British court decided that the landing was a deception since the duties on the cargo were rebated to the ship's owners. Conceivably, had they been collected in good faith there would have been no grounds for seizure. In reality, American ships were carrying enemy goods (from Spain as France's vassal) from the West Indies directly to European ports. As a consequence American re-exports rose from $40 million in 1800 to over $60 million in 1805.

It was now obvious that a sea change was taking place in Britain's conception of the neutral rights of the United States. This was reflected in a pamphlet widely circulated in 1805, *War in Disguise, or the Frauds of the Neutral Flags*, by James Stephen, which was appreciated sufficiently by the Pitt ministry in London to secure the author a seat in the House of Commons. Stephen's argument had two major points: 1) that the United States was serving as a willing partner in Napoleon's war against Britain in defiance of the Rule of 1756, which prohibited trade closed in peacetime to be opened in wartime; and 2) that the United States should not be allowed to profit from enemy commerce except by stopping in Britain to pay import taxes en route to the Continent. Neutral ships would be allowed to take enemy goods provided that they paid for a license for the privilege, Stephen argued. Americans would thereby help to pay for their colonial commerce with the enemy on terms that served the British belligerent. This interpretation of neutral rights went far beyond the judgments of the *Essex* decision in the damage it would inflict on American commerce. Fittingly, as Bradford Perkins has pointed out, publication of Stephen's pamphlet "appeared on Trafalgar day."[3]

The name of Trafalgar, site of Admiral Horatio Nelson's great victory in the Bay of Biscay over the combined fleets of France, Spain, and the Netherlands on October 21, 1805, must be joined with that of Austerlitz, site of Napoleon's smashing victory over Austria on December 2 of that year. Together these victories helped to direct the war from confrontation between the principals on the high seas or on the battlefields of Europe to a war of attrition waged primarily against neutrals. Although Prussia and then Russia in the next few years joined with Britain to challenge Napoleon, they were quickly routed, Prussia at Jena in 1806 and Russia at Friedland in 1807, leaving the Continent under French control and the oceans under British command. In essence, during Jefferson's second administration neither belligerent could strike directly at the other; France lacked naval power, and Britain lacked armies. Economic warfare made the neutrals a surrogate for direct confrontation, and before the end of Jefferson's term the United States was the only neutral remaining in the western world. This was hardly the situation the president had envisioned when he anticipated America profiting from Europe's wars.

## The Monroe-Pinkney Mission

America's major adversary in this war of attrition inevitably was Britain. There was always a streak of venom in its behavior toward its former colonies that can be traced to the American Revolution. It was manifested in Whitehall's reluctance to part with the Northwest posts, its encouragement of Indian resistance to American sovereignty, and its continuing refusal to permit its subjects to renounce their allegiance and become citizens of another nation. Impressment was more than an effort to reclaim renegade sailors; it was also a means of expressing contempt for the new nation. Stephen's pamphlet, after all, did not really break new ground. It followed a tradition of the Earl of Sheffield's *Observations on the Commerce of the American States*, which had urged the British government in 1783 to deny American ships entry into British West Indian ports. Ousting Americans from their prewar domination of that trade was an appropriate retribution for their revolution as well as an occasion to cultivate Canadian and Irish sources of provisions for the islands. Economic opportunity for Britain would accompany punishment for American competitors in both instances. If there was a difference between 1783 and 1805, it was in Britain's recognition that its independence as a nation was at stake. It was less than a year beforehand that Napoleon had prepared a naval buildup in Boulogne in preparation for an aborted invasion of the island.

This subtext in British attitudes toward the United States was not unfamiliar to Jefferson. He had commented frequently on British malevolence during his service in France in the 1780s and in the State Department in the 1790s. But his criticism had been muted since 1801 by Britain's relative moderation on the high seas, by the highly visible problems with France, and by the euphoria resulting from the acquisition of Louisiana. It took time for him to realize that renewed war in the Old World would not be translated into opportunity for the New World.

His fifth annual message to Congress in December 1805 reflected some confusion about the course now open to the administration. In general terms the president excoriated Britain for "the oppression of our commerce" and for injecting the law of nations with new principles "founded neither in justice, nor the usage or acknolegement of nations."[4] But his denunciation of British practices contained no immediate call for action, whereas his references to Spain were specific and bellicose. Referring to Spain's harassment of Americans living in West Florida, he "found it necessary at length to give orders to our troops on that frontier to be in readiness to protect our citizens, and to repel by arms any similar aggression in future."[5] He still had expectations that the war would induce Spain into yielding to American demands. "The present crisis in Europe is favorable for pressing such a settlement: & not a moment should be lost in availing ourselves of it," he advised Congress. "Should it pass unimproved, our situation would become much more difficult. Formal war is not necessary. It is not probable it will follow. But the protection of our citizens, the spirit and honor of our country, require that force should be interposed to a certain degree. It will probably contribute to advance the object of peace."[6]

These confident words were written in December 1805, at the end of the year that encompassed the *Essex* decision and Trafalgar and in the same month that Napoleon won his greatest victory at Austerlitz. The president was slower than Congress to recognize that "the present crisis" in Europe was unfavorable to American interests. It was the British threat to American shipping rather than impressment that aroused the mercantile community to demand action, and its spokesmen in Washington responded with the Non-Importation Act, which included the dispatch of a special mission to London empowering James Monroe and William Pinkney, a prominent Maryland lawyer, to treat with the British on seizures of American ships and impressment of American sailors.

Monroe was already on the scene, and not pleased with having Pinkney, a former Federalist, forced on him as a fellow commissioner. The president himself seemed curiously passive as Congress, particularly the powerful Senator Samuel Smith of Maryland, took the initiative. Against Jefferson's wishes, Congress passed a mild nonimportation law, "a milk-and-water bill, a dose of chicken broth to be taken nine months hence," according to Representative John Randolph of Virginia.[7] By omitting such imports from Britain as cottons, woolens, and iron, and then suspending the act until British reaction had been measured, Congress assured its ineffectiveness. Jefferson did not want confrontation with the belligerent powers, nor a mission that could lead to confrontation. Economic coercion was always a favorite weapon in his arsenal, but it was to be used advisedly, as a last resort. Open war was not even conceivable, at least not against the superpowers of Europe. He would have preferred to wait until the European conflict forced its participants to bid for American support rather than risk an arrangement that could be as explosive as Jay's Treaty had been a decade before. That treaty may have served the Federalists, but it was a disaster for the Republicans.

Jefferson's caution seemed to have been justified by the sudden death of William Pitt in January 1806 and the replacement of his hostile government with an old friend of America, Charles James Fox, as minister of foreign affairs. The new minister had been opposed to the *Essex* decision and was prepared, it was hoped, to modify the draconian policies of his predecessor. Fox seemingly pointed the way to the rapprochement sought by the Monroe-Pinkney mission by replacing the British minister to Washington, Anthony Merry, with David Erskine, a younger and more liberal figure married to an American. When a British naval ship fired at an American vessel in American territorial waters, killing a crew member, Fox apologized, and recalled the captain of the H.M.S. *Leander*. Little came of these gestures of conciliation, in part because Monroe chose to wait for Pinkney's arrival before he began negotiations. Whether a different treaty would have resulted if it had been concluded earlier is questionable. It is clear, however, that Fox's death in September 1806 deprived the United States of an accommodating partner.

The president had great expectations of Fox, in whom he claimed "to have more confidence than in any man in England, and it is founded in what, through unquestionable channels, I have had opportunities of knowing his honesty and good sense. While he shall be in the administration, my reliance on that government will be solid."[8] But, given the instructions that Secretary of State Madison imposed on Monroe, it was unlikely that Fox could have accepted the terms had he been alive to receive them. In addition to asking reparations for damages to American shipping inflicted since the *Essex* decision, Monroe and Pinkney were to demand severe limitations on British impressment of sailors from American ships and a return to the re-export practices under the old "broken voyage" arrangements. These were "two *sine qua nons*," as Bradford Perkins noted, that "really meant that the United States demanded a return to the halcyon days before seizures and impressment became serious problems."[9]

These instructions raise a legitimate question about whether the administration anticipated, and perhaps even welcomed, the failure of the mission. Monroe, in retrospect, was suspicious about Madison's motives as a political rival. It was more likely that the president was still hopeful that the military scene in Europe would force Britain to accommodate American demands. The administration expected Napoleon's exploits not only to weaken Britain's resolve but also to support America's hopes for the Floridas.

Negotiations proceeded smoothly for the most part, with Britain making more concessions than might have been expected from Lord Auckland, the president of the Board of Trade and a veteran of the putatively hostile Pitt-Grenville ministries. They were helped by the surprisingly good relations between Monroe and Pinkney. For a time it even seemed that the British negotiators would yield on impressment, particularly when Monroe and Pinkney did not object to impressment in British ports. They recognized that no genuine rapprochement could be made between the two countries without resolving this issue. But the British ministry rejected the possibility of a genuine compromise over impressment; it did not trust Americans to take measures preventing British sailors from jumping to American ships. More important, concessions over impressment, it thought, might lead to wholesale desertions from the navy, the mainstay of Britain's war against Napoleon.

The result was a treaty that ignored the major sine qua nons of Madison's instructions. But the terms were so favorable in other respects, even more than Jay's Treaty a dozen years earlier, that Monroe and Pinkney believed that the document would be acceptable to the president. The re-export trade was confirmed, with only a modest duty to be paid in the course of the "broken voyage." The British accepted a narrow definition of contraband and agreed to give appropriate notice of blockades. And as a further mark of accommodation they agreed to indemnify any merchant whose ship was detained in violation of the treaty. The price for these concessions was minimal. The United States would issue no commercial sanctions against Britain that were not applied to other nations. The doctrine of "free ships, free goods" and the denial of American ports to Britain's enemies had been in place since Jay's Treaty. Aside from the issue of sanctions, nothing was new.

According to historian Donald Hickey, the president's rejection of the treaty was "a great turning point in the Age of Jefferson. . . . By rejecting this treaty the United States missed an opportunity to reforge the Anglo-American accord of the 1790s and to substitute peace and prosperity for commercial restrictions and war."[10] This is a serious, but plausible, charge. The abortive Monroe-Pinkney Treaty was followed by a breakdown of relations with Britain that led to war less than six years later. Why, then, did Jefferson refuse even to submit the treaty to the Senate?

Jefferson's explanation was clear and simple. Having warned the negotiators against signing a treaty containing no provision against impressment, he said he would suspend it unless changes were made. When he learned that the article on impressment was left to further consultation, he wrote to Madison in April 1807 that "I am more and more convinced that our best course is, to let the negotiation take a friendly nap, and endeavor in the meantime to practice on such of its principles as are mutually acceptable." This was not written out of a sense of betrayal—either by the American or British negotiators. A month earlier he had been willing to continue the suspension of the nonimportation law "as a proof of the continuance of friendly dispositions."[11]

The nub of his problem may have been impressment, but it was also the Monroe-Pinkney Treaty's abandonment of sanctions that distressed the president. The Napoleonic Wars were very much on his mind as he decided against submitting the treaty to the Senate. The signing of the treaty in December 1806 was preceded by Napoleon's Berlin Decree, declaring the British Isles in a state of blockade. Consequently, any American ship that put into a British port would be excluded from ports on the French-controlled Continent or be subject to seizure upon docking. Britain's response was an Order in Council on January 7, 1807—exactly one week after the Monroe-Pinkney Treaty had been signed—that asserted its right to retaliate against the Berlin Decree. Britain proceeded to act on this assertion, as the practice of impressment was reaffirmed and American ships were seized. In brief, the successive acts by the two European belligerents struck hard at the American neutral.

In this context the president's refusal to submit the Monroe-Pinkney Treaty was understandable. Not only was it unlikely that the treaty would have passed the Senate given the increasingly hostile environment in Europe, but it was even more unlikely that the British government would have abided by the liberal articles of the agreement. Napoleon was intent on isolating and destroying the island kingdom, and with survival at stake the Orders in Council affecting the American neutral would follow. By the same token, the United States would have been forced to violate the article denying it the right to issue sanctions—nonimportation, embargo, or any such punitive measure—in order to cope with British behavior. And while the Berlin Decree would have had a devastating effect on Anglo-American commerce, the French did not put the decree into effect immediately. Jefferson still had hopes of playing the French card, if not against Britain, at least against Spain.

Jefferson's reasons for rejecting the treaty were clearly expressed in a letter to Robert Livingston in March 1807, when he appeared more exercised over Britain's "reserving the right, if we did not oppose the French decree to their satisfaction, to retaliate in their own way, however it might affect the treaty; so that, in fact, we were to be bound and they left free." This concern seemed to carry more weight with him than the failure of the treaty to condemn impressment. In the same letter the president's intention to exploit France was also clear: "I think, upon the whole, the Emperor cannot be dissatisfied at the present state of things between us and England, and that he must rather be satisfied at our unhesitating rejection of a proposition to make common cause against him, for such in amount it was."[12] The significance of this sentiment was the president's recognition that relations with Britain were deteriorating, and would grow worse. Passing a nonimportation or nonintercourse act "may bring on a war of commercial restrictions," he informed James Bowdoin in April 1807. His seeming complaisance about this prospect was based on an assumption that France and Russia would establish neutral rights as a key element in a peace treaty, a conclusion that also assumed the ultimate defeat of Britain. While he continued to suspend the ineffectual Non-Importation Act of 1806, he expected that "the state of things should be understood at Paris."[13]

## The *Chesapeake* Affair

The "state of things," regrettably for Jefferson, was well understood both in Paris and London, but at the expense of the United States. After Trafalgar and Austerlitz, the two superpowers, unable to strike directly at each other, intended to use the neutrals to serve their respective war aims. After Britain destroyed Denmark's neutral fleet in September 1807, the only viable neutral was the United States. With its control of the seas and its insulting policy of impressment, the Royal Navy, not surprisingly, was the prime offender in 1807. While the British government never asserted a right to impress American-born citizens, it refused to acknowledge the right of naturalization of its subjects, and was not particularly scrupulous about distinguishing between American and British sailors. As Samuel Flagg Bemis once noted, "A Cockney accent might cost an American months of involuntary servitude or even his life."[14] Inevitably, fraud was practiced. Ten dollars could secure illegal documents attesting to citizenship, and the United States contributed to this practice by furnishing sailors with official statements whether they were natives or naturalized citizens. For Britain, impresssment of neutral ships was a necessary means of procuring manpower as well as curbing desertion in its epic struggle with France. For the United States, resisting impressment was an assertion of its pride as a nation.

On June 22, 1807, an especially outrageous example of British arrogance aroused the American public. It arose from desertions of British seamen from warships blockading two French naval vessels undergoing repairs at Annapolis and Norfolk. As the American frigate *Chesapeake* sailed from Norfolk, the British man-of-war *Leopard* followed it, stopped it, and demanded the right to search for deserters. When U.S. Commodore James Barron refused, the *Leopard* opened fire, killing three and wounding eighteen sailors. Lining up the crew after Barron lowered the colors, the British seized four alleged deserters. The incident ignited a firestorm of anger and protest. Americans were so indignant that Jefferson might have led a more united nation to war than Madison would command five years later.

Public reaction against Britain was strong and immediate. The president's proclamation ordering British warships out of American waters and cutting off supplies to British ships did not go far enough to suit angry Virginia militiamen patrolling the coast. In New York, the British consul's house required police protection from menacing mobs. Federalist opponents, usually solicitous of British sensibilities, were also carried away by the emotions of the moment. In Boston, two thousand people attended a town meeting at which a young Federalist denounced British behavior. A declaration of war seemed imminent.

Jefferson decided against this path. It was not that he failed to register his own indignation at this act of contempt for American sovereignty, the assault on an American ship in American waters. Rather, it was a question of an appropriate response to the outrage. A declaration of war was obviously an answer, but it was not his answer. He had a better solution. Inasmuch as a decision for war belonged "exclusively to Congress, it is our duty not to commit them by doing anything which would have to be retracted." But in the next sentence of his letter to Governor William Cabell of Virginia, he suggested two simultaneous responses: "We may, however, exercise the powers entrusted to us for preventing future insults within our harbors, & claim firmly satisfaction for the past."[15]

The latter approach required some wishful thinking. Conscious of dealing with a superpower, Jefferson's language suggested that national revulsion against British behavior might induce "the aggressor to do what is just, and abstain from future wrong."[16] There was an intimation here that Britain would realize the damage it was inflicting on Anglo-American relations, and that the exigencies of its war with France might yield concessions on impressment. Foreign Secretary George Canning, at least, expressed regrets and promised punishment if British officers were to blame. Negotiations involving reparations were undertaken but with no success. Impressment remained in place, as the war of attrition against neutrals worsened during 1807.

The other course of action short of war was a stiff warning to Britain. Three weeks after the incident the president issued a proclamation barring British naval vessels from American waters. If any vessel violated the terms of the proclamation, "I do in that case forbid all intercourse with either or any of them, their officers or crews, & prohibit all supplies & aid from being furnished to them or any of them."[17] This warning was hardly a declaration of war or a call for war. At most, it was designed to calm popular anger by expressing presidential disapproval in what he hoped would be considered strong language. There were no plans to interpret the *Chesapeake* debacle as a call for a deepwater navy. Instead, the president asked for more gunboats. While he did not exclude the possibility of war if no reparations were made or if new depredations were committed, his mind was still on the utility of gunboats to protect the nation. "Believing, myself, that gun-boats are the only *water* defence which can be useful to us, & protect us from the ruinous folly of a navy, I am pleased with everything which promises to improve them."[18]

But just as his hopes for a British retreat were in vain, so his faith in gunboats appeared faint. When Captain John Rodgers's gunboats set out to intercept two British frigates off New York harbor in September, the president chose not to risk force and stopped a confrontation with the British ships. What then was left for a leader who did not want war and yet wanted to punish the offending power for its insults to American sovereignty and damage to American property? Jefferson had an answer, but it was complicated by the presence of not one offender, but two. France under Napoleon was a lesser danger only because it lacked Britain's naval power.

## The Embargo

While the president was pondering the means of coping with the effects of the *Chesapeake* incident, the war of the lions and the tigers escalated. In Britain the disciples of James Stephen wanted more than merely denying the United States vast profits from its neutrality; they also wanted to profit from American trade with the Continent. Napoleon in turn sought to prevent the United States from breaching the Continental System that would seal all European ports against British commerce. The result was intolerable pressure on the Jefferson administration in the second half of 1807.

The British issued a new group of Orders in Council on November 11, prohibiting all trade with territories controlled by France unless neutral ships obtained a special license. By this arrangement American exports to Europe would be allowed, but under British control. Unlike France, Britain had no interest in boycotting the Continent; its object was to exploit the American trade with the Europeans to penetrate the Continental System. Napoleon responded immediately with his Milan Decree of December 17, which stated that any ship that permitted a British warship to examine its cargo, or that stopped in Britain and paid duties to that government, would be denationalized. Having forfeited protection of its own flag, the ship would be considered British property and hence a lawful prize in a continental port or on the high seas. Although Napoleon's inability to control the seas could not prevent neutral goods from reaching Britain, he could seize a neutral vessel should it venture into a continental harbor.

Jefferson had few resources to cope with the worsening international environment. What had been a last resort—the Non-Intercourse Act that had been in suspension since its passage in 1806—became the only resort by the end of 1807. The descent of the president's fortunes had been swift since his reelection. Britain had resumed depredations that had not been encountered since Jay's Treaty a decade earlier; France had done nothing to advance American hopes for the Floridas, and it had undertaken a tactic in its economic war against Britain that was as damaging to American trade, not to mention sovereignty, as anything the British had done. The result was the Embargo Act of December 22, 1807, a self-blockade prohibiting the departure of all ships in American harbors for any foreign ports.

The embargo did not represent a pacifist streak. Jefferson's reluctance to engage in war with one or another of the European belligerents was based on a pragmatic weighing of costs to the nation and recognition of the folly of a declaration of war. Given his treatment of a navy composed largely of gunboats unable to cope with British sea power and an army reduced to dependence on state militias, economic coercion was a reasonable path to follow. The initial impulse was isolationist and defensive. If American ships did not ply the seas, there would be no occasion for cargoes to be seized or sovereignty to be insulted. Jefferson was concerned that merchants and shipowners seeking exemption would endanger "the great object of the embargo in keeping our ships and seamen out of harm's way."[19]

While preventing a *casus belli* was a defensive object of the embargo, it was hardly the only one. To some degree the embargo was the realization of an old dream that Jefferson shared with other Founding Fathers—namely, the isolation of the United States from the evils of the Old World. As such, it was a measure that conformed easily to a pattern of behavior that he periodically advocated when the "common herd" was endangered in the jungle world of international politics. Britain and France having virtually banned American commerce from the high seas, the embargo was a face-saving means of giving their decrees the force of American law, thus removing a source of conflict with the belligerents.

This conception of the embargo was fitting for a small nation endangered by the great powers, but it coexisted with an equally long-standing Jeffersonian objective of using an economic weapon to extract concessions from the belligerents. The embargo in this sense was an extension of the nonimportation principle that would deny the adversary vital supplies, such as foodstuffs and naval stores. Secretary of State Madison agreed with this interpretation and pressed for its adoption with more vigor than Jefferson had demonstrated. As early as 1794, Madison had considered an embargo the appropriate weapon in dealing with British depredations. It was left to a skeptic, Secretary of the Treasury Albert Gallatin, who was distressed by the indefinite time frame of the embargo, to carry out its provisions.

Superficially, the embargo itself made no distinction between the two warring parties. Both violated neutral rights, and stopping trade with both presumably was designed to force the revocation of their decrees. In fact, Jefferson's embargo message made a point of directing the act against France. Three of the four documents attached to the message dealt with French violations of American neutrality. This impression was deliberately misleading. The president knew very well that the first effect of the embargo would be to give teeth to the Non-Importation Act against Britain that had gone into effect eight days before the embargo. He was convinced that if Britain were deprived of its food imports and of raw materials for its industries, powerful manufacturers would force the government to yield to American demands. By April his optimism seemed confirmed from reports that "our embargo, added to the exclusions from the Continent, will be most heavily felt in England and Ireland. Liverpool is remonstrating, & endeavoring to get other ports into motion."[20] One of Jefferson's primary aims was to strike a hard blow against Britain without bringing upon himself the charge of being a French agent.

Jefferson was fully aware that the embargo constituted a service to Napoleon. He admitted that it would not hurt France when he went out of his way to convince Louis Marie Turreau, the French minister in Washington, that the United States had no intention of treating both countries alike. "The embargo which appears to hit France and Britain equally," he told the envoy, "is for a fact more prejudicial to the latter than the other by reason of a greater number of colonies which England possesses and their inferiority in local resources."[21] France, unlike Britain, was reasonably self-sufficient; the supplies it needed from abroad could be obtained for the most part from its continental satellites. Although Federalist leaders saw through Jefferson's public pose of equal treatment and immediately sought political advantage from his aid to Napoleon, they were mistaken in interpreting his behavior as evidence of a belief that France was more benevolent toward the United States, or that French violations of neutral rights were less hateful.

Jefferson did not deny Napoleon's malevolence. He confessed that it was "mortifying that we should be forced to wish success to Bonaparte, and to look to his victories as our salvation."[22] But the alternative seemed to be British domination, and France was unwittingly serving the cause of neutral rights. To another correspondent in the difficult summer of 1807 he exclaimed: " I never expected to be under the necessity of wishing success to Buonaparte. But the English being equally tyrannical at sea as he is on land and that tyranny bearing on us in every point of honor or interest, I say 'down with England' and as for what Buonaparte is then to do with us, let us trust to the chapter of accidents. I cannot with the Anglomen, prefer a present evil to a future hypothetical one."[23] He had triumphed over Napoleon once before, when an "accident" led to France's sale of Louisiana to the United States. It was not unreasonable for him to expect similar results from the embargo.

Because he was convinced that France was not an immediate threat to the security of the United States, Jefferson envisioned the embargo as an offensive as well as a defensive weapon. Remembering the emperor's pose as a champion of neutral rights, he equated America's various acts against British behavior on the seas as blows on behalf of maritime liberty and as America's equivalent of joining the Continental System. In return, the president hoped that Napoleon would force Spain to cede the Floridas and rectify the western boundary—a hope based on the emperor's promise to John Armstrong, the American minister in Paris, that if the United States made an alliance with France against Britain, Jefferson would be free to intervene in Spanish America. Thus, the embargo should be sufficiently painful to force Britain to revoke its Orders in Council; and at the same time it would inveigle France into working for America's territorial expansion, all without the loss of a single American life. If a French victory was the consequence of his policy, the Atlantic Ocean would prevent Napoleon from attacking the United States unless some other obstacle in the "chapter of accidents" did not stop him first.

Unfortunately, Napoleon outplayed Jefferson in this dangerous game. The Embargo Act, proffered as a fair exchange for the Floridas, in effect made the United States an ally in the Continental System without securing one square foot of Florida soil. Instead, the emperor's price kept rising: repeal all restrictions against French commerce, accept France's right to seize American ships in European ports, and ultimately join openly in the war against Britain. As a first step, Napoleon issued the Bayonne Decree in April 1808, ordering the confiscation of any American ship found in European harbors on the spurious grounds that any such vessel was violating American law. Perhaps with tongue in cheek, Napoleon claimed he was helping Jefferson enforce the embargo. When Americans complained about France's maritime restrictions or about its procrastination over Florida, they were told that the president himself had announced that the embargo was aimed at France, and hence the emperor's measures were a logical reprisal. In the same facetious manner, French officials refused to listen to American designs on the Floridas, arguing that Spanish law prevented the king from alienating any part of his territory. The king of Spain in 1808 was Joseph Bonaparte, whose younger brother Napoleon had put him on the throne and presumably exercised considerable influence over his actions.

Jefferson naturally resented this cavalier treatment. But his response seemed petty and inadequate in view of the provocations. He annoyed Minister Turreau by his refusal to capture French deserters in the United States and by the strict accountability to which he held any ship leaving an American port for France on a special mission. Aside from these pinpricks the president did nothing to hurt France's war effort. To the very end of his administration he maintained that Britain's sea power made it the greater danger to the United States.

The Spanish uprising against French domination in 1808 only served to convince him that Napoleon could never carry out a program of overseas aggression. Indeed, Jefferson even wondered whether France's difficulties in Spain might facilitate American action against Spanish America. "Should England make up with us, while Bonaparte continues at war with Spain," he speculated, "a moment may occur when we may without danger of commitment with either France or England seize to our own limits of Louisiana as of right, and the residue of the Floridas as reprisal for spoliations."[24] Not that he anticipated reconciliation with Britain. What he continued to anticipate as late as the summer of 1808 was ultimate profit for America from the struggle in Europe. He was willing to accept a French victory over Britain on the assumption that it would remain the lesser evil.

If this was his assumption, his French friends bore a responsibility for nourishing it. At a time in his second administration when he needed a clear understanding of the emperor's intentions, the silence of his liberal colleagues about the significance of Napoleon's tyranny helped to confirm his conviction that Britain was the primary threat to America's security. Lafayette and Du Pont gave their opinions in good faith. They saw no conflict between the aims of France and the interests of the United States. Lafayette in particular encouraged Jefferson to believe that Napoleon could be persuaded to understand the common ground of both nations. On the problem of Napoleonic harassment of American commerce, Lafayette asserted that the emperor was merely misinformed. Writing in 1809, he told the squire of Monticello that "I every day hope his [Napoleon's] great powers of sagacity and calculation will at last discover that in his plan to bring about Great Britain he has taken the wrong end."[25] Jefferson's French friends believed that a British victory in the war would be a greater disaster to France and to the United States than the realization of Napoleon's plans for world conquest.

Jefferson, in fact, needed little encouragement to tilt the embargo away from France and against Britain. There was nothing Francophilic in his posture. It was simply that Britain was the more immediate danger to his nation's interests, and France seemed to have more to offer. Had the British government yielded on the Orders in Council, if not on the principle of impressment, the president would have turned an Anglo-American accord into a Francophobic policy, with the aim of using British power to remove the punitive Berlin and Milan decrees and, above all, to acquire the Floridas.

Failure of the embargo was equated with failure to coerce Britain, not France, and by the end of 1808 the policy of economic coercion was in shambles. The severing of American markets and American exports from Europe should have fulfilled the long-standing expectations of Jefferson and Madison that economic coercion could substitute for armed force as well as cut ties with the corrupt Old World. It did not. Napoleon had no need for American supplies; his Europe was self-sufficient, and Jefferson's embargo was designed primarily to hurt his enemy. As for Britain, some damage was done, but not enough to require a change in policy. Perhaps, as Bradford Perkins observed, Britain might have been concerned about the loss of American markets if the embargo had prohibited British exports in foreign ships.[26] Instead, American merchants, farmers, and ship owners suffered from the disruption of their livelihoods. Britain held fast in good part because of breaches of the Embargo Act: New England maintained a Canadian trade, and ships restricted to coastal voyages defiantly crossed the Atlantic.

For the embargo to have a chance of success, full support of the American people was necessary. This was never available to the president. While he could dismiss the more rabid Federalist charges of subservience to France, he was unable to convince the citizenry that the drastic self-denial required by the embargo was commensurate with the defense of the nation's honor. New England's endemic Anglophilia quickly became manifest. In Massachusetts the Federalists recaptured the legislature from the Jeffersonians. Moreover, John Quincy Adams's senatorial career came to an untimely end after he had voted for the Embargo Act. But Republicans as well as Federalists suffered from the privations caused by the embargo and joined with their political opponents in resenting the administration's dispatching of troops to the frontiers and gunboats to the harbors to prevent evasions of the embargo.

As violations of the Embargo Act became more numerous in the spring of 1808, the president employed strict measures of enforcement, giving collectors in ports the authority to seize goods suspected of being illegal. The navy was used to stop ships, again simply on suspicion of violating the embargo. Constitutional protections against unreasonable search were disregarded. The administration controlled the embargo without interference since Congress did not meet from the end of April until October 1808. Jefferson's zeal took the form of advising Gallatin that "agriculture, commerce, navigation" should defer to the objectives of the embargo. Given the "power of detentions as the panacea. . . . I am clear we ought to use it freely that we may, by a fair experiment, know the power of this great weapon, the embargo."[27] The weapon failed to hit its mark.

The consequence of this miscalculation was public disaffection. It was also the apparent abandonment of all that Jeffersonian republicanism stood for: harsh treatment of offenders against the embargo undermined strict construction of executive authority; promotion of manufactures to foster self-sufficiency undermined the primacy of an agrarian society; subordination of domestic polity to foreign affairs undermined the emphasis on isolation from European politics. Jefferson had overreached himself in assuming he could manipulate the superpowers to America's advantage. As his term drew to a close he seemed to surrender his leadership. Small wonder that a discouraged president accepted the repeal of the Embargo Act three days before Madison assumed the presidency. As he exclaimed the day before Madison's inauguration, "Never did a prisoner, released from his chains, feel such relief as I shall on shaking off the shackles of power."[28]

## Notes

1. TJ to Benjamin Rush, October 4, 1803, in Andrew A. Lipscomb and Albert E. Bergh, eds., *The Writings of Thomas Jefferson*, 20 vols. (Washington, DC: Thomas Jefferson Memorial Association, 1903–04), 10:422 (hereafter cited as Lipscomb and Bergh).

2. TJ to Edward Rutledge, July 4, 1790, in Julian P. Boyd, ed., *The Papers of Thomas Jefferson*, 24+ vols. (Princeton: Princeton University Press, 1950), 16:601 (hereafter cited as Boyd).

3. Bradford Perkins, *Prologue to War: England and the United States, 1805–1812* (Berkeley and Los Angeles: University of California Press, 1961), 78.

4. Draft of Fifth Annual Message, December 3, 1805, in Paul L. Ford, ed., *The Works of Thomas Jefferson*, 12 vols. (New York: G. P. Putnam's Sons, 1904–05), 10:188 (hereafter cited as Ford).

5. Ibid., 189–90.

6. TJ, "Confidential Message on Spain," December 6, 1805, ibid., 204–5.

7. *Annals of Congress*, March 26, 1806, 9th Cong., lst sess., 851.

8. TJ to Monroe, May 4, 1806, Lipscomb and Bergh, 11:109.

9. Perkins, *Prologue to War*, 119.

10. Donald R. Hickey, *The War of 1812: A Forgotten War* (Urbana and Chicago: University of Illinois Press, 1989), 16.

11. TJ to Madison, April 21, 1807, Lipscomb and Bergh, 11:193.

12. TJ to Livingston, March 24, 1807, Ford, 10:377.

13. TJ to James Bowdoin, April 2, 1807, ibid., 381.

14. Samuel Flagg Bemis, *A Diplomatic History of the United States*, 3d ed. (New York: Henry Holt and Co., 1950), 145.

15. TJ to Cabell, June 19, 1807, Ford, 10:433.

16. Ibid.

17. TJ, "Chesapeake Proclamation," July 2, 1807, ibid., 445–46.

18. TJ to Thomas Paine, September 6, 1807, ibid., 493. Italics included.

19. TJ to William H. Cabell, March 13, 1808, Lipscomb and Bergh, 12:12.

20. TJ to Caesar Rodney, April 24, 1808, Ford, 11:29.

21. Turreau to Jean-Baptiste de Champagny, June 28, 1808, France, Archives du Ministère des Affaires Etrangères, Correspondance Politique, Etats-Unis, vol. 61, pp. 166–67, photocopy in Library of Congress, Washington, DC.

22. TJ to John Taylor, August 1, 1807, Lipscomb and Bergh, 11:305.

23. TJ to Thomas Leiper, August 20, 1807, Ford, 10:483–84.

24. TJ to Secretary of War Henry Dearborn, August 12, 1808, Lipscomb and Bergh, 12:125.

25. Lafayette to TJ, November 18, 1809, in Gilbert Chinard, ed., *Letters of Lafayette and Jefferson* (Baltimore: Johns Hopkins University Press, 1929), 294.

26. Bradford Perkins, *The Cambridge History of American Foreign Relations*, Vol. 1, *The Creation of a Republican Empire, 1776–1865* (New York: Cambridge University Press, 1993), 130.

27. TJ to Gallatin, May 6, 1808, Lipscomb and Bergh, 12:52–53.

28. TJ to Du Pont, March 2, 1809, ibid., 259–60.

# 8

## The View from Monticello

### 1809–1826

Jefferson went home to Monticello convinced that the experiment might have worked if it had been continued over a longer period. And he may have been right. Britain did capitulate, even if too late, on the eve of the War of 1812. In the seventeen years between his retirement from office and his death in 1826, as well as during the tension-filled years of Madison's first administration, Jefferson's interest in foreign relations remained as alive as it had been in the past. While the retirement was permanent and unmarked by the reservations that had accompanied his resignation as secretary of state in 1793, it did not signify abdication of his concerns for America's relations with the familiar triad of Britain, France, and Spain.

He was convinced that Spain sooner or later would have to cede the Floridas, and perhaps Cuba as well, to the United States. If Napoleon should not be the instrument, then Spain's endemic weakness, particularly in the face of ongoing European wars, would effect this result. Writing to President Madison in 1809, he granted that Napoleon's "policy is so crooked that it eludes conjecture." But at the same time he envisioned the emperor consenting "to our receiving Cuba into our Union, to prevent our aid to Mexico and the other provinces." As for the Floridas, "they are ours in the first moment of the first war."[1] It is worth noting that he used much the same language in corresponding with President James Monroe in 1820, as Spain was hesitating over the cession of Florida: "Florida, moreover, is ours. Every nation in Europe considers it such a right. We need not care for its occupation in time of peace, and, in war, the first cannon makes it ours without offence to anybody." War was not needed over Florida; the threat of war was sufficient after the termination of the War of 1812. And Jefferson looked beyond Florida to Texas, which would be "the richest State of our Union, without any exception."[2] Jefferson may never have left Virginia after his return from Washington, but his vision of the American empire continued to expand.

It did not extend, however, to the new states of Latin America. Although he suggested that Spain would be wise not to follow the British precedent in holding back the independence of the new states, there was little ardor in his views on Latin America. Remembering the experience of revolutionary France, he had some doubts about their ability to replicate the North American experience. Moreover, as he observed to the Spanish minister in Washington in 1814, he was not sure "that the United States would find an interest in the independence of neighbor nations, whose produce and commerce would rivalize ours."[3] But he shared John Quincy Adams's reservations about recognizing the new republics until the cession of Florida had been secured—Jefferson's eye remained fixed on the Floridas. The Adams-Onís Treaty of 1819 was a surrogate triumph for Jefferson. Once the cession of Florida was complete, the squire of Monticello was as opposed as President Monroe or Representative Henry Clay to the return of those territories to Spain.

In the immediate aftermath of his presidency, Jefferson's attention understandably was directed to supporting France against Britain in the ongoing war. He bombarded Madison with advice urging the president to stand fast against British power. Still smarting from his humiliation by the British, he was willing to overlook Napoleon's cavalier treatment of Americans and his cynical exploitation of variations on nonimportation, even though the emperor continued to be as great an offender as his British rival. The War of 1812 against Britain appeared to Jefferson to be a logical extension of the embargo program, and the results he expected from the Embargo Act of 1807 were just those he hoped war would bring in 1812. He rationalized favoring France not only because Napoleon lacked the navy needed to invade the United States, but also because the French empire lacked the stability and permanency of Britain.

The former president was no more deceived than Madison by Napoleon's putative revocation of the Berlin and Milan Decrees in 1810. If Madison was willing to accept French professions of accommodation to American demands for revocation of their restrictions on American commerce, it was to exert maximal pressure on Britain. Jefferson and Madison both shut their eyes to reality by allowing the crimes of the British to push Napoleon's rapacity into the background.

Once war had been declared, Jefferson's concern centered on the service France might render to the United States. To equate cobelligerency with a new Franco-American alliance was the furthest thing from his mind. Napoleon's invasion of Russia served the war effort against Britain by adding the "closing of the Baltic" to the exclusion of British commerce from the United States. But once Britain was defeated, "I should be for peace with England and then war with France. One at a time is enough, and in fighting the one we need the harbors of the other for our prizes."[4]

Jefferson's attitude toward the two major adversaries in 1812 was more confused than subtle. Singlehandedly, it seemed, the American David could take on the two Goliaths of Europe, and defeat them each in turn! But first the French Goliath should play the role Jefferson had sought and failed to achieve in his second term as president—namely, to win America's objectives without the entangling alliance that had been forced on the new nation in 1778. He had no interest in either party winning ultimate victory over the other. Rather, the interest of the United States, he believed, was to let the two powers battle themselves into a state of mutual exhaustion so that neither would have the strength left to hurt smaller countries. To help this process along he urged the dispatch of grain to British forces in Spain, since "she is fighting our battles there, as Bonaparte is on the Baltic." If Napoleon gained full control of the Iberian peninsula, he would exclude America from the "greatest and surest of all our markets." Moreover, Jefferson noted that if the British armies were pushed out of Spain, they would be sent to America, concluding that "I think we had better feed them there for pay, than feed and fight them here for nothing."[5]

Jefferson did not lose sight of the possibility that despite all the obstacles Providence might throw in the way of Napoleon's conquest of the United States, a victorious emperor might take over the British fleet and all the resources of their empire. The result would be the worst of all possible outcomes: war against a brilliant military leader animated by lust for world conquest that could leave the United States in the position of a French satellite. All that had been won in Louisiana might be forfeited if Napoleon mastered the sea as well as the land. So difficult was the choice, he lamented in 1814, that "we know not what to fear, and, only standing to our helm, must abide, with folded arms, the issue of the storm."[6]

While the devious course of Jefferson's opinions on foreign policy pointed to a stalemate in Europe as the desirable outcome for the United States, the logic of his position indicated service to French interests. Understandably, his followers were never so mystified about his views on the war as they were at this time. If a French conquest of Europe were inimical to the United States, why make common cause in war? How was he to explain a policy that advocated a French victory, but not too much of a victory? The old statesman was forced to make explanations, for even in retirement he was assumed to exert considerable influence on the Madison administration.

For the most part he was able to reconcile the intraparty confusion on war aims that his own ambivalence helped to create. But in one instance he feared that his professed hostility to France would induce the French minister in Washington to accuse him of lending comfort to the common enemy. The cause of the embarrassment was the controversial George Logan, an ardent supporter of the French Revolution until the appearance of Bonaparte. Logan was the idealistic, if naive, Philadelphia Quaker who had made a visit to Europe in the summer of 1798 to find out for himself the extent of France's hostility to the United States. Although the Federalists had reprimanded him by passage of the Logan Act penalizing private citizens undertaking such missions to foreign governments, Logan's account of the openness of the Directory to American concerns influenced many Republicans, including Jefferson. Fifteen years later Logan's missionary zeal was no less strong, except that his Francophilia had been converted into hatred of the emperor. On another visit to Europe, this time to Britain in 1810, he confirmed his prejudices, just as he had in 1798. Great Britain was a free society much less under the control of the sordid commercial class than most Americans believed. And so, when the Anglo-American war broke out, Logan considered it his duty to inform Jefferson that an honorable treaty could be made with the British if the former president exerted his influence on Madison.

Jefferson had standard answers for Republican critics who opposed America's fighting France's enemy. He would marshal his old arguments admitting the villainies of Napoleon and France's animosities toward the United States, while asserting at the same time that British enmity was more immediate and more threatening to the nation's security. Possibly in deference to Logan's emotional state, he expressed his horror of the imperial regime more forcefully than usual: "No man on earth has stronger detestation than myself of the unprincipled tyrant who is deluging the continent of Europe with blood." The letter to Logan also contained qualifying remarks about his hope of "seeing England forced to just terms of peace with us," a hope that could be realized only through the agency of Napoleon.[7] Whether Logan misunderstood the qualification or purposely misconstrued the letter is not clear. What is clear was his release to the press in December 1813 of an excerpt that presented the former president as an enemy of France and an opponent of the war against Britain.

Publication of Jefferson's condemnation of Napoleon antagonized Republican friends such as Thomas Leiper of Philadelphia, who considered the French to be performing a noble service, even if unwittingly, in fighting the forces of monarchical reaction. Leiper rebuked Jefferson for failing to see the consequences of a British victory. The triumphant British, he foresaw, "would not suffer a Cockboat of any other nation to swim the Ocean."[8] The only consolation he could take from the old statesman's uncharacteristic Anglophilia was the possibility that the letter was a forgery. Jefferson did not fail him. He professed to be shocked "by the infidelity" of an old friend who now showed himself to be a "bigoted partisan of England, and malcontent of his own government." Logan seized on "two little sentences of the printed extract . . . and exactly these two little sentences, from a letter of two or three pages, he has thought proper to publish, naked alone, and with my name." Jefferson remained convinced that as evil as Napoleon was, he could help America bring Britain to reason by "the complete exclusion of England from the whole continent of Europe."[9]

Jefferson's long letter of explanation to Leiper underscored the incoherence of his policy toward the belligerents. His disdain and fear of Napoleon were genuine, as was his visceral anger over Britain's behavior. And his effort at detachment was equally genuine. He wished to have Napoleon succeed "so far as to close the Baltic against her. This success I wished him the last year, this I wish for him this year; but were he again advanced to Moscow, I should again wish him such disasters as would prevent his reaching [Saint] Petersburg. And were the consequences even to be the longer continuance of our war, I would rather meet them than see the whole force of Europe wielded by a single hand."[10] Yet Jefferson was just as insistent on identifying Britain as the greater threat because Napoleon was only one mortal man; Britain's tyranny was in the hands of many men, an entire Parliament. If that "single hand" should take over all of Europe, there was still the "chapter of accidents" that the elder statesman believed would intervene to protect America.

It was a dangerous policy that Jefferson was advocating, whether or not a beleaguered President Madison could, or would, pay attention to the stream of advices that he offered from the day he left office until the war ended on Christmas Eve 1814. To manipulate the balance of power in such a way as to immobilize both belligerents was beyond the capacity of any American leader, and in 1814 it appeared that Jefferson's worst fears would be realized. With Napoleon brought to heel and banished to Elba, Britain was master of Europe as well as of the high seas and hence in a position to impose its will upon France's hapless cobelligerent. America's war with Britain had gone badly enough before Napoleon's abdication. The burning of the White House and the Capitol in the summer of 1814 could have been an augury of further humiliation to follow. The victorious British armies that took the measure of the Grande Armée were now free to complete the conquest of France's informal ally.

This catastrophe did not take place. The fact that four months after the sacking of Washington the Treaty of Ghent ended the war without entailing the loss of any U.S. territory testified to the essential truth of one of Jefferson's favorite theses: Europe's troubles were America's opportunities. If Britain did not complete its reconquest of America, a prominent deterrent arose in the problems it encountered in the redivision of Napoleon's Europe. Exhausted by long years of warfare, Britain envisioned sufficient obstacles at the peace tables of the Vienna conference—squabbles over spoils among the victorious allies and the potential return of Napoleon to power—to dampen its ardor for revenge upon the country that effectively joined its European enemy.

The retired statesman of Monticello initially saw none of this. When the emperor departed for Elba in the spring of 1814, Jefferson anticipated the worst-case scenarios. His voice grew shriller as the year advanced. To John Adams he confided in July that he watched "with anxiety the tyrant of the ocean remaining in vigor, and even participating in the merit of crushing his brother tyrant."[11] After the devastation in Washington "by means of their force," he claimed that "we can burn their St. James' and St. Paul's by means of our money, offered to their own incendiaries, of whom there are thousands in London who would do it rather than starve." If we do not take such action, it is only because "we think it more honorable to set a good example, than follow a bad one."[12] A week after the peace treaty was signed, but before news had reached America, Jefferson was still fretting over the burning of Washington: "diabolical as they paint that enemy [France], he burnt neither public edifices nor private dwellings. It was reserved for England to show that Bonaparte, in atrocity, was an infant to their ministers and generals."[13]

As soon as the United States was released from war, Jefferson's attitude toward France gradually became more hostile. Not that he admitted his mistake in having supported the imperial regime in the past. On the contrary, his disgust for the stupidity of the Bourbons made him welcome for a moment the return of Napoleon from Elba as a defender of "the cause of his nation, and that of all mankind, the rights of every people to independence and self-government."[14] But with the British threat removed, these thoughts were no more than passing expressions of anger at the greed of the former Coalition partners and their Bourbon puppet; he knew that France could never enjoy lasting peace under a Bonaparte. No matter how democratic the guise, the result would be military despotism in France and renewal of conflict for the world.

Jefferson did not regret Waterloo for long. Had he still been disturbed by the specter of another British war with its implications for neutral rights, he might have felt more solicitous about the fate of the exiled emperor on Saint Helena and for the country that once made a revolution under his guidance. But the government that succeeded Napoleon would have been an inadequate shield even if he had been inclined to look to France for protection or for influence. Under the feeble but oppressive leadership of the Bourbons, France after 1815 was just one of a group of continental powers that, according to Jefferson, dedicated themselves to the eradication of the liberal ideals America represented.

Still, in his ruminative correspondence with John Adams over the last years of his life, Jefferson exhibited optimism about the ultimate destiny of France. The French Revolution had given his disciples a taste for freedom and some experience in self-government. As long as they did not try to proceed too quickly, the France of Lafayette, Du Pont, and Destutt de Tracy might yet lead Europe along the path of liberty. But nothing in the reflections of his old age indicated a recognition of error in his treatment of the two great European powers. While he excoriated the evils of the dictator's regime, he saw an imbalance in the comparative positions of

France and Britain which allowed diplomatic maneuvers that would not have been ventured had he genuinely believed that he was dealing with two countries equally dangerous to the United States.

He was not without doubts about his balance-of-power policies. Periodically, he expressed fear concerning the consequences of a victory for either belligerent, but even in his darkest moods he would still take his chances with a victorious France, if such a choice had to be made. Those rare occasions when he spoke in favor of an alliance with Britain or on the usefulness of British sea power were prior to the intensification of the European wars and reflected either a devious gambit designed to extract concessions from the French or an errant faith in the friendliness of a particular British ministry.

Jefferson's tilt toward Napoleon in Britain's struggle for survival is explicable largely on the basis of faith in the ultimate defeat of France. As to Napoleon's intentions after victory he had no illusions, whatever he may have felt about the emperor's ability to realize them. Granting the material and psychological damage done by British maritime practices and granting also the insult to American sovereignty inherent in such actions, Britain's war was essentially a defense against the continuous pressure of Napoleonic imperialism, and the policies injuring Americans were primarily by-products of Britain's response to that pressure. In this circumstance, did the United States go to war on the wrong side? To illustrate the differences between the two nations, one need only speculate as to what Jefferson's foreign policy might have been if France, and not Britain, had been a neighbor in Canada during the reign of Bonaparte. The president's behavior in the Louisiana crisis suggests that he would have been far more disturbed over potential French aggression than he had been over the reality of Britain's invasion of the Northwest Territory in 1812. Its war with the United States was fought reluctantly—despite the malevolence of such figures as Foreign Minister George Canning—and its war aims were limited.

But there is also the question of the wisdom of a weak power, one of the "common herd of cattle" attempting to pit a lion against a tiger without being mortally wounded. W. Stull Holt once likened the young republic to a jackal picking up the spoils it steals from the more powerful animals diverted by fighting among themselves.[15] The United States picked up Louisiana in this fashion in Jefferson's first administration, but it failed to win any of its objectives in his second administration, and tumbled into a destructive war under Madison's. Only by keeping out of Europe's wars could the plan of playing one country against the other be executed with any real hope of success. Jefferson's only objection to the declaration of war in June 1812 was its timing; he felt that war should have been declared when the weather first permitted entrance of U.S. troops into Canada. But by engaging in war as a cobelligerent, if not as an open ally of France, the country deprived itself of the advantages he had anticipated. Once caught up in war, the danger of being overwhelmed by the superior force of the enemy or of being treated as a satellite by the powerful "ally" was far greater than the opportunity for making gains at the expense of either of them.

Most of the foregoing considerations may be found in the corpus of Jefferson's letters and commentaries over the many years of his political life. His Anglophobic sentiments were often couched in more hyperbolic, if not more paranoid, language than his Francophobic opinions. His personal history in the American Revolution, his animus against Federalist "monocrats," and the immediacy of British naval power combined with the putative advantages a French connection might bring led him to weigh Britain's depredations more seriously than France's, at least until the end of the War of 1812.

As the British menace receded into the past, Jefferson saw the island kingdom in a very different perspective. Despite its odious government and the persistence of supercilious anti-American sentiment, he was satisfied that the long and hard wars of the past had weakened Britain's economy to such an extent that it had lost its ability to hurt the United States. Jefferson felt that the root of the problem with Britain had been in the fundamental immorality of its government and economy, which poisoned its relations with the United States. The avarice of its merchants and the piratical spirit of its navy had damaged America in the past, but a day of reckoning was at hand. He concluded in 1816 that excessive development of an economy based on finance and commerce, overexpansion of major industries, ruinous taxation, and dangerous extremes of wealth would generate a crisis that would overthrow the ruling class. When this happened, the virtues of Britain—the vital elements of a free society, such as freedom of the press and representative government—would make its people "probably turn their eyes to us, and be disposed to tread in our footsteps, seeing how safely these have led us into port."[16]

John Adams's skepticism about this hopeful projection did not deter Jefferson from envisioning a reformed British nation that would restore the natural ties between Britons and Americans. When he was seeking professors for the new university in Charlottesville, he looked to Britain for their supply. It was, after all, "the land of our own language, morals, manners and habits."[17] These were the cultural links that would bind America to Britain once the latter was ruled by a government that would treat Americans with justice and equality. If Britain could break up "the consuming circle of extravagance, debt, insolvency, and revolution" as well as renounce "eternal war," then it would "again be in the degree of force which nature has measured out to it . . . a respectable station in the scale of nations, but not at their head."[18]

Once again, Jefferson was indulging in illusions. But the thrust of his judgment was not to launch another tirade against Britain's past sins. Rather, he wished to enlist a reformed Britain as a counterpoise to continental powers, since "the present prospects of southern Europe seem to need the acquisition of new weights in their balance."[19] A year later the prospect of Spain or France employing force to suppress the independence of Latin America convinced Jefferson that Britain was already reformed. When President Monroe asked him and Madison in 1823 for their view of an alliance with Britain to deter a European reconquest of Latin America, Jefferson and Madison reiterated a familiar call for nonentanglement with Europe, but with a difference. Both former presidents urged an entangling connection with Britain. Jefferson reasoned that if there should be conflict with Europe over the continued independence of the Americas, Britain's support would be invaluable: "With Great Britain withdrawn from their scale and shifted into that of our two continents, all Europe combined would not undertake such a war."[20] In this response to the president, Jefferson seemingly abandoned not only his Anglophobia but also the American conception of the division between the Old and New Worlds. Britain had become metamorphosed into an American power.

Had the sage of Monticello in his dotage repudiated the opposition to British imperialism that had characterized his political life? In fact, he considered cooperation with Britain on this issue to be perfectly consistent with his hope of keeping America out of the clutches of Europe. Close ties with Britain were advisable because "the war in which the present proposition might engage us, should that be its consequence, is not her war, but ours."[21] But the need for such links to Britain, or to any other nation, would not last indefinitely. Britain's service would be temporary, of far less importance than France's was during the American Revolution. He exulted in a letter to Du Pont in 1815 that the time was coming when the United States would be strong enough to sever all ties with the rest of the world and announce itself militarily and economically self-sufficient. In twenty years, "we shall be twenty millions in number, and forty in energy," and masters of our own destiny.[22] The Monroe Doctrine dispensed with a formal British connection, even if the British had been willing to pursue it. Secretary of State John Quincy Adams made it clear in his contribution to President Monroe's address to Congress in December 1823 (the Monroe Doctrine) that the United States alone would keep Europe from interfering with the independence of American republics. At Jefferson's death in 1826, on the fiftieth anniversary of the signing of the Declaration of Independence, America was more secure from European interference than it had been since the nation's founding.

The failure of the embargo of 1807 did not define Jefferson's presidency, or his foreign policy over a quarter of a century. His faith in the efficacy of economic coercion was shaken but not destroyed. His belief in the civic-mindedness of his fellow citizens was strained, but his optimism about the future of America, revealed repeatedly in his correspondence with John Adams over the last decade of his life, remained alive. It is tempting for the historian to join with Bismarck in attributing America's success and the statecraft of Thomas Jefferson to the notion that Providence has a special place for fools, drunkards, children, and Americans. Yet the Virginia statesman's optimism was based on more than divine intervention or dumb luck. The nature of the balance of power in Europe and the advantageous geographic position of the United States made credible not only the survival of the fragile republic but also the creation of an American empire.

The crises accompanying the course of events in the Jeffersonian era often obscured this reality. The euphoria resulting from the easy acquisition of Louisiana led to an overestimation of Jefferson's ability to control the lions and the tigers of the European jungle, which in turn has led to an exaggeration of the inconsistencies that historians have identified over the years. These inconsistencies were observable in his decision to annex Louisiana by treaty rather than by constitutional amendment and in the contrast between his conceptual benevolence toward Indians and the harsh reality of his support for their removal from the path of westward expansion. His second term witnessed an apparent abandonment of Republican principles in favor of Federalist policies toward commerce, toward manufactures, and toward expansion of presidential powers.

Were Jefferson's foreign policies more than a mass of inconsistencies, with the accumulation of power his objective, as many of his enemies asserted and some of his friends feared? Or was he essentially a pragmatist employing whatever tactics he could muster to keep America free from the corruption and the control of the Old World while exploiting that world's weaknesses to fashion a new kind of empire? He envisioned an America imbued with agrarian values—free men living on terms of equality unsullied by the vices of urban society. For this empire of liberty to be achieved, the westward movement of a growing population was vital for the strength of the nation. His hope for the future, he noted in 1817, was "built much on the enlargement of the resources of life going hand in hand with the enlargement of territory, and the belief that men are disposed to live honestly, if the means of doing so are open to them."[23] There were cataracts in this vision, particularly in the roles blacks and Indians would play. There was also a need for Jefferson to shut his eyes to divisions in America, to the class divisions growing in cities and regional divisions growing in the nation.

Caveats notwithstanding, Jefferson's foreign policies contained a consistent pattern of movement toward his goal. Recognizing that the nation was caught up in a global economy, he sought the best terms possible for its prosperity. There was nothing new about his support of American trade with Europe; this was the essence of his service as minister to France. Nor was there a deviation from his conception of the office of the chief executive in his exercise of power as president: witness his views of the Constitution from Paris, or of the presidency from his position as secretary of state. His advocacy of limited government in 1787 and 1798 was based less on principle than on concern in 1787 about the cult of Washington and in 1798 about a potential Hamiltonian man on horseback. His use of the presidency resulted in spectacular success and in dismal failure, but it was in aid of the most consistent of his objectives—namely, freeing America from the constraints imposed by Britain, France, and Spain and expanding the new nation at the expense of these European powers. He lived long enough to witness their achievement.

## Notes

1. TJ to Madison, April 27, 1809, in Andrew A. Lipscomb and Albert E. Bergh, eds., *The Writings of Thomas Jefferson*, 20 vols. (Washington, DC: Thomas Jefferson Memorial Association, 1903–04), 12:276–77 (hereafter cited as Lipscomb and Bergh).

2. TJ to Monroe, May 14, 1820, ibid., 15:251.

3. TJ to Chevalier Luis de Onís, April 28, 1814, ibid., 14:131.

4. TJ to William Duane, August 4, 1812, ibid., 13:181; TJ to Robert Wright, August 8, 1812, ibid., 184–85.

5. TJ to James Ronaldson, January 12, 1813, ibid., 206.

6. TJ to Mrs. Elizabeth Trist, June 10, 1814, Reel 8, Thomas Jefferson Papers, Massachusetts Historical Society, Boston.

7. TJ to George Logan, September 18, 1813, Reel 46, Jefferson Papers, Library of Congress, Washington, DC.

8. Thomas Leiper to TJ, December 9, 1813, Reel 47, ibid.

9. TJ to Leiper, January 11, 1814, Lipscomb and Bergh, 14:41–42.

10. Ibid, 44.

11. TJ to John Adams, July 5, 1814, ibid., 146

12. TJ to Thomas Cooper, September 10, 1814, ibid., 186–87.

13. TJ to Monroe, January 1, 1815, ibid., 226.

14. TJ to John Adams, August 10, 1815, ibid., 345.

15. W. Stull Holt, "Uncle Sam as Deer, Jackal, and Lion; or The United States in Power Politics," *Pacific Spectator* 3 (January 1949): 47–48.

16. TJ to John Adams, November 25, 1816, in Lester J. Cappon, ed., *The Adams-Jefferson Letters*, 2 vols. ( Chapel Hill: University of North Carolina Press,1959), 2:496–97.

17. TJ to Samuel Parrs, April 26, 1824, Lipscomb and Bergh, 18:329.

18. TJ to Edward Everett, March 2, 1822, ibid., 15:356.

19. Ibid.

20.TJ to Monroe, October 24, 1823, ibid., 478.

21. Ibid.

22. TJ to Du Pont, December 31, 1813, ibid., 14:371.

23. TJ to Barbé de Marbois, June 14, 1817, ibid., 15:131.

# Bibliographical Essay

Thomas Jefferson's role as the symbol of America's legacy to the world is enshrined on the face of Mount Rushmore, in the words on his tombstone, and in the writings of admiring historians from George Tucker's *The Life of Thomas Jefferson*, 2 vols. (London: Charles Knight and Co., 1837) and Henry S. Randall's *The Life of Thomas Jefferson*, 3 vols. (New York: Derby and Jackson, 1858) to Dumas Malone's *Jefferson and His Time*, 6 vols. (Boston: Little, Brown and Co., 1948–1981) and Merrill D. Peterson's *Thomas Jefferson* (New York: Oxford University Press, 1970). But for every favorable study of his life and works there has been a negative verdict beginning with harsh Federalist critics such as Stephen Cullen Carpenter, *Memoirs of the Hon. Thomas Jefferson* (New York, 1809) to the equally critical treatment by Conor Cruise O'Brien, *The Long Affair: Thomas Jefferson in the French Revolution, 1785–1800* (Chicago: University of Chicago Press, 1996). Both accuse Jefferson of being a captive of dangerous French revolutionary ideals. The wide variety of interpretations, as seen over the years, is best viewed in Merrill D. Peterson, *The Jefferson Image in the American Mind* (New York: Oxford University Press, 1960).

Collections of Jefferson's papers have been available in print since his grandson, Thomas Jefferson Randolph, edited four volumes of his papers in 1829. The most authoritative is Julian P. Boyd et al., eds., *The Papers of Thomas Jefferson* (Princeton: Princeton University Press, 1950–). Regrettably, this definitive edition has progressed only through 1793; the work should be completed in the middle of the twenty-first century. In the interim, scholars depend principally on Paul Leicester Ford, ed., *The Works of Thomas Jefferson*, 12 vols. (New York: G. P. Putnam's Sons, 1904–05), or the more voluminous but less reliable Andrew A. Lipscomb and Albert E. Bergh, eds., *The Writings of Thomas Jefferson*, 20 vols. (Washington, DC: Thomas Jefferson Memorial Association, 1903–04). The two hundred volumes of Jefferson's correspondence in the Library of Congress are available in microform. Other papers may be found in the

Massachusetts Historical Society, the University of Virginia's Alderman Library, the Virginia State Library, and the Missouri Historical Society Library.

If a negative image of Jefferson's foreign policies predominates in Jeffersonian historiography, the long shadow of Henry Adams's magisterial *History of the United States During the Administrations of Jefferson and Madison*, 9 vols. (New York: Charles Scribner's Sons, 1889–1891), accounts for the tone of many of the critical studies of his statecraft in the twentieth century. There have been few important commentaries on this aspect of his life in the past decade, but those that have appeared are cast in the Adams mold. It is not that they accuse Jefferson of being an unregenerate Francophile, as Federalist and neo-Federalist historians would have it; or that he was a traitor to Virginia cuisine, as Patrick Henry once suggested. The Adams influence may be found in criticisms of Jefferson's presumption that he could outwit Napoleon. His policies were confused, and his successes were products of luck rather than wisdom. Such is the verdict of Robert W. Tucker and David C. Hendrickson, *Empire of Liberty: The Statecraft of Thomas Jefferson* (New York: Oxford University Press, 1990). Doron S. Ben-Atar, *The Origins of Jeffersonian Commercial Policy and Diplomacy* (New York: St. Martin's Press, 1993), concentrates on Jefferson's pre-presidential years, viewing his foreign economic policies as a consequence of a Virginian perception of a British conspiracy to exploit innocent planters. Jefferson's exaggeration of America's power to coerce foreign powers by withholding agricultural exports led to the misjudgments culminating in the embargo.

A different angle of observation of Jefferson's foreign policies appears in Marie-Jeanne Rossignol, *Le ferment nationaliste: Aux origines de la politique extérieure des Etats-Unis, 1789–1812* (Paris: Belin, 1994). Rossignol too is influenced by Adams, but as an adversary rather than as a guide. She contends that American nationalism was responsible not only for war in 1812, but also for a westward expansion that defined the nation. Contemporary awareness of racism in the Jeffersonian years, as manifested in the treatment of Native Americans and in the formulation of policies toward Haiti, makes this study a fuller treatment of American foreign relations than may be found in the work of earlier historians. It is worth noting that the issues of slavery and racism in other chapters obscure Walter LaFeber's reasonable effort in Peter S. Onuf, ed., *Jeffersonian Legacies* (Charlottesville: University Press of Virginia, 1993) to resolve apparent contradictions in Jefferson's foreign policies. These studies comprise the major additions to the literature of Jefferson's diplomacy produced in the last decade. Although Bradford Perkins, *The Creation of a Republican Empire, 1776–1865*, in *The Cambridge History of American Foreign Relations*, ed. Warren I. Cohen (New York: Cambridge University Press, 1993) covers much more ground than the Jeffersonian era, his balanced judgments make this volume a useful introduction to the subject.

For insight into Jefferson's early views on British relations see Anthony M. Lewis, "Jefferson's *Summary View* as a Chart of Political Union," *William and Mary Quarterly*, 3d ser., 5 (January 1948): 34–51. Three major studies of the Declaration of Independence offer differing judgments on the Enlightenment's influence on Jefferson. Carl Becker's classic *The Declaration of Independence and What It Means Today: A Study in the History of Political Ideas* (New York: Alfred A. Knopf, 1945) gives major credit to John Locke, while Garry Wills, *Inventing America: Jefferson's Declaration of Independence* (Garden City, NY: Doubleday and Co., 1978) identifies the Scottish moral philosophers of the commonsense school as the primary influence. The most recent entry into this field is Pauline Maier. *American Scripture: Making the Declaration of Independence* (New York: Alfred A. Knopf, 1997) downplays Jefferson's role—and the role of European philosophers—and emphasizes the document as the expression of America's colonial experience.

Mary Giunta and J. Dane Hartgrove, eds., *The Emerging Nation. A Documentary History of the Foreign Relations of the United States under the Articles of Confederation, 1780–1789*, 3 vols. (Washington, DC: National Historical Publications and Records Commission, 1996) is an important guide to Jefferson's progress and problems in Europe. Norman A. Graebner, Peter P. Hill, and Lawrence S. Kaplan provide essays based on the documents. Robert R. Palmer, "The Dubious Democrat: Thomas Jefferson and Bourbon France," *Political Science Quarterly* 72 (September 1957): 388–404 observes Jefferson's doubts about French abilities to make too drastic a revolution. Merrill D. Peterson, "Thomas Jefferson and Commercial Policy, 1783–1793," *William and Mary Quarterly*, 3d ser., 22 (October 1965): 594–610 examines his valiant but failed efforts to use commerce as a weapon of foreign policy as minister to France and as secretary of state. Ben-Atar's monograph (cited above) is less appreciative of Jefferson's efforts in France or in Philadelphia. Herbert E. Sloan, *Principle and Interest: Thomas Jefferson and the Problem of Debt* (New York: Oxford University Press, 1995) perceptively links Jefferson's personal problems with debt to his consideration of the nation's debt during negotiations with Dutch bankers in the 1780s and with his Federalist opponents in the 1790s. William H. Adams, *The Paris Years of Thomas Jefferson* (New Haven: Yale University Press, 1997) is the most recent study of Jefferson and France.

Two master historians have examined Anglo-American relations and Franco-American relations in which Jefferson is the most significant actor. Bradford Perkins's trilogy—*The First Rapprochement: England and the United States, 1795–1805* (Berkeley and Los Angeles: University of California Press, 1955); *Prologue to War: England and the United States, 1805–1812* (Berkeley and Los Angeles: University of California Press, 1961); and *Castlereagh and Adams: England and the United States, 1812–1823* (Berkeley and Los Angeles: University of California Press, 1964)—is more sympathetic to British positions than to Jefferson's. Alexander DeConde's trilogy— *Entangling Alliance: Politics and Diplomacy under George Washington* (Durham, NC: Duke University Press, 1958); *The Quasi-War: The Politics and Diplomacy of the Undeclared War with France* (New York: Charles Scribner's Sons, 1966); and *This Affair of Louisiana* (New York: Charles Scribner's Sons, 1976)—focuses on domestic problems behind Franco-American relations and emphasizes Jefferson's expansionist aims in the Louisiana Purchase. Albert H. Bowman, *The Struggle for Neutrality: Franco-American Diplomacy During the Federalist Era* (Knoxville: University of Tennessee Press, 1974) presents American policy toward France from a Jeffersonian perspective. Mary P. Adams, "Jefferson's Reaction to the Treaty of San Ildefonso," *Journal of Southern History* 21 (Spring 1955): 173–88 relates Jefferson's militant response to Spain's retrocession of Louisiana to France.

Expansionism has been a major subject of American historians over the past generation. Donald Jackson, *Thomas Jefferson & the Stony Mountains: Exploring the West from Monticello* (Norman: University of Oklahoma Press, 1993) follows Jefferson's lifelong concerns with the American West. Reginald Horsman, *Expansion and American Indian Policy, 1783–1812* (East Lansing: Michigan State University Press, 1967) explores the tensions between Jefferson's expansionist interests and his desire for fair treatment of Native Americans. Bernard W. Sheehan, *Seeds of Extinction: Jeffersonian Philanthropy and the American Indian* (Chapel Hill: University of North Carolina Press, 1973) is the most authoritative account of Jefferson's Indian policies. A more positive gloss on western expansion is presented in Stephen S. Ambrose, *Undaunted Courage: Meriwether Lewis, Thomas Jefferson, and the Opening of the American*

*West* (New York: Simon and Schuster, 1996). William E. Weeks, *Building the Continental Empire: American Expansion from the Revolution to the Civil War* (New Haven: Yale University Press, 1996) gives Jefferson ample space but not a dominant role in the process. Frank L. Owlsey, Jr., and Gene A. Smith, *Filibusterers and Expansionists: Jeffersonian Manifest Destiny, 1800–1821* (Tuscaloosa: University of Alabama Press, 1997) focuses on an important aspect of expansionism.

The Barbary wars have been treated in Ray W. Irwin, *The Diplomatic Relations of the United States with the Barbary Powers, 1776–1816* (Chapel Hill: University of North Carolina Press, 1931), and in James A. Field, *America and the Mediterranean World* (Princeton: Princeton University Press, 1969). James R. Sofka, "The Jeffersonian Idea of National Security: Commerce, the Atlantic Balance of Power, and the Barbary War, 1786–1805," *Diplomatic History* 21 (Fall 1997): 519–44 sees the Barbary conflict as the culmination of a strategy that Jefferson had developed in the 1780s. Spencer C. Tucker, *The Jeffersonian Gunboat Navy* (Columbia: University of South Carolina Press, 1993) describes the useful function Jefferson's maligned gunboats played in the Barbary wars. For Jefferson's ambivalence toward the Haitian revolution see Rayford Logan, *The Diplomatic Relations of the United States with Haiti, 1776–1891* (Chapel Hill: University of North Carolina Press, 1941), and Tim Matthewson, "Jefferson and the Nonrecognition of Haiti," *Proceedings of the American Philosophical Society* 140 (March 1996): 22–47.

Jefferson's pursuit of the Floridas has received the attention of historians, with the president's positions criticized in Isaac J. Cox, *The West Florida Controversy, 1798–1813* (Baltimore: Johns Hopkins University Press, 1918), and in the more authoritative Clifford L. Egan, "The United States, France, and West Florida, 1803–1807," *Florida Historical Quarterly* 47 (Summer 1969): 227–53. See also Egan, *Neither Peace nor War: Franco-American Relations, 1803–1812* (Baton Rouge: Louisiana State University Press, 1983).

Jefferson's entanglement in the Napoleonic Wars during his second administration has been more thoroughly debated than any other aspect of his presidential tenure. Recently, Rossignol, as well as Donald R. Hickey, "The Monroe-Pinkney Treaty of 1806: A Reappraisal," *William and Mary Quarterly*, 3d ser., 44 (January 1987): 65–88, argue that Jefferson's failure to accept the treaty led to embargo and war. Louis M. Sears, *Jefferson and the Embargo* (Durham: Duke University Press, 1927) links his embargo to his pacifism. Reginald C. Stuart, *The Half-Way Pacifist: Thomas Jefferson's View of War* (Toronto: University of Toronto Press, 1978) concludes that

Jefferson saw war as a legitimate though limited instrument of policy. The most nuanced and most satisfactory treatment of the embargo is Burton Spivak, *Jefferson's English Crisis: Commerce, Embargo, and the Republican Revolution* (Charlottesville: University Press of Virginia, 1979). See also Richard Mannix, "Gallatin, Jefferson, and the Embargo," *Diplomatic History* 3 (Spring 1979): 151–72. Drew R. McCoy, *The Elusive Republic: Political Economy in Jeffersonian America* (Chapel Hill: University of North Carolina Press, 1980) offers insight into the influence of "republicanism" on the Jefferson-Madison foreign policies as well as a convincing explanation of the role of manufactures in an agricultural republic after the embargo.

Roy J. Honeywell, "President Jefferson and His Successor," *American Historical Review* 46 (October 1940): 64–75 and Adrienne Koch, *Jefferson and Madison: The Great Collaboration* (New York: Oxford University Press, 1950) observe the limitations in Jefferson's influence over President Madison. T. R. Schellenberg, "Jeffersonian Origins of the Monroe Doctrine," *Hispanic American Historical Review* 45 (February 1934): 1–34, identifies the doctrine of nonintervention as a Jeffersonian concept, influenced by the French philosophe Abbé de Pradt. My writings on the Monroe Doctrine and other aspects of Jefferson's positions on foreign relations are presented in the Preface.

# Index